আসসালামু আলাইকুম

সবাই স্বাগতম ประเทศจีน

ব্যালো

চীন। চায়না

مرحباً بالصين

САЙНУУ ХЯТАДАА!

안녕~중국!

こんにちは 中国

xin chào Trung Quốc

नमस्ते चाइना

MONI, CHINA

Halo TIONGKOK

Xin Chào, Trung Quốc

வணக்கம் சீனா

Xin chào trung quốc

สวัสดี ประเทศจีน

OLÁ, CHINA

안녕, 중국

Heniembah CHIMA

hello CHINA

Здравствуй, КИТАЙ

SALAM XITOY

안녕, 중국

Hello China

Здравствуй,Китай!

XIN CHÀO, TRUNG QUỐC

안녕, 중국

Xin chào Trung Quốc

শালা চীন

こんにちわ 中国

Apa Khabar China

HOLA CHINA

چین

Salam, Kjnaŭ!

G'DAY~ CHINA

Здравствуй, Китай!

谨以此书献给改革开放四十年
This book is dedicated to the 40th
anniversary of China's reform and opening-up.

我与中国的美丽邂逅

来华留学生讲述改革开放的中国

My Beautiful Encounter with China

International Students' Stories on China's Reform and Opening-up

教育部国际合作与交流司
教育部留学服务中心 编

Compiled by

Department of International Cooperation and Exchanges,

Ministry of Education of the People's Republic of China

Chinese Service Center for Scholarly Exchange,

Ministry of Education of the People's Republic of China

人民日报出版社

People's Daily Press

图书在版编目（CIP）数据

我与中国的美丽邂逅：来华留学生讲述改革开放的中国：汉英对照 / 教育部国际合作与交流司，教育部留学服务中心编 . -- 北京：人民日报出版社，2018.11（2022.11 重印）

ISBN 978-7-5115-5743-8

Ⅰ.①我… Ⅱ.①教… ②教… Ⅲ.①留学生－学生生活－文集－汉、英 Ⅳ.① G648.9-53

中国版本图书馆 CIP 数据核字（2018）第 261879 号

书　　名：我与中国的美丽邂逅：来华留学生讲述改革开放的中国
WO YU ZHONGGUO DE MEILI XIEHOU: LAIHUA LIUXUESHENG JIANGSHU GAIGE KAIFANG DE ZHONGGUO

编　　者：教育部国际合作与交流司　教育部留学服务中心

出 版 人：刘华新
责任编辑：翟福军　梁雪云
封面设计：春天书装工作室

出版发行：人民日报出版社

社　　址：北京金台西路 2 号
邮政编码：100733
发行热线：(010) 65369509　65369527　65369846　65363528
邮购热线：(010) 65369530　65363527
编辑热线：(010) 65369517　65369526
网　　址：www.peopledailypress.com
经　　销：新华书店
印　　刷：炫彩（天津）印刷有限责任公司

开　　本：710mm×1000mm　1/16
字　　数：356 千字
印　　张：24
版次印次：2019 年 1 月第 1 版　　2022 年 11 月第 2 次印刷

书　　号：ISBN 978-7-5115-5743-8
定　　价：98.00 元

序言
Preface

Over 2,100 years ago, a Chinese envoy named Zhang Qian in the Han Dynasty, a "pioneer of the ancient Silk Road", travelled westward, spreading Chinese civilization and promoting cultural exchanges between the East and the West. Through his routes, grape, alfalfa, pomegranate, flax and other products entered China.

More than 1,300 years ago, in the Tang dynasty, China began to welcome the envoys from other countries. It was an unprecedented event in the history of cultural exchanges between China and the world that lasted for over 260 years. China's culture, art, science and technology, and customs were introduced to East Asian countries, pushing the social development of neighboring countries and regions.

Over 400 years ago, Matteo Ricci, an Italian missionary, came to China, becoming the first Western scholar who read Chinese literature and studied Chinese classics. At the same time, he actively promoted Western astronomy, mathematics, and geography, making important contributions to the scientific and cultural exchanges between China and the West.

两千一百多年前，中国汉代的张骞出使西域各国，他将中华文明传播至西域，又从西域诸国引进葡萄、苜蓿、石榴、胡麻等物种到中原，促进了东西方文明的交流，成为"古丝绸之路的开拓者"。

一千三百多年前，中国开始接受遣唐使赴华学习，持续达二百六十余年，成为中外文化交流史上的空前盛举。中国的文化艺术、科学技术以及风俗习惯传入东亚各国，推动了周边国家和地区的社会发展与进步。

四百多年前，意大利人利玛窦来到中国，成为第一位阅读中国文学并对中国典籍进行钻研的西方学者。与此同时，他积极传播西方天文、数学、地理等科学技术知识，对中西科学文化交流作出了重要贡献。

四十年前，中国实施改革开放并做出派遣留学生的战略决策，推动形成了中国历史上规模最大、领域最多、范围最广的留学潮和归国热；与此同时，中国与世界各国的教育交流与合作日益紧密，逐步成为了国际学生流动舞台上的重要一员。越来越多的外国学者和青年学生把目光投向中国，中国也以愈发开放的姿态吸引和培养了大批来自世界各国的留学生。2017 年，中国出国留学人数达 60.84 万人，持续保持世界最大留学生生源国地位。中国接受的来华留学人员达到 48.92 万名，来自

40 years ago, China adopted the reform and opening-up policy and made a strategic decision to send students to other countries, on a scale of which had been unprecedented. So were the students returning to China. In the mean time, the educational exchanges and cooperation between China and the rest of the world became increasingly closer, making China an important destination for international students. A growing number of foreign scholars and young students have focused on China, and China, with an open mind, has also attracted and cultivated a large group of international students. In 2017, the number of Chinese students studying abroad reached 608,400, making China the largest overseas student pool. In addition, China embraced 489,200 international students from 204 countries and regions, making itself the largest destination in Asia for overseas students and one of the largest in the world.

In all ages, different countries and nations have conducted cultural and people-to-people exchanges and learned from each other; in particular, international student exchanges not only have carried forward the diversity of human civilization and richness of national culture, boosted the progress of science, technology and civilization in all countries, but also deepened the friendship among all.

This year marks the 40th anniversary of China's reform and opening-up. On one hand, international students serve as envoys of friendship, showing their home countries to Chinese people. On the other hand, they convey to the world the achievements and a real China in reform and opening-up, enabling people around the world to witness China's changes and the Chinese people's good wishes for building a community of shared future for mankind. The Chinese people stand firm to harmonious coexistence, mutual benefit and win-win results, and seek openness, innovation as well as inclusiveness and reciprocity. The Chinese people also promote harmony in diversity, draw on the best of other cultures, respect

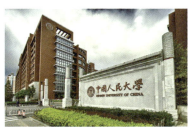

204 个国家和地区。中国已成为亚洲最大、世界主要的留学目的地国。

自古至今，不同国家和民族之间的人文交流与互相学习，尤其是留学人员的往来不仅传递了人类文明的多样性与民族文化的丰富性，促进了各国科技与文明的进步，而且深化了各国人民之间的友谊。

今年，适值中国改革开放四十周年，各个国家的留学生来到中国学习，一方面作为友谊的使者，向中国人民展示着自己国家的风采，另一方面也把中国改革开放的成就和真实风貌传递给世界，让世界人民感知中国的变化以及中国人民希望构建人类命运共同体的良好愿望。中国人民坚持和谐共生，互利共赢，谋求开放创新，包容互惠，促进和而不同、兼收并蓄，尊崇生态自然、绿色发展，中国人民的梦想同各国人民的梦想息息相通。

为了传递这样的梦想，增进中国人民与来华留学生的友谊，分享中国改革开放四十年的成就和经验，促进不同国家留华学生之间的交流，受教育部委托，教育部留学服务中心组织

the nature, and pursue green development. The dream of the Chinese people has always been in line with the dreams of people in the whole world.

To convey Chinese people's dreams, enhance the friendship between the Chinese people and international students in China, share China's experience and achievements in reform and opening-up in the past 40 years, and promote the cultural and people-to-people exchanges among international students in China, the Chinese Service Center for Scholarly Exchange (CSCSE), entrusted by the Ministry of Education, organized the second essay competition for international students. This competition received positive response from universities, as well as international students and graduates in China, with many outstanding works emerged. we have received over 800 essays submitted by 108 colleges and universities, education sections of China's embassies and consulates, associations of international alumni in China, as well as individual international students from over 100 countries. After being reviewed by the judging panel, the CSCSE chose 5 first prizes, 8 second prizes, 16 third prizes and 32 recognition awards. All prize-winning essays, rich in content, were written in Chinese with ease and grace. As a companion piece of *My Beautiful Encounter with China—the Chinese Story Told by Foreign Students*, these essays will be published in collection with the title of *My Beautiful Encounter with China—International Students' Stories on China's Reform and Opening-up*.

In this book, international students in China, by telling stories, described their experiences, and shared their perception on the changes and achievements China has made in reform and opening-up. The authors included young international students studying in China and some elder international graduates studied in China in the 1980s and 1990s. In their essays, they described their confusion caused by different lifestyles

举办了第二届来华留学生征文大赛。征文大赛得到了中国各高校、广大来华留学生和留华毕业生的积极响应，涌现出了一大批优秀的作品。据统计，征文期间共收到来自108所高校、驻外使（领）馆教育处组、留华校友组织以及个人投稿800余篇，文章作者来自100多个国家。经过征文比赛评委会的评审，最终评选出一等奖5名，二等奖8名、三等奖16名、优秀奖32名。获奖的作品均以中文写就，文章流畅优美，内容丰富多彩，并作为去年出版的《我与中国的美丽邂逅——来华留学生讲述中国故事》的姐妹篇，以《我与中国的美丽邂逅——来华留学生讲述改革开放的中国》为书名结集出版。

书中，来自不同国家的来华留学生用讲故事的方式，讲述自己的来华留学经历，畅谈在华留学的感受，并通过自身视角看中国改革开放的发展变化、取得的成果，分享自己的体验和感想。其中，有目前正在中国学习的年轻一代留学生，也有毕业于20世纪八九十年代的老来华留学生。在他们的笔下，有面对生活方式与文化习惯不同的困惑；有

and cultural habits, their delight in overcoming difficulties, gradually adapting to and blending with surroundings , their love for Chinese culture generated through learning Chinese language, their beautiful memories of their study life, as well as their willingness to become an envoy linking China and the rest of the world after experiencing China's economic development and the Chinese people' enthusiasm and friendship. This book will provide international students in China with a window showing their study and life here and also a bond for them to connect with China.

Looking into the future, the Chinese government will continue to pursue greater opening up, strengthen international educational cooperation and exchanges with the rest of the world, welcome and encourage excellent international students to further their studies in China. By 2020, the estimated number of international students in China is expected to amount to 500,000. The Chinese government as well as colleges and universities will take more measures to create a better environment for them, integrate more high-quality educational resources and provide more internationalized educational services.

As a Chinese poem goes, "If you have a friend afar who knows your heart, distance can't keep you two apart." Dear international students and friends, wherever you are in the future, the nearly 1.4 billion Chinese will always be your sincere friends and partners, and China's development will provide and create a broader stage for you to show your talent. It is hoped that all of you will continue to pay attention to China's development, and make greater contributions to the exchanges and cooperation in economy, education, culture, diplomacy and other fields between China and your country.

Editorial Committee

November 6, 2018

克服困难、逐渐适应并融入环境的喜悦；有通过中文学习而产生的对中国文化的喜爱；有对于在中国留学的似水年华的美好追忆；以及感受到中国经济的发展和中国人民的热情友善，而积极成为沟通中国和世界使者的愿望。此书的出版为各国的来华留学生提供了一个展示在华学习风采、交流来华留学生活感受的窗口，同时也为大家提供了一条与中国联系的纽带。

展望未来，中国政府将继续扩大开放，加强与世界各国的国际教育合作与交流，欢迎和鼓励各国优秀学子来华学习深造。到 2020 年，来华留学生的人数预计达到 50 万，中国政府和高校将继续采取一系列措施，致力于营造更加优化的留学环境，整合更加优质的教育资源，并提供更加国际化的教育服务。

"海内存知己，天涯若比邻"，留学生朋友们，无论你们以后走到世界的任何一个地方，近 14 亿中国人民都将是你们真诚的朋友和友好的伙伴，中国的发展将为你们提供和创造展示才华的更为广阔的舞台。希望广大留学生朋友继续关注中国的发展，继续为增进中国与你们祖国的经济、教育、文化、外交等方面的交流与合作做出更大的贡献。

编委会

二〇一八年十一月六日

目 录

CONTENTS

Contents

/ 目 录 /

Contents

/ 目 录 /

Contents

/ 目录 /

Contents

/ 目 录 /

七年之仰慕
Seven-Year Admiration

[孟加拉国]　木森　山东大学

[Bangladesh] Muhsin Billah Bin Khashru, Shandong University

I have been in China for seven years. Chinese people always like to use "the seven-year itch" to describe such a long relationship, but for me "the seven-year admiration" would be a better phrase for my days in China. During this period, I have never gotten tired of this country but become increasingly obsessed with its beauty and vastness.

As spring has gone and autumn come for seven times, I have witnessed how this ancient country started shining the light of a new era while maintaining the dignity of its five millennia-long culture. Her beauty shaped in thousands of years and her strong capabilities to advance its high-tech industry in the information era have made me unable to put into words the vitality I have seen. I remember there is a slogan describing Yangzhou, a famous city along the Yangtze River, as a place where ancient culture and modern civilization illuminate one another. This best represents the country's achievement. The collision between ancient culture and modern civilization presents us with glamour.

When analyzing all of this, I take serenity first as example. Every morning,

　　来中国已有七年之久，中国人有个说法叫"七年之痒"，可是我和中国的七年时光却可以用"七年之仰慕"来形容，对这个广袤而美丽的国家我不但没有"审美疲劳"，对她的热爱反而与日俱增。

　　时间轴上走过七年，我也用自己的脚步和眼睛见证着这个古老的国家散发出新时代的光芒，同时又不失自己千年文化的端庄。回首她历经千年而沉淀出的岁月静好之美，展望她面对高科技信息化时代而表现出的强劲发展力，我不得不感叹，这是一个生命力何等强大的国家。记得形容江南名城扬州时是这样说的："古代文化与现代文明交相辉映的名城，"想来，这用来形容中国也极其恰当。古代文化与现代文明在这里碰撞，让我们看到一个魅力无限的大国。

　　先看这里岁月静好。晨光初起，一缕阳光叫醒一座古城。霞光洒在大运河边上，千年古城准时从静谧中醒来，又准备走向新一天的喧嚣。老巷里偶尔有车子颠簸而过，行人走得不疾不慢，步履悠然。老人提着早市里精挑细选来的新鲜时蔬，向坐在家门旁择菜的街坊问声早。狗儿知道是熟人，轻轻摇晃尾巴，偶尔顽皮追赶一二陌生路人，路人也并不懊恼。我喜欢这个国家，喜欢她安详的模样。

the first rays of dawn awake the ancient city. When the sunlight sprinkles over the Grand Canal, the ancient city completely wakes up from the tranquility and readies for another bustling day. In the old alley, you see pedestrians walking leisurely and sometimes cars bumping along the gravel road. After carefully examining the morning market's produce, the elderly take fresh vegetables back home and greet neighbors who are sitting by their doors and trimming vegetables for cooking. The dogs know that he is one of old friends, so they just wag tails gently. But sometimes they also chase strangers for fun but not in an annoying way. I love this country for her serenity.

Next that comes to mind is enthusiasm, which is ebullient on this land. The crazy rollercoaster takes brave young men whizzing past. On the square, middle-aged and aged people infect me with their impassioned dance and music. In the shopping mall, various restaurants and recreational facilities are open to citizens, presenting a scene of jollification. I love this country for the convenient life, the rapid growth rate and the optimism about the future she so ardently creates.

Let us move on to elegance and dignity. This thousand-year-old city wall still stands erect. Although the wall is no longer used for defense, its majesty shows no signs of waning. The ancient palace retains its magnificence, silently recounting those old glories. In a hundred-year-old temple, burning incense is continuously curling upwards, bearing locals' aspiration for peace and prosperity. I love this country for her majesty and ancient beauty.

Finally, I shift my focus to advancement. As a leader in information technology, China is proof of how technology reshapes lives. High-speed trains, running at speeds of over 300 km/h, lead the country to embark on the track of

再看这里热情奔放。疯狂的过山车载着胆量过人的年轻朋友呼啸而过，广场上感染着我的是中老年人富有激情的舞步和歌声。商业中心里有着让人眼花缭乱的餐饮娱乐设施，这个国家呈现着让人目不暇接的热闹景象。我喜欢这个国家，喜欢她便捷的生活方式，喜欢她的速度与激情。

又看这里庄重典雅。千年的古城墙依旧屹立城边，没有了戍守的作用，却依旧还有威严不可触犯的气场。古时宫殿气宇轩昂，无声诉说着曾经的辉煌。百年寺庙中香火不断，它庇佑的是一方平安，更是一方民众对安定吉祥的愿望。我喜欢这个国家，喜欢她的庄重，喜欢她的古色古香。

还看这里前卫时尚。走在科技化信息时代的前端，这个国家向我们

第一次到山东大学

山东大学提供

rapid development. Sharing economy is her new exploration in pursuit of low-carbon and green development. E-commerce is not only changing people's lifestyle, but also reshaping the country's economic structure. I love this country for her advancement.

This country, with her beauty shown in thousands of postures and extremely fascinating charm, awaits on your exploration. Welcome here to find a different China in your eyes.

在中国的第一天（右三为作者）

证明了现代化科技手段可以给我们的生活带来多少改变。时速超过 300 千米的高铁拉动着这个国家高速前进，共享经济方式是这个国家在低耗绿色发展上做出的新探索，电子商务正在改变着所有人的生活方式，乃至改变着经济发展结构。我喜欢这个国家，喜欢她先进，前卫，时尚。

　　这个美丽的国家，值得看的地方还远不止这些。看不够，爱不够。这个国家千种姿态，这个国家万种风情。欢迎你来，发现你眼中的，中国。

中国，这里有我深深的爱
China, Things I Love Here

［巴基斯坦］　婷韩　中国科学技术大学

[Pakistan] Tasneem Akhtar, University of Science and Technology of China

Two years ago (2016), thanks to the Chinese Government Scholarship, I came along the bridge of China-Pakistan Friendship, travelled over mountains and rivers and finally ran into your arms. At that time, you had been an amazing fantasy in my mind, woven by your five-thousand-year history, your solid and rolling Great Wall as well as the University of Science and Technology of China,

where I would study for my doctorate.

In the past two years, you gave me the same kind of care as my hometown Jhang did. As a matter of fact, at times you would make me feel more loved. Your care and love deeply moved me, an outsider—every scholarship granted by the Chinese government, every considerate service provided by my university during the summer and winter

　　两年前（2016 年），我乘着"中国政府奖学金"的东风，顺着"中巴友谊"的桥梁，翻越千山万水拥入你温暖的怀抱。那时的你，在我心里满满的都是神奇的幻想，这幻想，来自 5000 年源远流长的历史，这幻想，来自坚固而又连绵不断的万里长城。当然，这幻想也来自我即将攻读博士学位的中国科学技术大学。

　　两年来，我在你的怀抱里感受着和巴基斯坦 Jhang 市（我的家乡）一样的关怀。哦不，有时候，我甚至会觉得，在你的怀里有着比 Jhang 市更浓的爱意。这浓浓的关怀和爱意，使身在异国他乡的我心里感到深深的眷恋——政府发给我的每一份奖学金，学校在寒暑假提供的每一项贴心的服务，干净卫生的穆斯林食堂，导师点点滴滴的教导和鼓励，同学之间不求回报的帮助和支持，陌生人不经意间的微笑……

　　若有人要问我，关于中国，你深深的爱意源自哪里？那么，我想为他（她）分享我在中国所看到的，所听到的，所感受到的一切。

　　我曾经是一名大学教师，对教育的关注就像我必须保证一日三餐一样重要。巴基斯坦是一个重视教育的国家，可是当我走近你，我才知道你对教育的关注远远超过很多国家。农村孩子九年义务教育期间的"两

vacation, every meal cooked in the clean Muslim canteen, every guidance and encouragement given by my supervisor, every help and support from my selfless classmates, and even every smile from strangers...

If someone asks me what makes me love China so much? I would answer by sharing what I have seen, heard and felt here.

I had been a university teacher, so for me, focusing on education is as important as taking in necessary nutrients. Pakistan is a country that values education, but when I get close to you, I found that your investment in education surpassed that of the majority of countries in the world. Children living in rural areas can enjoy the policy of waiving tuition and miscellaneous fees, supplying free textbooks, and granting living allowances for boarders from financially disadvantaged families as well as nutritious breakfast provided by schools. If they get admitted to a university, they could apply for student loans, scholarships and grants. All of these measures are guaranteeing the right to education for children from all backgrounds. In my two years studying at the University of Science and Technology of China, I witnessed how Chinese students exert tremendous focus on their researches and studies. Many of them study in labs at night and usually don't go back to their dormitory until very late.

Over the past two years, I have visited Beijing, Xi'an, Wuhan, Yangling and Chaohu. During these trips, I have had the pleasure of touring by plane, train, high-speed train and car. Then I found that, in China, regardless of your transport means, the trip is always a comfort. When I took high-speed train from Hefei West Railway Station to Xi'an for the first time, I was amazed that the station was as well-equipped as the Islamabad Benazir Bhutto International Airport. It was a magical experience.

In Pakistan, a great many commodities that people use everyday are

免一补",农村学校里每天配备的营养早餐,大学里提供的助学贷款、奖学金、助学金,这所有的一切都在保证着所有孩子的受教育权。在中国科学技术大学学习的这两年,我也看到,中国的学生是那么专注地做研究,很多学生晚上在实验室学习,直到很晚了才回宿舍。

在中国的这两年,我去过北京、西安、武汉、杨凌、巢湖。我所乘坐的交通工具有飞机、火车、高铁、汽车,我发现在中国,每一个交通工具都是如此便利舒适。第一次在合肥西站坐高铁去西安时,我感觉合肥高铁站可以和伊斯兰堡的首都机场相媲美,这真是一个神奇的体验。

在巴基斯坦,人们生活中所使用的很多产品都来自中国,因为中国的产品质量都很好,巴基斯坦人总是很赞赏。而且,在巴基斯坦,越来越多的人开始学习汉语,也有越来越多的巴基斯坦人因为得到中国政府提供的奖学金而来这里学习。关于这一点,我常常在祷告的时候说,感谢你,亲爱的中国,为我们提供一切的便利,我都在心里一遍又一遍地

imported from China. They are welcomed and praised for their high quality. Nowadays, more and more Pakistanis have started learning Chinese and come to China to further their study with the help of the Chinese Government Scholarship. In my prayer, I always say, thank you, my dear China, for all the convenience you give us. I express my gratitude over and over in my mind.

In China, people use WeChat to contact their families, pay bills, order take-outs as well as send and share locations. What's more, on WeChat, people can send stickers, which are very interesting and can help you easily express your feelings. From Taobao. com, we can buy everything we need for daily life, including clothes, shoes, backpacks and suitcases. China's express service is very convenient as it helps us to send and receive packages in no time. My friends, both Pakistanis and friends from other countries, often do online shopping.

Words can hardly express my love for you, but I still want to take from the lyrics to express myself: dear China, my love for you is just like the spring breeze that will never stop; dear China, my love for you is just like the sun and the moon that will be there day and night.

在中国科学技术大学

中国科学技术大学提供

说，谢谢你，亲爱的中国。

在中国，人们使用微信可以和家人联系，购买东西的时候支付费用，可以订外卖，可以发送位置，共享位置，尤其微信表情包，很有趣也很方便。在淘宝网我们可以买到所有的日常用品，衣服、鞋子、背包、皮箱，快递也很方便，无论任何时候，快递都可以帮助人们收发各种东西，非常方便。我身边有很多的朋友，不仅仅是巴基斯坦的朋友，其他国家的朋友，也经常在网上买很多非常有用的东西，而且价格也很便宜。

再多的言语，也无法表达我对你深深的爱意，但我依然要借一句中国的歌词，我爱你，亲爱的中国，如春风十里，不问归期；我爱你，亲爱的中国，如日月升起，不问朝夕。

给爸爸妈妈的一封信

——我在中国的生活

A Letter to My Parents

— *My Life in China*

［韩国］ 洪起熊 武汉大学

[Republic of Korea] Hong Giung, Wuhan University

Dear mom and dad:

It has been a long time since our last meeting. I miss you so much. Is everything going well?

I have been in China for almost two years now. During this period, I have gradually become accustomed to the pace of life here and found that China is a country full of surprises, completely different from what we had known before. So I really want to share my experience here with you through this letter.

The first thing I would like to share is diet, because food is the paramount necessity of people. Before my coming to China, what concerned you the most was that I might not get used to the food here, so you mailed a large amount of packaged food to me. However, later I found it to be unnecessary. I believe you certainly remember that my favorite food is tofu. Back home, the variety of tofu is scarce. But in China, I find there are various types of it, such as dried tofu and tofu skin and they all come with different flavors for you to choose.

亲爱的爸爸妈妈：

你们好！好久不见啦，十分思念你们，一切都还顺利吗？

我来中国已经快两年了，慢慢习惯了这边的生活节奏，发现中国是一个非常有意思的国家，跟我们之前所了解的情况完全不一样，想跟你们分享一下。

第一，民以食为天。来中国之前你们最担心的是我不能习惯这边的食物，给我邮寄了很多包装好的食品。但是这完全是多余的担忧。我在韩国的时候，不是很喜欢吃豆腐吗，但是韩国的豆腐种类太少了，我每次问有没有别的豆腐，但是也都差不多。当我来到中国之后发现这里有各种各样的豆腐，比如豆干、豆皮，口味也有很多选择。别的菜也特别特别好吃！虽然我有的时候不能看懂菜单，但是通过点评软件可以看到不同菜的图片和别人的介绍，所以总是可以选到喜欢的菜。有时候比较忙想叫外卖也很方便，在韩国需要先看资料，然后打电话给他们之后才可以叫外卖，但是中国一个软件就可以搞定，对喜欢吃美食的我而言，真的太棒了！

Beyond that, China has many other delicacies! Although sometimes I could not understand the menu, I could still pick up what I might like by referring to pictures and introductions of various dishes posted by other foodies on those review apps. When I am busy, I order take-outs, a convenient indulgence here. Back home, we need to read the menu and then call the restaurant, but in China, people just need an app. It is amazing for foodies like me.

The second thing I would like to share is China's transportation. As a Chinese saying goes, "One needs to not only read 10, 000 books, but also travel 10, 000 miles to know the world around us." Coming to China has enabled me to learn abundant knowledge. Meanwhile, China's convenient transportation system helps me have a deep understanding of China's vast territory and abundant resources. Shortly after I arrived in Wuhan, I needed to apply for various documents at different places, such as Wuhan Citizens Home and the hospital for physical examination. For a newcomer like me, who did not know much about the city and how to use public transit, the car-hailing app works wonders. No matter where I am or where I want to go, I can hail a car by the app, which is very cheap. More importantly, it frees me from getting lost with the complicated map. China's high-speed train is also very impressive, featuring high speed and good service. Foreigners can buy tickets with their passports. I have taken the high-speed train for several trips and enjoyed a good time.

The third thing I would like to share is those kind friends I made in China. As an ancient Chinese proverb says, "Isn't it a delight should friends visit from afar." My Chinese friends helped me a lot in my study and life. When I was majoring in international economy and trade, I got familiar with my classmates in professional courses. I didn't have a very good academic record, but they

　　第二，读万卷书，行万里路。来到中国让我有机会学习到丰富的知识，通过便捷的交通深刻了解到中国的地大物博。刚到武汉的时候，我经常要去不同的地方办理各种需要的证件，比如要去市民之家和体检医院，虽然这边公共交通很方便，但是还不太熟悉环境的我选择了使用更为省心的打车软件，这个简直太神奇了。不管我在哪里，想去什么地方，使用一个打车软件定位一下，就可以打到车，而且不用看地图，也不用担心迷路，价格还很便宜。中国的高铁也让人佩服，速度快，服务也很好，使用护照就可以买票，我几次旅行都是坐高铁去的，每次都玩得非常开心！

　　第三，有朋自远方来，不亦乐乎。在中国我交了许多很善良的朋友，他们在学习和生活方面帮助了我许多。我学习国际经济贸易专业期间，认识了一起学习专业课的同学，虽然我的学习成绩不是很优秀，但是他们愿意相信我，与我合作完成小组作业。他们告诉我"三人行，必有我师"，小

在宜昌旅游

all trusted me and were willing to team up with me to do group assignments. They told me: "When I walk along with two others, they may serve me as my teacher." Group assignments can give everyone the opportunity to learn from someone else, which should be cherished by all.

The fourth thing I would like to share is the inclusiveness of China. China is a diverse country, advocating seeking common ground while shelving differences and pursuing inclusiveness. Although China's political and economic system is different from that of Republic of Korea, Chinese people treat different races and cultures around the world with an inclusive attitude and are willing to know about and respect our customs. For example, in Wuhan University, there are many international students coming from different countries. While we are learning Chinese language and culture, we are also introducing our own country to one another. Last autumn, Wuhan University held the International Cultural Festival, establishing a great platform for both international students and Chinese students to know more about each other's cultures.

I really enjoy my days in China. My teachers and friends are all very hospitable. China is developing very fast and has become a completely different country from what you fathom. For us, there are so many aspects worth learning in China. I do hope one day you can visit China and you will definitely be surprised. Please don't worry about me. I will study hard here and I wish you all good health.

武汉大学提供

组合作能让大家有机会学习别人的优点，我们都应该好好把握这一机会。

第四，求同存异，兼容并包。中国是一个多元的国家。虽然跟韩国相比，中国有着不一样的政治经济体制，但是中国对世界各个国家的人民和文化都很包容，愿意了解、尊重我们的风俗习惯。比如在我们武汉大学，就有来自世界各地的留学生同学，大家共同学习汉语和中国文化的同时，也互相介绍自己国家的情况。去年秋季，我们学校举办了国际文化节，为外国留学生提供了文化交流的机会，也帮助中国学生了解更多其他国家的文化。

我在中国这边真的过得非常开心，中国的老师和朋友都很热情，现在中国发展速度飞快，已经不是你们所了解到的中国了，很多方面我们需要向中国学习，真希望你们以后有机会可以来中国旅游，一定会让你们感到惊喜。在这边我会努力学习，请爸爸妈妈不要担心。祝你们身体健康！

北京欢迎你
Welcome to Beijing

[越南] 罗氏云 北京理工大学
[Vietnam] La Thi Van, Beijing Institute of Technology

"Here comes another dawning filled with refreshing air. Our love for Beijing stays the same whatever changes. Our friendship grows in savoring the fragrant tea. "

In 2008, during that hot and humid summer, when I first heard this song, "Welcome to Beijing" , I started to be interested in Chinese and thought about visiting China.

As a kid, I loved Chinese costume drama and was highly impressed by the Palace Museum and the Great Wall. Though I was young at that time, I would sit down and watch Chinese TV series whenever it was on TV, having no idea where that place on screen was. Since then, those Chinese TV series have been deeply rooted in my mind and are still there.

In 2016, after graduation, I came to Beijing to study at Beijing Institute of Technology for my master's degree. I came across a myriad of troubles during my adaptation process. The main problem was the weather. The climate here is much drier than that of my hometown, I finally adapted to it after several times of nosebleed. When I studied my bachelor's degree back home, there

"迎接另一个晨曦，带来全新空气。气息改变情味不变，茶香飘满情谊……"

2008 年，这首《北京欢迎你》让我在那个潮湿、闷热的夏天喜欢上了中文，也让我萌生了来中国的念头。

我从小就爱看中国古装片，故宫和长城很早就在我脑海中留下了印象。那时候的我虽然还很小，不知道哪儿是哪儿，但家里只要放中国电视剧，我就坐在小椅子上看，看得多了，它们就不知不觉地钻进了我的记忆中，到现在也未曾消失过。

2016 年，大学毕业后的我来到北京，在北京理工大学读硕士。刚来时不免遇到很多麻烦，其中最主要的就是这里的天气比我家乡的天气干燥得多，我流了几次鼻血后才适应。我在国内读本科时，学校的食堂非常小而且是唯一的一个食堂，所以我很少去那里吃饭。来到北京后，我才知道什么是大学里的食堂，黄焖鸡米饭、北京烤鸭、小笼包……各地的美食应有尽有。更让我吃惊的是北京的每所大学都很大，里面像个小社区一样：操场、宿舍、食堂、超市、医院、花园，甚至连小学都有。可见，中国教育是系统而完善的，为学生提供了很多便利条件。

was only one tiny cafeteria in my school which I seldom visited. But here in Beijing, I got to know what college cafeteria looks like. We have all kinds of local delicacies, such as braised chicken and rice, Beijing roast duck, small steamed bun, etc. I was more surprised to find that every university in Beijing is like a small community with playground, dormitory, cafeteria, supermarket, hospital, garden, and even elementary school. It can be seen that Chinese education is systematic, providing all kinds of convenient services to students.

I love life in Beijing. In Vietnam, I seldom wear sneakers or sports shoes to go to classes. Whenever I go out, I always ride a motorcycle. However, things changed when I came to China. In Beijing, the pace of life is quite fast. Wherever I go, I wear sports shoes. Whenever you look around, the streets are always filled with cars. Some people hurry to get home, while others are busy at work. Pedestrians walk quickly without a moment of rest. My fondness for sports shoes has been growing. The high-heeled shoes I brought from home are put aside, and my shoe rack is full of sports shoes. I like Beijing, a "world of sneakers" , where I could enjoy much more convenience and greater efficiency. I also like myself better when I put head down and run at full speed.

Beijing is a well-developed city. With all these cameras, I feel safe even when walking alone at night. Besides, the transportation here is very convenient, especially the subway. As long as you have 4G access, you can go anywhere with the help of the navigation provided by Baidu Map without being lost. What's more, the advanced online shopping and take-out services bring me much convenience. I don't even have to go out as one-click will get my package and food delivered to me.

I love the ancient architecture in Beijing. Many thoughts came to my mind

北京理工大学 / 柴运春摄

　　我喜欢北京的生活。在越南时，我上课或出门很少穿平底鞋或运动鞋，一出门就骑摩托车，很少走路，但来到北京之后一切都变了。北京的生活节奏很快，只要出门，不管去哪儿，我都穿运动鞋。放眼望去，无论何时，北京的路上总是车水马龙、川流不息。有的人忙着回家，有的人忙着工作，路人总是脚步匆匆，没有片刻的休憩。我越来越喜欢运动鞋，以前从国内带过来的高跟鞋都不穿了，整个鞋架都是运动鞋。我喜欢北京这个"穿平底鞋的世界"，这让我的生活更加方便、高效，奔跑时的速度更快。我也越来越喜欢这个脚踏实地、全力奔跑的自己。

　　我喜欢北京的发达。这里很安全，到处都有摄像头监控，就算夜晚走在路上也会觉得很安心。北京的交通工具也非常方便，特别是地铁。出门只要有4G，用百度地图导航，想去哪儿都很方便，不会迷路。除

when I first visited the Palace Museum and the Great Wall I had been dreaming about for quite a long time. I love ancient royal gardens. The Summer Palace, the Old Summer Palace, and the Fragrance Hill took my breath away. Every season presents different beauty. People can enjoy the scenery of the lotus in summer and red maple leaves in autumn. As for spring, all kinds of flowers bloom and compete with each other in every garden. My favorite season is autumn when I can enjoy the red maple leaves on Fragrance Hill. Looking down from the top, I saw thousands of hills in crimson dotted with evergreen. What is more interesting is that many people wear ancient costumes to take photos there. You may also find some ladies wearing ancient costumes on the subway. Whenever I see them, I, a super fan of ancient costume, suppose they may be disciples of Little Dragon Girl or Emei School.

I love every street and every corner of Beijing. All the places I ever visited give me a sense of belonging. Although I haven not been here for a very long time, the longer I stay, the more unwilling I am to leave. If people ask me, "What kind of city Beijing is?" I would tell them, "It is a city well worth visiting. China is a great country and you may want to come here in person."

此之外，我更是享受到了中国发达的网购和外卖带给我的便利，下楼取快递，下楼取外卖，整天不出门也无所谓，因为很多问题只要动动手指就可以解决。

我喜欢北京的古老建筑。我第一次去参观故宫和长城时，心中感慨万千，这是我一直以来都梦寐以求的事情。我喜欢以前的皇家园林，我去过颐和园、圆明园、香山，那里的风景十分美丽，每个季节都有着不同的美。夏看荷花，秋看红叶。待到春暖花开时，每个公园都可以看见百花盛开、争奇斗艳。秋天，我最爱到香山上赏红叶。瞭望山下，满山一片火红，偶尔几点翠绿，那是常青的松柏。真是"万山红遍，层林尽染"。更有趣的是有很多帅哥美女穿着古装去那里拍照，非常有意思。在地铁里也能经常看见美女们穿着古装，每每这时，都会让我这个古装片迷猜想，也许她们是小龙女或峨眉派的弟子吧。

我爱北京的每一条街，每个角落，每处我去过的地方，它们给了我强烈的归属感。虽然我在这里生活的时间还不是很长，但是相处的时间越久，越给我一种不想离开的感觉。我舍不得离开这里。若是有人问我："北京是个怎样的城市？"我一定会说："她是非常值得你亲自来感受的一座城市。中国，也是非常值得你来的伟大国度！"

我的中国之路
My Journey to China

［巴布亚新几内亚］ 卡迈　中国石油大学（华东）

[Papua New Guinea] Nakemai Aileen Swawe Wangihomie, China University of Petroleum (East China)

Traveling from my country to China is no short journey. It is even longer to learn Chinese from scratch and to finish school and get employed in China. My journey to China started here three years ago.

I am very grateful that the Chinese government provided me with a full scholarship to study. On September 9, 2015, I left my country Papua New Guinea. After flying for six hours with a transfer in Singapore, I finally arrived in Beijing, a brand new world. Such a long road!

After arriving in Beijing, I needed to go to my next stop, Tianjin University. After doing a lot of research, I found several ways to Tianjin. It takes two hours to get there by taxi, 30 minutes by high speed train, and about 5 hours by bus. The ways are endless. With the help of warm-hearted Chinese people, I finally took the bus leaving for Tianjin. When I arrived at the Tianjin Bus Station, a taxi took me to my would-be university.

What struck me most was the good road condition. Many cars drive at high speeds on the wide and straight highways. The mountainous landscape of my country makes the road building extremely difficult. But Chinese people did

从我的国家来到中国，是一条很长的路；从不会说一个汉字到用汉语学习我的专业，是一条很长的路；从完成我的学习到以后在中国工作，又是一条很长的路。这就是我的路，我的中国之路，一条开始在 3 年之前的中国之路。

我非常感激中国政府提供全额奖学金让我来中国学习。2015 年 9 月 9 日，我离开了我的国家巴布亚新几内亚，飞行了大概 6 小时，经过新加坡抵达中国北京，到达了一个完全陌生的世界。这真的是一条非常远的路。

到了北京后，我需要去天津大学。在不知疲倦地寻找信息之后，我找到了几条"路"可以去天津：大约 2 小时的时间乘坐出租车，需要 30 分钟乘坐快速列车，需要大约 5 小时乘坐巴士。哇，有这么多"路"可以带你到另一个地方。在热心人的帮助下，我最后登上了巴士出发去天津。抵达天津巴士站后，我被一台非常舒适的出租车送到了天津大学。

给我印象最深的是一路上中国的路太好了。高速路很宽很直，很多车以很快的速度前进。在我的国家巴布亚新几内亚有很多很多的山，这使得修路成为一件很难的事情。但是中国太厉害了，路修得真是太好了，我对这个印象非常深刻。

a really good job, which really impressed me.

I love Tianjin, but I had to leave for another city after finishing my language course. On August 30, 2016, I moved to Qingdao and started my study in China University of Petroleum.

On campus, my professors and classmates always talked about "Lu" (road, way, or journey in English). For example, there is no royal road to learning but diligence; traveling thousands of miles is better than reading thousands of books; all roads lead to Rome; the road is under foot... I could not fully understand them at first, but later I knew that what they talked about was not literal but transcended words.

Gradually, I found my own way for learning and for living. Words can hardly express my gratitude to my professors and classmates. With their help, I avoided detours and found the most efficient way to live and study. I saved a lot of time and energy making new friends, from whom I learned how to shop online and pay bills by WeChat and Alipay.

Three years ago, before I came to China, I only knew a little about this country. For me, it was an Asian country more advanced than my own. Along my way to many Chinese cities, such as Beijing, Tianjin, Jinzhou and Hefei, I have witnessed China's soaring economy. Over the past three years, I have also seen how advanced China's high-speed trains, planes, highways and online shopping are. All Chinese people I see are always busy with something, and I believe that they too are walking their road, or "Lu".

I do love China. I love China's traditional culture and I have gradually fallen in love with delicious Chinese food, but what I love most are the kind Chinese people. Just as I said before, after graduation, I hope to live here and find an ideal job so as to continue my journey.

我喜欢天津，但是完成我的汉语学习后我不得不离开去另一个城市。2016 年 8 月 30 日我移居青岛，在中国石油大学开启了我的专业学习之路。

在中国石油大学，老师们和同学们经常说的很多事情就是"路"。书山有路勤为径，学海无涯苦作舟；读万卷书，行万里路；条条大路通罗马；路在脚下……我都不懂他们说的"路"的意思。后来，我懂得了他们说的"路"不是"马路"，而是方法、办法和思路。

慢慢地，我在学校和城市生活中找到了自己的"路"。我很感谢我的老师们和同学们，因为他们的帮助，我找到了最短的路去学习和生活，这使得我避开了一些错路，我省下了很多时间和精力。我也交了很多朋友，学会了网购、使用微信和支付宝支付，生活变得更加轻松了。

3 年以前，就是在我来中国之前，我对中国只了解一点点，我只能说我知道中国是比我的小岛县更发达的亚洲国家。我去过中国好多地方，比如北京、天津、锦州、合肥等。现在我知道了中国的经济很厉害，中国的高铁、飞机、网购、高速公路都很厉害。当中国人走在路上的时候，他们看起来都很匆忙，他们肯定都在为中国梦忙碌，我觉得这就是中国人正在努力走的自己的"路"。

总的来说，我非常喜欢中国。我喜欢中国的传统文化，并且我慢慢习惯了丰富美味的食物，但是我最喜欢中国的还是这里友善的人们。就像我之前所说的那样，我希望毕业后能生活和工作在中国，继续我的中国之路。

中国石油大学（华东）提供

迅速发展的中国
Booming China

[印度尼西亚] 林贤真 华南师范大学

[Indonesia] Giovanny Ariesta Hermanto, South China Normal University

I am a Chinese-Indonesian. My grandfather, a native Chinese, left China in 1931. Since China had not yet opened up to the outside world at that time, he was unable to return home. In 1978, upon hearing that China launched the reform and opening-up policy, he tried his best to get in touch with relatives in the mainland of China but to no avail. Our straitened circumstances back then made it impossible for him to get back to his motherland. He could only cling to his memories, wishing to go back in dreams. Not long after, he passed away with regret. For us, our vague impression about China and how Chinese people live only came from the elder generation, newspaper, TV programs and magazines. It was not until 2010 that my parents and I got the chance to visit some cities in south China. In my eyes, the mainland of China and Indonesia's major cities was then at a similar development stage, while Hong Kong and Macao, the two Special Administrative Regions, were at stages above.

In September 2017, I furthered my study in Guangzhou. I found it incredible that this city was far different from the place I lived 7 years ago. Now, Guangzhou is bristling with skyscrapers and enjoys orderly road networks

我是一名印尼华裔。我的爷爷从 1931 年离开中国后，就再也没能重返家园，因为当时中国还未对外开放。1978 年，中国打开了国门，开始实行改革开放政策，当时爷爷立即想方设法联系在大陆的家人，可惜一无所获。由于当时家境困窘，无法回到中国，爷爷只能在回忆中，在梦中重回祖国，他最终带着遗憾离开了人世；而子孙也只能在老一辈人的谈论中，在报纸、电视、杂志中了解中国以及中国人的生活。直到2010 年，我和父母才有机会来到中国南部的一些城市旅游。在我看来，当时中国内地的发展水平与印尼的大城市差不多，而香港和澳门两地相对来说更发达一些。

2017 年 9 月，我来到广州留学。当时我对这个城市的变化感到难以置信，这儿完全不像我 7 年前来过的地方。现在的广州到处都是高楼大厦，交通和城市规划都非常整齐，而最令我感到惊叹的是中国科技的发展。中国科技的迅速发展引领着中国高铁的"飞奔"。我曾从广州乘坐高铁到桂林，这真是一个令人难忘的旅程：快捷的速度，舒适的环境，单独提供的电源及 USB 接口等，都让我享受到了一场不一样的美妙旅行。中国科技的快速发展引领着中国互联网经济和移动支付的迅速普及。在

and sound urban planning. However, what impressed me most was the technological advancement in China which supports high-speed trains run across the country. I once took the train from Guangzhou to Guilin. The rapid speed, the comfortable environment, the charging station and USB port for every passenger all made this journey wonderful and unforgettable. Meanwhile, the fast-developing technology has driven the development of internet economy and the application of mobile payment. In China, you do not need to carry your wallet because most transactions can be concluded on your mobile phone. Payment can be easily made in two steps: scanning the QR code and entering your password. The user does not have to be bothered with looking for changes in wallet, which saves time for both sellers and consumers and avoids the circulation of counterfeit money. Beyond that, the rapid technological development has also encouraged the growth of sharing economy. Beautiful shared bikes are everywhere on the streets. Scan the QR code by mobile phone, and you are ready to go.

A safe environment matters the most. China gives me a real sense of security. Here, I do not need to worry about theft, robbery, terrorist attack and shooting. I dare go out alone at night because surveillance equipment is installed every corner, such as roads, subways, cars, buses and skyscrapers, with guard and police protecting us.

As an ethnic Chinese, I am amazed by the phenomenal changes that have taken place in China since the implementation of the reform and opening-up policy and truly proud of its prosperity. It is a pity that my grandfather could not see all of these by himself. I hope to tell my grandpa what I have seen here after I return back, and I believe he would be delighted.

华东师范大学提供

中国，几乎在大部分地方买东西时，都不需要带钱包，只需要用手机扫二维码，输入一下密码，支付的过程就完成了。既不用麻烦掏口袋，又不用找零。这样一来不但省了买卖双方的时间，还避免了假币的循环。中国科技引领着共享经济的飞速发展。我们在马路上走着就可以看到路边排着颜色艳丽的共享单车。人们用手机扫一下二维码，就可以马上使用，极其方便。

　　千好万好不如安全好！中国是一个让我感觉最安全的地方，不用担心偷盗与抢劫，不用担心恐怖袭击，不用担心枪击事件。中国城市许多角落，道路、地铁、公交、高楼都安装了监控设备，保安和巡警也容易找到，在中国我敢一个人晚上出门。

　　身为一名华裔，看到改革开放后中国的巨大变化，惊叹于中国的巨大变化，同时也为中国的繁荣昌盛感到自豪。只可惜爷爷没来得及看到这一切。我心里抱着一个愿望，就是回国祭拜爷爷时一定要告诉他这一切，让他在九泉之下也感到欣慰。

美丽的缘分
Blessed Fate

[泰国]　谢曼蓉　西北大学
[Thailand] Sanamad Nidchakan, Northwest University

Rainy Xi'an in July is not as hot and dry as before. It is the first time that I see such long rainy days in Xi'an after being in China for more than two years. Though I have got my master's degree, I cannot find it in my heart to leave China for all those joyful memories, days of learning and people I love . The sky should have no emotions, but why does it rain for days in the time of parting? I'm saddened by the rain and my leaving.

I'm amazed by the pace of Xi'an toward modernization. Surrounded by high-rise buildings, people are busy at work to keep this city bustling with life. Cars, benefited by the convenient transportation network, drive orderly and slow down to give way to approaching pedestrians. SAGA International Shopping Mall boasts the first escalator in Asia which can carry shoppers non-stop to the sixth floor. Only smart and diligent Chinese people have the ability of building such feats. At night, Xi'an puts on its colorful night garment. After a busy day, people can have a moment of peace here. The yellow lamps light up the city wall. On the square near Yongning Gate, the grand dancing performance Chang'an Impression is put on display; the height of Asia's largest water fountain, at the south square of Dayan

　　进入七月，西安突然阴雨绵绵，没有了之前的燥热。我在中国两年多，这么久的阴雨天，在西安还是第一次见到。我已硕士毕业，将要离开这个美丽的国家，这里有我太多的欢乐和牵挂，我不想离开。天空应该没有感情吧？但它为什么在我要离开的时候，下起这场连阴雨？雨淋湿了地面，也淋湿了我的心情。

　　我惊叹西安高速的现代化发展。街上到处是高楼大厦，人们忙碌在自己的岗位，维持着这座城市的活力。交通很方便，宽阔的马路上，虽然车辆很多，却始终没有混乱；遇到行人，车辆都主动停下来让行。在小寨的赛格商城，有着亚洲第一梯，一条扶梯从一楼直到六楼，只有聪明勤劳的中国人，才能创造出这样的奇迹。夜晚时，西安开始了灯红酒绿的夜景，忙了一天的人，可以享受片刻的悠闲。黄色的彩灯把城墙的棱角照得更清楚；永宁门的广场上，正在进行着大型的歌舞表演——梦长安；在大雁塔南广场，喷泉伴着欢快的音乐有节奏地变化着水柱的高度；在德福巷的轻酒吧，年轻人小饮一杯，分享生活的喜悦和忧愁；宽阔的环城公园沿着护城河建立，给喧闹的城市保留了一块安静的土地。

　　听人说：五岳归来不看山，黄山归来不看岳。不管是五岳，还是黄

Pagoda, is changing to the rhythm of joyful music; youth in bars of Defu Lane share the joys and pains of life in toasts; the wide City Park is built along the moat, saving a piece of quiet land for the bustling city.

Some people said that the landscape of the Five Great Mountains belittles those elsewhere, and the landscape of Huangshan tops that of the Five Great Mountains. I thought about visiting these five great mountains and Huangshan, but I underestimated the broadness and richness of China. Though I have only been to Sichuan, I was highly impressed and fascinated by its natural beauty. Chinese pandas there captured my heart with their cuteness. A group of naughty monkeys sometimes would play with visitors and even steal stuff without anyone's notice. What impressed me the most was Leshan Giant Buddha. It sits quietly among mountains and rivers, guarding all ships passing under its feet. When visiting this place, people can't help but be left in awe. It is regretful that I haven't had time to visit other such sceneries across China.

When the leaves turn yellow next year, I will be back to China to keep my promise to him. Buddha once said it takes 500 times of look-back in the past lives to come across with each other in this life. We, born in different countries, must have kept looking back into our past lives to meet and fall in love with each others. Though lovesickness is painful, I am only on a temporary leave. On the wishing wall of Da Xingshan Temple, we wrote down our best wishes and promises. Even though the wind and rain may blur out those words, they are still engraved in our hearts.

It's still raining, just like my mood of leaving. However, this is just a temporary leave, and I will be back to this beautiful country next year, because there is someone waiting for me. After then, I will enjoy this wonderful city life, travel around China with him, and write our story together.

山，我曾经都打算去拜访。我低估了中国的辽阔和丰富，仅仅去了四川，我就惊叹于自然的神奇，三月不知道肉味。这里有中国的大熊猫，它们憨厚的动作俘获了我

西北大学提供

的心；一群调皮的猴子，偶尔会去和游客打闹，趁人不注意，抢了他们手中的东西，让人哭笑不得。更让我震惊的，是那座乐山大佛，它端坐在山水之间，默默地守护着脚下过往的船只。分不清哪里是山，哪里是佛，佛就是山，山也是佛。中国还有很多山川，很遗憾我没有时间去拜访。

明年树叶变黄的时候，我还会回到中国，只为与他之间的约定。佛说，前世的五百次回眸，才换来今生的擦肩而过。我们生长于不同的国家，却能相遇、相知、相恋，前世一定都在不停地回头吧？相见何如未见时，感叹相思的无奈，但离别是暂时的，我不后悔这美丽的缘分。在大兴善寺的许愿墙上，我们曾经写下了美好的愿望和誓言，即使风雨模糊了字迹，它也深深地刻在我们的心里，字字清晰。

雨依然不停地下，像离别的心情。这只是短暂的离开，明年，我还会回到这个美丽的国家，因为这里有一个人在等我。从此，和重要的人，一起享受这繁华的都市生活，一起走遍中国的山山水水，一起书写我们的故事。

我要看看中国的模样

—— "洞察中国" 全球胜任力社会实践

See What China Embodies

—*"Insight into China" Global Competency Social Practice*

[哥伦比亚] 大卫海纳 清华大学

[Colombia] David Janna David, Tsinghua University

After participating in the "Insight into China, Global Competency Social Practice" organized by the Practice Department of Graduate Youth League Committee of Tsinghua University, not only were my impression and understanding about the development of contemporary China and its long cultural history deepened, but also my longtime dream came true. This is one of my most memorable experiences in China.

With careful organization and arrangement of the sponsor, we visited some very important and interesting places, such as the headquarters of LAIX, the Shanghai Stock Exchange, Fudan University, and the CPC Committee of Shanghai Pudong New District, which I really longed for. Even the leaders and members of the CPC, whom we encountered later, said they themselves had yet to visit these places; thus, I felt honored. The leaders also shared their own stories with us, and exchanged their views on China's development and the 19th National Congress of the CPC, from which I really benefited.

　　通过参加清华大学研究生团委实践部组织的"洞察中国，全球胜任力社会实践"活动，我不但加深了对当代中国经济发展和悠久文化历史的感受和体验，而且也圆了长期以来的梦想。这是我在中国最难忘的经历之一。

　　在主办方的精心组织和安排下，我们参观了一些十分重要和有意思的地方，比如英语流利说的总部、上海证券交易所、复旦大学以及我最为向往的中国共产党上海市浦东新区委员会，就连后来与我们偶遇的领导和共产党员都说他们未能有机会进入这些地方，我因此而倍感荣幸。领导们还和我们分享了他们自己的故事，并和我们交流了对于中国发展、对于十九大的看法，我感到受益匪浅。

　　在清华大学"洞察中国，全球胜任力社会实践"活动的准备过程中我学到了很多。为了参加这个活动我花了很长时间学习中国共产党十九大报告，特别是"一带一路"的相关部分。我们周日晚上跟复旦大学的研究生一起进行了十九大报告的座谈会，在座谈会上我做了一个关于

I learned a lot during the preparation for the "Tsinghua University, Insight into China, Global Competency Social Practice" . In order to participate in this activity, I spent a long time studying the Report of the 19th CPC National Congress, especially the relevant parts of the Belt and Road Initiative. On Sunday night, we had a symposium of the report to the 19th CPC National Congress with the graduate students of Fudan University. At the symposium, I made a sharing about the Belt and Road Initiative. We visited many important places, for example, the CPC Committee of Shanghai Pudong New District and Shanghai Stock Exchange. I asked government leaders the same question: "What's the role and contribution of Shanghai Stock Exchange and the Pudong New District for the Belt and Road Initiative?" Though the question was the same, their answers varied within the spectrum. As a very comprehensive plan, it will affect all industries in China.

I asked Cai Min, Deputy Director of Human Resources and Social Security Bureau of Shanghai Pudong New District: "As a student, I spent a long time learning Chinese culture, and 'Do in Rome' took me a long time. 'Do in Rome' includes learning Chinese, understanding ancient culture and so on. Learning about the Chinese government is also an important attempt for me to do as the Romans do. One of my favorite things about the Chinese government is its 'core socialist values'. One of my favorite values is 'patriotism'. No doubt, all values are important, but I'm curious, and I want to know which value do you think is the most important one? Why?"

Ms. Cai's answer was interesting. First, they were surprised at the fact that I knew these values. Then they explained to me how important these values are to Chinese society. They are all special and valuable. These values coexist and

"一带一路"的分享。通过这个活动，我更为深入地学习了"一带一路"，最重要的是了解了"一带一路"的全面性。这几天我们参观了很多十分重要的地方，比如，中国共产党上海市浦东新区委员会和上海证券交易所，我在两个地方都问过政府领导们一模一样的问题："上海证券交易所浦东新区在'一带一路'中有什么贡献和充当什么样的角色？"最有意思的是，虽然我问的问题是一样的，但是两个地方领导的答案是不同却相关的：作为一个非常全面的计划，它会影响中国的各个产业。

　　我曾询问上海市浦东新区人力资源和社会保障局副局长蔡敏女士，"作为一名留学生，我花了很长时间学习中国的文化，花了很长时间'入乡随俗'。入乡随俗包括学习中文、了解古代文化等。通过学习了解你们的政府也是我入乡随俗中的重要尝试。我最喜欢中国政府的一点是：中国的'社会主义核心价值观'。其中，我最喜欢的价值观是'爱国'。毫无疑问，所有的价值观都很重要，但是我很好奇，我想知道你觉得哪

作为华东师范大学 2017 届优秀留学生代表在毕业典礼上发言

together constitute the values of Chinese society.

When we arrived at the Shanghai Urban Planning Exhibition Hall and saw the photos of Wenchuan Earthquake in the exhibition, I realized for the first time what a special school Tsinghua University is. In those photos of the earthquake relief, I saw many people in Tsinghua University who left their jobs, their schools and cities immediately for Wenchuan and help their country overcome one of the worst natural disasters in history. For the first time, I experienced the feelings of home and country of Tsinghua people. No matter how big the challenges faced by Tsinghua people are, they are willing to take on the responsibilities of the country and society, go to the most dangerous and critical front line and make their own contributions to the homeland. Tsinghua

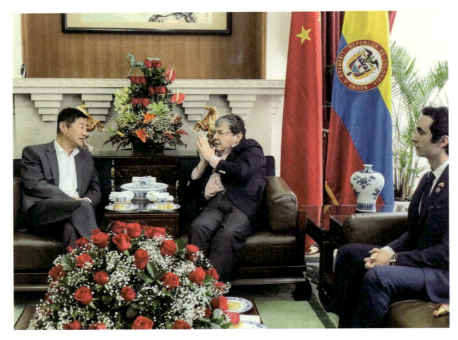

参与中国驻哥伦比亚大使与哥伦比亚外长的会晤

清华大学 / 吴璟薇摄

一个价值观是最重要的？为什么？"

　　蔡敏女士的答案是非常有趣的。领导们先是很诧异：我居然能知道这些价值观，随后他们向我深入浅出地解释了这些价值观对中国社会的重要性。他们告诉我们，没有一个价值观比另一个价值观更重要，相反，它们都是有价值的特别的存在，这些价值观共存，共同构成了中国社会的价值观。

　　当我们到达上海城市规划展示馆，看到展览中的汶川地震照片时，我第一次意识到清华是一所多么特别的学校。在这一张张抗震救灾的照片中，我看到了许多清华人的身影，他们在第一时间离开自己的工作岗位，离开自己的学校和城市，来到汶川一线，去帮助自己的国家克服历史上最严重的自然灾害之一。第一次，我体会到清华人的家国情怀，不

University is the place cultivating the future national pillars. Tsinghua alumni are not only intelligent, but also always remember their own social responsibility.

Finally, I want to express my thanks to the "Insight into China, Global Competency Social Practice" : first of all, I would like to thank this country and the city of Beijing, for its openness and inclusiveness, providing international students the opportunity to learn, experience, become a part of China's progress and development, and participate in China's social development. I would also like to thank every student in the Practice Department of the Graduate Youth League Committee of Tsinghua University for providing us with opportunities and building a platform for us to have a deeper understanding of China. I also sincerely call on all international students. Let us study together in China, live in China, and explore and practice our overseas students' own "Chinese dream" !

清华大学 / 吴璟薇摄

管清华人面对的挑战有多大，他们愿意担任起国家和社会的责任，到最危险、最危急的前线，为国家尽一份自己的力量。清华大学培养的是未来的国家栋梁，他们不仅十分聪慧，还时刻谨记自己身上的社会责任。

最后，我想表达对于参加此次"洞察中国，全球胜任力社会实践"活动的感激之情：首先我想感谢中国这个国家，感谢北京这个城市，这里是如此开放包容，才让我们国际学生有机会来学习，来体验，成为中国进步和发展的一部分，参与到中国社会发展变革的重要时期当中。我也想感谢清华大学研究生团委实践部的每一位学生，感谢他们为我们提供了机会，为我们搭建了深入了解中国的平台。我也衷心呼吁所有国际学生，让我们一起乐学在中国，乐活在中国，一起探究并实践我们留学生自己的"中国梦"！

留学散记
Recollection of Studies in China

[日本] 高野梓　北京师范大学
[Japan] Takano Azusa, Beijing Normal University

In 2016, I was admitted into the School of Chinese Language and Culture, Beijing Normal University. At the very start, I encountered so many fantastic things, some of which were kind of confusing while others quite surprising. However, as I gradually got used to the lifestyle of Chinese people, I found many life aspects which are worth of trying and learning. As far as I am concerned, making friends and mobile phone operating are two aspects that impress me a lot.

Making Friends

"Hey, what college are you in? May I have your WeChat?" is what I heard most frequently since the first day of my university life. Most Chinese people will say something similar to people they meet for the first time and become friends with them really quickly. In contrast, Japan attaches special importance to etiquette, thus being impolite to people whom you have just met is a taboo. In Japan, dealing with the relationship between superior and subordinate and between colleagues is especially a minefield, because if one is not polite enough, the other will feel offended. Therefore, we Japanese are meticulous

2016 年的中国高考季，我考入了北京师范大学，入读文学院。留学生活开始后，我遇到了许多"不可思议"的事情，它们有时让我无法理解，有时又让我措手不及。但是在我逐渐习惯了留学生活后，我发现其中有许多值得一试、值得学习的地方。在我的心目中，它们就是交友方式和手机操作。

交朋友

"同学，你是哪个学院的？我们加一下微信吧。"这是我进了大学以后常常听到的一句话。大多数中国人都会对初次见面的人说类似的话，而且认识之后很快就能成为朋友。日本是一个很重视礼仪的国家，对初次见面的人一定不能做出失礼的行为。上下关系和同事关系更是严格，如果一方的礼节不到位，另一方会感到不舒服，嫌他没有礼貌。所以日本人第一次与别人见面时，对鞠躬、说敬语和礼貌性的问候等所有的言谈举止都很在意。有时这种行为甚至会导致两个人的关系永远停留在点头打招呼的阶段，这对我们来说很正常。但是在逐渐习惯了与中国人打交道之后，我发现中国人的那些"无礼"其实并不是没有礼貌，而是中

when it comes to behaviors like bowing, honorific words and polite greeting. It is the norm for us. On my first interactions with Chinese people I realized the rudeness I felt at first was but a misunderstanding. It is their unique way to interact. Naturally engaging with someone else is the way the Chinese people express their friendliness and getting into someone's private space could be understood as their desire to know more about you or a kind curiosity. Once, facing a problem that I was unable to solve, I, an introvert, plucked up my courage and asked a Chinese girl for help. She taught me patiently and exchanged her contact details with me. I had never known before that making friends could be so easy!

While politeness is important, it must be used appropriately. If people are always bound by etiquette when they get along with each other, they could never become true friends.

Almighty Mobile Phone

In my first several days in Beijing, what surprised me most was the way that Chinese people did shopping. Usually, they could check out by just scanning the QR code with their mobile phones. In China, from fruit stalls to shopping malls, almost no one pays with cash. I came to find that the app used for the purchases was Alipay, by which you can withdraw the amount of money you entered from your bank card if the card has been tied to the app. Hearing all these procedures, many questions came into my mind, such as how to tie my bank card to the app, what else I needed to do and how to operate it... Besides, I also found that Chinese people use various apps, such as Taobao, Dianping, Meituan and Yongche. Even chat tools like WeChat and QQ allow users to

国人特有的交际方式。中国人的"自来熟"是友好和亲切的表现，希望能踏入别人的空间则是因为想要了解对方，或者可以理解为善意的好奇心。有一次，我遇到一个不理解的问题，不善于交朋友的我也在课后鼓起勇气向一个中国女孩子请教。她不光耐心地教我，还主动和我交换了联系方式。我以前不知道，原来交朋友竟然这么简单！

礼貌固然重要，但一定要恰当。人与人之间一直受到礼仪的束缚，你让我、我让你的话，永远也成为不了好朋友。因此我认为中国人的交友方式是最值得我们学习的地方。

万能的手机

刚来北京时，最让我感到新奇的是中国人购物的场景。他们拿起手机，对着商店的二维码"扫一扫"，完成付款，没有人用现金支付，而且这种场面从卖水果的摊位到大型百货店，比比皆是。后来，我才知道那些人使用的是一个叫支付宝的软件，可以从绑定的银行卡直接提取输入的金额。听到这些，我脑子里产生了许多疑问，"怎么绑定银行卡""需要什么手续""怎么操作"……而且，我发现中国人手机里面的软件也不止这一个。他们的手机里有淘宝、大众点评、美团外卖、易到打车等各种各样的应用软件。原以为只是聊天工具的微信和 QQ 也有互相转账、发红包的功能。我有点纳闷儿，手机是这么万能的东西吗？

我渐渐对手机软件使用产生了兴趣，开始陆续下载这一系列的软件。绑定了银行卡之后，我尝试着用微信支付买东西。第一次用的时候很紧张，于是我先观察了一会儿别人付款的样子，然后自己也试着操作一下再去付了款。没想到，整个过程比我想象得简便好几倍！从此以后，我陆续地掌握了许多应用软件的操作。终于有一天我发现，我也会像中国人那样熟练地运用手机上的应用软件了。在使用手机软件的过程中，我

transfer money to each other and send red envelopes. I was wondering that whether the mobile phone is so almighty?

Since then, I have been so interested in these apps and use them regularly. After tying my bank card to WeChat Pay, I had my first paying experience. Since it was my first try, I was very nervous and tried with caution. Unexpectedly, the whole process was much easier than I'd imagined. Since then, I have learned to use more and more apps. Meanwhile, mobile apps have changed my life unconsciously. For example, when I go out, I only take my phone with me rather than my wallet and band cards; when I have a dinner with my friends, I can transfer my share of the money to my friend on the spot rather than find change in the restaurant; and when I want to manage my finances, I can check my shopping records in my phone conveniently. Mobile apps have changed my habits, making consumption more convenient, getting out quicker, study more efficient and chatting with friends hassle-free.

In China, I often meet fantastic things like I mentioned above. If I am too scared to try out new things, I could never enrich myself from it. My experience tells me, as long as I can have a try when encountering different cultures, I may surprise myself.

北京师范大学提供

发现我的生活也发生了种种变化。比如，出门不再必须带钱包和银行卡，一部手机都能搞定；朋友聚会一起吃饭，到付账时不必再凑钱买单，事后转账就行了；想管理财务的话随时用手机查询自己的购物记录等。手机软件改变了我的一些生活习惯，它让我消费更方便，出行更快捷，学习更高效，交友更快乐！

　　在中国，我会常常遇到以上这些对我来说稀奇古怪的事情。如果我畏惧新鲜事物，不去体验，不去学习，就永远不能从中获益。我的经历告诉我，面对任何一种异国文化和不同的社会现象，只要能勇敢地踏出一步去尝试，就能得到意外的收获。

在中国实现梦想
Realizing My Dream in China

［莫桑比克］ 毛思 复旦大学

[Mozambique] Hilton Michel Rogerio Mausse, Fudan University

The value of a dream should not be measured by its size or in wealth. Dream encourages us to march forward and turn it into reality. My dream is closely intertwined with Fudan University, Shanghai and China.

I am Maosi (Hilton Michel Rogerio Mausse), a Mozambican student studying at Fudan University.

Though many foreigners favor Chinese traditional culture, they do not have access to study in China. It was only after China's reform and opening-up that all these things started to change. The exchanges between other countries and China have become more convenient, providing foreigners with opportunities to experience the inclusiveness of Chinese culture themselves.

Studying in China must have been one of the most memorable experiences of my life. I used to have a very narrow view of the world, which was never expanded until I came to China. When I first arrived in China a few years ago, I was very frustrated. Since I could not speak Chinese, I was not even able to order food. Intimidated by diet culture differences, I ate nothing but biscuits for a whole week, which is embarrassing to look back. But now things

梦想没有大小之分，也没有贫富之分，它的意义在于鞭策我们不断进步，将梦中所想变为现实之事。我的梦想与中国、与上海、与复旦大学密不可分。

我叫毛思，来自莫桑比克，是复旦大学的一名留学生。

一直以来，很多外国人都对中国的传统文化相当有好感，但是外国人来中国留学曾经是非常困难的事。中国改革开放以后，这一切才得以改变，世界各国和中国的交流变得更加方便，许多外国人有机会亲身感受到中国文化的包容。

在中国留学的经历一定是我一生中最深刻的经历之一。曾经的我好比井底之蛙，来中国以后，才拥有了全球视野。几年前我刚到中国的时候曾经非常沮丧：语言的障碍让我无法顺利点餐，饮食的差异又让我无从选择，为此我连吃了一个星期的饼干，现在回想起来真是恐怖。可现在的我，中文已经十分熟练，饮食也早已入乡随俗。这与我在复旦大学的语言学习，与复旦大学师生对我的关心与帮助密切相关。

从复旦出发，我开始了解上海，这个城市的活力和亲和力使我很快适应了环境，融入了周围的世界，我甚至在学习的同时尝试创业。

have changed. I am fluent in Chinese, and I have long been used to eating Chinese food. None of these would have been possible without my experience of learning Chinese at Fudan University and the care and help of teachers and students there.

Starting from Fudan, I began to understand Shanghai. The vitality and inclusiveness of this city saved me a lot of trouble in quickly adapting to the new environment and integrating into the society. I even tried starting my own business while studying at Fudan.

In Mozambique, people told me, "You'd better study hard and land a good job. " I saw my future self in them somehow. I dreamed of starting my own business. Though I am not sure what life will be like when I'm 30, 40, or 50, this is exactly the way I choose to live. However, in Mozambique, a college student without background has a rare chance to start a business.

After coming to Shanghai, I found that the Chinese government encourages mass entrepreneurship. Moreover, Shanghai is such a vibrant city where you can achieve whatever you want and always have someone to help you realize your dream as long as you really want it and try hard enough. I feel that Shanghai is where my dream will come true. While attending classes, I also pay attention to China's various policies to deepen my understanding of it. In the hardest days of starting my own business, the teachers at Fudan University encouraged and helped me overcome difficulties and keep trying. I have always been grateful for what they did for me. As I go further down the road of starting my business, my dream is getting bigger and closer to reality as well.

I have been asking myself a question, "What can I do for my country?" I did not have a clear answer to it before. Now I can say with certainty that, "Through

复旦大学提供

　　在莫桑比克的时候，人们告诉我："你好好读书，找一个好工作。"
从他们身上，我看到了自己未来的样子。我却梦想可以自己创业，这是
一条前途未卜的道路，我无法看到自己三十、四十、五十岁以后的生活，
这正是我想要的生活方式。可是在莫桑比克，一个没有任何背景的在校
大学生几乎不可能有机会创业。

　　来到上海后，我发现，中国政府鼓励大众创业。而且，在上海这个
充满生机的城市，只要你真心愿意并且足够努力，就一定可以找到你要
的东西，找到有经验的人来帮你实现心愿。我感觉到，上海就是我实现
梦想的地方。我在课业学习的同时，关注中国的各种政策，加深对中国
的了解。在我创业最艰难的日子里，复旦大学的老师们给我很多鼓励，
帮助我克服困难，坚持下来。对此我一直心存感激。我在创业的路上越
走越远，我的梦想也越来越大，越来越接近现实。

what I have learned in China and the experience I have accumulated, I can help more people." Although I am still nothing but a very ordinary person without any background, I will work hard to improve the lives of my own and others. I believe that every progress starts from something small and basic. In the future, I should take on more social responsibilities and help more people.

As time goes by, the memory of striving for dream is the most special gift that we get in our life. Although there will still be many difficulties lying ahead, I believe that the power of dreams will be strong and long-lasting enough to get us through one difficulty after another, and secure us a place in a progressive society. I am proud of myself because I started pursuing my dream amid China's reform and opening-up. I admire China for its achievements. I hope to seize this valuable opportunity and continue to work hard to realize my dream of starting my own business in China!

　　我一直问自己一个问题："我能为我的国家做些什么？"以前我不知怎么回答，现在我可以肯定地说：通过在中国学到的东西和积累的经验，我可以去帮助更多的人。虽然我现在还很普通，没有任何背景，但我会努力奋斗，改善自己和别人的生活。我相信，成长都是从基础开始的。未来，我应该承担更多的社会责任，帮助更多的人。

　　在时间的流逝中，为梦想而奋斗的生活带给我们最特别的礼物就是不同常人的回忆。前路还有很多困难，但我相信，梦想的力量是强大的，长久的，它会帮助我们跨越一个又一个困难，使我们都生活在进步的社会中。我为自己感到骄傲，因为我在改革开放的中国开始了梦想的旅程。我现在对中国的一切都非常钦佩，希望抓住这个难得的机会，继续努力，在中国实现自己的创业梦想！

复旦大学提供

中国，我要和你在一起
China, I Want to Be with You

［越南］ 潘氏秋　北京工业大学

[Vietnam] Phan Thi Thu, Beijing University of Technology

Time is a river, while memory is the water, what I scoop up from the river is all wonderful memories of you, Beijing.

Four years ago, I was an innocent girl in Vietnam who knew nothing beyond there. Sudden departure from family, relatives and friends left me at a loss. When I left home, everyone was worried about me. They were afraid that I would be alone, that I would be deceived and unable to adapt to the new environment. To be honest, I was also a little bit afraid, because I had always had the impression that China lacked in many aspects. I was afraid nobody would know if I was kidnapped as there were a lot of people in Beijing. Under such condition, I came to Beijing with anxiety. However in spite of all uncertainty I came, settled and have gotten used to life here. And now I see that all my worries had no grounds. Beijing is so safe and flourishing, and I really fell in love with this city.

Beijing really overwhelms me with its prosperity, modernization and rapid development. Sometimes I cannot even tell whether I am living in a dream or in reality. My imagination of China before I came was totally backwards.

时间是河，记忆是水，北京，我从河里捞起来的都是对你的回忆——优美的回忆。

四年前的我在越南还是一个天真纯朴的姑娘，什么都不懂，一下子离开家庭、亲人和朋友，使我思绪纷乱。当我离开家的时候大家都很担心我，怕我一个人孤单，怕我会被别人欺骗，怕我接受不了新的生活。说实话我也有点害怕，因为印象里中国不是很发达，人那么多，万一被绑架也没有人知道。胡思乱想的我忐忑地来到北京。真的开始生活以后才发现原来北京那么安全，那么发达，我也爱上了这里。

北京的繁荣、现代化和高速发展，让我应接不暇。有时候分不清我活在梦里还是活在现实，到中国之前的想象和之后的发现真是天壤之别！

这些年中国发展很快，高楼大厦鳞次栉比，新鲜事物层出不穷，人们衣着得体，脸上散发光彩。在中国一切似乎都是快的，快递是快的，便捷支付是快的，网速是快的，高铁是快的，人们的步伐也是快的。

只要你手里拿着一部智能手机有 4G 网络就可以迅速上淘宝网购，同城购中午买一副耳机，下午就能戴在头上听音乐了。

China has developed rapidly in recent years, with numerous skyscrapers and emerging new things. People with smiling face all dress well. Everything seems fast in China, including express delivery, convenient payment, internet speed, high-speed train and even people's walking speed.

As long as your smartphone is 4G-enabled, you can directly shop on taobao. com. If you buy a pair of headphones in the city you live at noon, then you can listen to the music with it in the afternoon.

A bag of fruits, 178. 6 yuan, can be paid for in one second just by scanning the code with your phone. No change is needed.

It only takes you a chatting time to order takeout online, the delivery person will send you hot soybean milk and refreshing ice cream in no time.

To have some fun at night, you can download a HD movie online within a minute.

It takes more than 1, 000 kilometers to go on a business trip to Shanghai, and with just five hours of high-speed rail, I can eat Beijing roast duck at noon and enjoy delicious bamboo shoot soup with fresh and pickled streaky pork, a traditional Shanghai cuisine, and the Oriental Pearl Tower in Shanghai at night.

China is not only fast, but also more open, especially Beijing.

When I first came to Beijing, I always pretended to be a Chinese on the subway, because I was afraid that people would look at me strangely had they known I was from abroad. Now, you can find faces of all colors everywhere, including black and white, not only on the subway. Everybody's attitude is easy and natural, and you won't have the feeling of being treated as a foreigner.

I made a lot of foreign friends here. They all want to stay in China after graduation, just like me. Beijing can offer competitive salary, just as it does with

北京工业大学提供

买了一兜水果，用手机扫码，178 块 6 不到一分钟支付完成，不需找零。

饿的时候可以在网上点外卖，跟朋友聊个天的时间，送餐员就会在规定的时间准时送给你热腾腾的豆浆和冒着白烟的冰激凌。

晚上想消遣一下，上网下载电影，几个 G 的容量不到一分钟显示下载成功。

去上海出一趟差，1000 多公里的路程，中午在全聚德吃了北京烤鸭，坐上高铁 5 小时即可到达，下车去外滩时间刚刚好，可以边吃腌笃鲜边看东方明珠。

不只是快，中国，尤其是北京还更开放了。

刚来北京的时候，在地铁上我常常假装中国人，害怕别人用异样的眼光看我。现在呢，不光地铁上，到处都是各种颜色的面孔，黑的、白的。

comfortable working environment, and Beijing is a particularly inclusive city for foreigners. In one of the companies I worked at as an intern, the employees came from all over the world. We cooperate for the common task in a really harmonious atmosphere.

My school once organized us to visit a company that mainly deals with the African market. Their aim is to make digital TV available to every African family. Sitting in the spacious studio, I thought I belonged. The company welcomes foreign employees. As long as we have good foreign language skills and professional knowledge, they will provide us with superior conditions. I really want to seize this opportunity, because I am good at Chinese, English and French. I hope to work for this company after graduation.

I deeply love such an international, open and inclusive Beijing. I want to stay here with the Chinese people and create a bright future with my own wisdom and hard work. China is moving forward, and so am I. I am fully confident about the future, and I believe that China will surely bring light and hope to the world.

大家态度从容自然，一点也不会有"瞧那是个外国人"的感觉。

在这里我交了好多外国朋友，他们都跟我一样，想毕业后找一份工作留在中国。北京不仅能提供高工资，也能给予我们舒适的工作环境。北京对外国人的包容度真的特别高。在我实习的一家公司里面，员工全是来自各个国家的。大家为了共同的任务分工合作，气氛十分融洽。

学校曾组织我们参观过一家公司，这家公司主要面对非洲市场，它的宗旨是让每个非洲家庭都能享受数字电视的美好。坐在敞亮的直播间，我觉得这是属于我的地方。这家公司非常欢迎外国人参与他们的工作。只要具有良好的外语水平和专业知识，他们将为我们提供尽可能优厚的条件。我非常想抓住这个机会，我的中文不错，英语也很好，还会法语。我希望毕业后可以去这家公司谋职。

我深深地喜爱这里，这样一个国际化、开放、包容的城市，我要留在这里，和中国人一起，靠着自己的智慧和勤劳，开创美好的未来。中国在前进，我也在前进，我对未来充满了信心，我相信中国一定能给世界带来光明和希望。

我记忆里的中国
China in My Memory

［澳大利亚］ 倪珂 云南大学
[Australia] Nicole Elizabeth Brigg, Yunnan University

When I was eight, my parents gave me a book, *Young Marco Polo*. I was fascinated by his magical experiences in China. Then on February 7th, 1992, I finally had the opportunity to study in China. From then on, I fell in love with Chinese delicious food, charming scenery and friendly people.

I felt the hospitality of Chinese people as soon as I got off the plane. In 1992, the Chinese lunar new year fell in February. It was the first time I had seen so many people queuing up to buy tickets. I did not know much about Chinese language, but a kind and enthusiastic policeman helped me find my carriage and sleeping berth, and put away my luggage.

During my trip in China, I also met Cui Jian, who was known as the "father of Chinese rock and roll" . He gave me a piece of paper with his name on it. I didn't realize how special the paper was until I arrived at a video shop, where someone pointed to a tape with the name of Cui Jian, then it dawned on me I had met China's Mick Jagger!

During my studies, I had to learn a lot of new Chinese characters every day and practice using them, and I also learned a lot about Chinese history. In

　　8 岁时，我的父母送给我一本《少年马可波罗》，我着迷于书中马可波罗在中国的神奇经历。直到 1992 年 2 月 7 日，我终于有机会去中国学习，从此我爱上了中国的美食，爱上了中国迷人的景色，更爱上了中国友善的人们。

　　刚下飞机的我就感受到了中国人的友好。1992 年的 2 月是中国农历新年，我第一次看见如此多的人在排队买车票，当时语言不通的我得到了一名善良警察的帮助，他热情地帮我找到了我的车厢和卧铺位置，并且帮我放好了行李。

　　在中国的旅途中，我还遇见了被称为"中国摇滚之父"的崔健。他还给了我一张写了他名字的纸片，我当时并没有意识到这张纸有什么特别，直到我遇到一家音像店，有人指着标有"崔健"名字的磁带，我才知道我刚刚遇到了中国的 Mick Jagger！！

　　在学习期间，我每天要学习很多新的汉字并且练习使用它们，也学习了很多中国历史。为了学习高层次的词汇，我们要翻译报纸和文学名著，这种方法使我的中文写作水平提高得很快。我的老师鼓励我们到镇上和人交流，锻炼口语水平。我经常去百货大楼，虽然我滑稽的口音让

order to learn advanced vocabularies, we needed to translate newspapers and literary masterpieces. This method really improved my Chinese writing ability. My teacher encouraged us to communicate with people in town to improve our spoken English. I always went to the shopping mall, and though my funny accent was hard to understand, the eager salesman was still willing to help me.

I especially prefer the street food in China, and am still fond of it. At that time, I liked eating a kind of sweet potato that is baked in a 44-gallon keg and roasted stinky tofu skewered with bamboo sticks. I was also attracted by a Yunnan snack called Er Kuai, which was filled with air-dried beef and vegetables and topped with sauce. It was hard to imagine that such a delicacy existed.

I am glad to be back in Kunming again after more than 20 years. Kunming is still that beautiful and friendly city in my memory. But 20 years later, great changes have taken place in China. I do not have to wait in line to buy tickets as I just need to log on to a mobile APP to buy all the tickets I want. Twenty years ago, I spent 100 yuan on a three-minute phone call to my parents in Australia. Now, I can talk to them for free anytime, anywhere through WeChat. Classrooms are all equipped with multimedia, which allows students to learn through audio, video, and various methods, even receive bilingual and multilingual education.

China is attracting more and more foreign students. It is my great honor to be back in Yunnan University after more than 20 years, bringing cooperation in teaching and research. I hope my children will have the opportunity to study in China in the future.

云南大学提供

人难以理解，但热情的售货员依然愿意帮助我。

我特别喜欢中国街头的小吃，现在我依然热爱中国美食。当时，我喜欢吃一种用 44 加仑的圆桶烤出的红薯，还有用竹签串起来的烤臭豆腐。我还被一种叫"饵块"的云南特色小吃吸引，上面涂着酱料，中间还卷着风干牛肉和蔬菜，真难以想象世界上竟然有如此美味的食物！

20 多年后，我很高兴再次回到昆明。昆明依然是我记忆中那座美丽、友善的城市。但是，20 年后的中国发生了巨大的变化，我不用再排队买票，只需要在手机 APP 上操作就能把我之后所有行程的票都买好。20 年前我花了 100 块钱和"澳洲"的父母通了 3 分钟电话，而现在微信可以让我随时随地免费和家里通话。现在教室里都安装了多媒体，学生可以通过音频、视频和各种方法学习知识，甚至有双语和多语种教育。

中国正吸引越来越多的留学生来这里，我很荣幸能够在 20 多年后再次回到云南大学，这次我带来的是教学和科研的合作。我希望未来有机会，我的孩子也能来到中国读书。

空荡荡的白色墙壁
Blank White Wall

［加拿大 / 韩国］ 金珉志   南京大学
[Canada/Republic of Korea] Min Ji Kim, Nanjing University

When I first entered my new room, blank white walls surrounded me, like a new blank page in my life. At that time, the only contrasting tone was of my dusty luggage brought from Canada. The only things I was familiar with were my luggage and a piece of paper written with my address in Chinese and English, prepared by myself for the taxi driver. However, I still felt at ease, because I was excited to freely express myself in my new life, just as if freely practicing Chinese calligraphy on the blank white wall. I could enjoy my youth, my laughter and everything else unrestrained.

In no time, I developed a deeper appreciation for China. That was because I practiced Confucian values, which are common in China and the Republic of Korea (ROK), in my daily life. Though I grew up in Canada, I was born in South Korea and familiar with Confucianism. Life in China was full of surprises, but there were also many challenges. Anyway, whenever sharing all kinds of delicious Chinese food at table with friends I made in China, we were all very happy.

I have wanted to learn Chinese and Chinese culture as much as

当我走进我的新房间时，空空的白色墙壁围绕着我，就像一张全新的空白页。当时，我房间里唯一的颜色就是从加拿大飞来的尘土飞扬的行李袋。我的包和一张我用中文写的、为出租车司机提供拼音和英文翻译的地址的纸是我眼中仅有熟悉的东西。尽管如此，我还是感到非常自在，因为我的心中充满了能够在如空白墙面一般的新生活里像流畅而富有魅力的中国书法一般肆意挥洒的激动——我的肆意的青春、我的开怀大笑，等等。

我很快就对中国这个国家产生了更深层次的欣赏，因为我将中韩两国共同的儒家价值观的践行融入日常生活中。虽然在加拿大长大，但因为我在韩国出生，所以我对儒家文化很熟悉。虽然在中国的每一天都充满了惊喜，但也充满了语言障碍的挑战。很多时候，当我和我在中国认识的朋友们围绕在圆桌旁分享品尝各种各样丰富多彩的中国菜时，都充满着喜悦。

我的目标是尽可能多地学习中文和中国文化。我越努力练习汉字，我练习本上的笔记就越多。这些笔记充满了尝试的笔触，有时不是很工整，有时超出了格子。有志者，事竟成，我的努力得到了回报。我学会

possible. The harder I practiced Chinese characters, the more notes populated my exercise books. Those notes had a sense of experiment, so sometimes they were not neat, or even out of place. My hard work finally paid off. From my experience, I learned that the most important thing in life was people, people's stories, culture and relationships, instead of material pursuits. Soon, I learned to focus on important things in life and look beyond those imperfect characters in my practice books. I embraced everything surrounding me, including Chinese culture and spirit. I continued facing more challenges, coming out of my comfort zone, even when choosing tea. In this way, I was surprised to find some unique Chinese treasures, experiencing the Chinese way of exploring inner peace and comfort through tea. My experience in China has been an important step in realizing my dream of becoming a diplomat. Sometimes, I find that by discussion and activities, I can promote the friendship and cultural understanding between my foreign and Chinese friends to help them embrace differences and similarities, eventually building a bridge.

But time flew by me. Eight months transpired. When packing up and getting ready to go back to Canada, I noticed that I had acquired too much through Alipay and Taobao. At that moment, I realized that I had had an in-depth experience of Chinese life, especially its convenient modern online shopping system. Meanwhile, I also noticed that my room, which used to be blank, had turned into a colorful and energetic place. It was full of my memories, pictures with friends, tickets from different tourist attractions, and postcards from different cities. I was proud to check all these stickers with Chinese words labeled on many items. They proved how hard I had

提醒自己生命中最重要的事情，不是物体，而是人。他们的故事、文化以及人际关系。很快，我的眼界超越了笔记本中那些不完美的汉字，而专注于重要的事情。我拥抱周围的一切，中国人的文化以及精神。我继续迎接更多挑战，走出自己的舒适区，甚至在我进行茶叶选择的时候，我总是惊喜地发现中国独特的宝藏，体验中国人如何通过茶探索到内心的祥和和舒适。我体会到，通过额外的努力，我拥有最美好的回忆，收获友谊，学到更多道理。我在中国的经历是实现成为外交官理想的重要一步。很多时候，

在南京大学做交换生时的金珉志

我发现自己通过讨论和活动能促进我的外国朋友和中国朋友之间的文化理解，以接受差异和相似之处，最终建立桥梁。

时光飞逝，8个月很快就过去了。当我收拾行李，准备回加拿大的时候，我注意到我用支付宝和淘宝网采购了很多物品，我意识到我深入体验了中国的文化，特别是便捷而现代化的网购系统。与此同时，我还注意到当初空白的屋子现在变成了一个色彩缤纷，充满活力的房间，这里面充满了回忆，贴满了朋友的照片，不同文化景点游览的门票以及各个城市的明信片。我非常自豪地看到，我的许多物品上都贴着带有中文词汇的标签，这是我努力学习中文的一个表现。同时，我最喜欢的中国谚语和成语，让我感到安慰且激励我完成了中文学习。很明显，就像我

南京大学提供

worked to learn Chinese. I love Chinese sayings and proverbs, because they comfort and encourage me to study. Obviously, like that neat Chinese calligraphy in my practice books, my room also became fragments of my story of challenging myself and trying in China. As a better person, I left my room with pride.

(The author is currently studying in University of Ottawa)

金珉志在南京大学

笔记本中的中国书法已经变得更流畅一样，我空荡荡的房间也成了一个美丽的在中国的新冒险里挑战自己，不断尝试、努力的故事。作为比当初更加优秀的自己，我自豪地离开了我的房间。

（作者现就读于渥太华大学）

中国看得见和看不见的荣耀
Visible and Invisible Glory of China

［印度］ 李拯　中国科学技术大学

[India] Vithiyapathy Purushothaman, University of Science and Technology of China

Visiting China had been a dream that I realized in 2017. The Chinese Embassy in New Delhi organized a delegation of think tank researchers to pay a 10-day visit to Beijing, Shanghai and Chengdu. The visit not only opened a door to a new world for us, but also provided me with a more comprehensive and profound understanding of China. China has greatly improved through reform and opening-up and showed its reshaped nature in all respects. What China really looks like is different from the international media's portrayal, and only people in China can understand the big picture. Joining the doctoral program of the University of Science and Technology of China in Hefei offered me a platform to learn Chinese culture, traditions and scientific progress.

As one of the world's ancient civilizations, China has made great progress in social culture, science and technology through thorough reform. China's economy is in the midst of an innovation transition. Chinese society is moving towards a nearly cashless one with WeChat and Alipay making the need for carrying cash virtually obsolete, including online payments for all the basic necessities of daily life. In the past year alone, as a foreigner in Hefei, I could

　　访问中国是我在 2017 年实现的一个梦想。新德里的中华人民共和国驻印度大使馆组织了为期 10 天的智囊团研究员代表团，访问了北京、上海和成都。中国在各方面彰显出它的让人惊奇的荣耀。这次访问为我们打开了一个新世界的大门，为我提供了对中国更全面而深刻的理解。中国本土真正展现出的样貌与国际媒体的观点完全不同。只有身处中国的人才能理解这一重大差异。改革开放使中国的国情大为改观。加入地处合肥的中国科学技术大学的博士项目，为我提供了认识中国文化、传统和科学进步的真正的平台。

　　中国是世界上历史最悠久的文明古国之一，它的改革开放使社会文化和科学技术高度提升。中国的经济正处于创新转型中。中国人实际上是在将社会升级到一个无现金的社会，并通过微信和支付宝进行所有交易。这包括在线支付日常生活的所有基本必需品。这使得生活变得更加简单。在过去的一年里，在合肥，作为一个外国人，我可以清楚地看到中国城市的进步。合肥作为一个正在崭露头角的中国城市，已经适应了现代科学进步和未来研究的步伐。生活在一个发达的城市，给人带来生活的乐趣和舒适的感受。改革发展计划的成果在社会中是

clearly see the progress of the city. As an emerging city in China, Hefei has adapted itself to the pace of modern scientific progress and future research. Living in a developed city brings joy and comfort to people. Since the reform, China has made remarkable achievements. The hard work of all Chinese provinces has created the social total output. The reform and opening-up policy has improved the economy as well as the judicial and political systems. The export-oriented economic growth policies and the expected support for foreign investments are obvious in urban industrial parks.

China's infrastructure is incredibly convenient. China is utilizing solar energy as an alternative energy source. Solar panels can be seen on the roof of many buildings . Shared bikes are everywhere, which will hopefully reduce carbon emissions. China is trying to build clean, green and pollution-free cities. Social progress includes effective drainage systems, roads, railways, distribution of agricultural products and air quality control. China is a very green country and there is plenty of open space in cities. Convenient public transport facilities, abundant food supplies, advanced infrastructure and the use of freshwater resources have become the development policies in China. One can see that the security of the city is digital and highly regulated by cameras. China's modernization process is rapid, which benefits from the rapid development of science and technology. The scientific progress, such as quantum computing, artificial sun, digital economy and solar society, has largely guided the development of China. Even in the process of infrastructure construction and social modernization, China has kept its own culture and traditions. China is becoming an outstanding representative of the ancient civilization in the whole world.

非常明显的。中国各省（自治区、直辖市）的辛勤劳动共同创造了社会总产出。改革开放政策不仅影响了经济，也影响了司法和政治制度。在以出口为导向的经济增长政策和对外国投资的预期支持在城市工业园区中非常明显。

中国的基础设施的便捷是超乎想象的。在许多大楼的屋顶上都能看到太阳能电池板。中国正在把太阳能纯粹作为替代能源来利用。电动自行车、共享单车是最常见的，这有助于减少碳排放。因此，中国正在创造清洁、绿色和无污染的城市。社会的进步包括有效的排水系统、道路、铁路、农产品配送以及空气质量控制措施。中国是非常绿色的国家，城市有足够的开放空间。便捷的公共交通设施、丰富的食品供应、先进的基础设施和淡水资源的利用，已成为中国城市发展的标志。人们可以看到，城市的安全是数字化的，并被摄像头高度监管。中国的现代化进程非常快，这主要得益于科学技术的高速发展。量子计算、人工太阳、数字经济、太阳能社会等科学研究的进步，在很大程度上引领着中国社会

中国科学技术大学提供

Last but not least, the Chinese society embraces foreigners. Wherever you go, people are always willing to help foreigners reach their destination. Wherever you go, you will find that the Chinese, both the young and old, are hospitable. In general, as a foreigner, I can feel greater care and protection from the Chinese. Through interaction and cultural exchanges, the Chinese people have become increasingly intelligent.

China provides a friendly environment for foreign friends and improves itself through reform and opening-up, which in turn, works to its own favor.

中国科学技术大学提供

的发展。即使在基础设施建设和社会现代化的进程中，中国也保留着自己的文化和传统。中国正在成为世界文明古国的一个杰出代表。

最后一点，中国社会对外国人十分友好。无论你去哪里，人们都会愿意帮助外国人到达目的地。无论你走到哪里，他们都会挺身而出帮助外国人，不论老幼，他们非常热心地与外国友人交谈以及交流双方文化。总的来说，在初步观察中，作为一个外国人，我可以从中国人民那里感受到更大的关怀和保护。通过互动和文化交流，中国人民变得越来越聪明。

中国给外国友人提供了一个友好的环境，通过改革开放来提升自己。这一切反过来又使中国的前景变得越来越光明。

中国与梦想
China and Dream

[也门] 阿西末 南京理工大学
[Yemen] Jaidaa Asem Ahmed Moahammed Abdullah, Nanjing
University of Science and Technology

On my eighth birthday, my father gave me a special gift, and I could hardly tear myself away from it. I saw the words "Made in China" on it, but I didn't pay much attention at the time. One year later, on seeing the words "Made in China" again on the bike given by my father, I asked him curiously, "Why is China so extraordinary? Why are so many things in my life made in China?" My father replied, "China is the country with the largest population in the world, as well as one of the fastest developing countries. When you grow up, I will send you to study in China. " Since then, I have longed for the country and its culture. The Silk Road mentioned by the history teacher and the Chinese movies I watched on TV further made me look forward to coming to China. I have been studying hard in hopes to realize my childhood dream—go to China.

In 2014, the dream finally came true. When I got off the plane and entered the country, the immigration police greeted me with "Nihao" (hello in Chinese) and a bright smile. Walking out of the airport, I was amazed to find that the airport, the subway station and the high-speed train station were connected. Such a unique Chinese design had broadened my horizon. Then I took the bullet

　　八岁生日那天，爸爸送给我一份特别的礼物，我对它爱不释手。当时在上面看到"Made in China"，但是没有特别在意。一年后爸爸又送给我一辆自行车，我又看到了"Made in China"这句话，我就好奇地问爸爸："中国这个国家怎么那么厉害？我生活中的好多东西怎么都是中国制造的呢？"爸爸回答说："中国是世界上人口最多的国家，也是发展最快的国家之一，中国是一个无比神奇又魅力十足的国家。等你长大了，我就送你去中国留学！"从此我对中国和中国文化的向往与日俱增。不管是历史老师提的丝绸之路还是电视里面看的中国电影都让我更期待来中国。所以我不断努力学习，就是为了实现儿时的梦想：去中国留学。

　　2014年，我的童年梦想终于实现了。下飞机入境的时候，入境警察用灿烂的微笑与温柔的话语迎接了我，一句亲切的"您好"，给我留下了深刻的印象。出了机场，我震惊地发现：机场、地铁站和高铁站是相连的。在我印象中，这种设计是中国独有的，真让我大开眼界！接着，我又感受了"子弹头"高铁，感觉真是太棒了！

　　我先在湖南长沙学习了一学期的汉语。在这里，我发现中国人很努力，总是很勤劳，仿佛一直有用不完的精力。于是我意识到，其实中国

train for the first time, and it proved to be a great experience.

I first learned Chinese for a semester in Changsha, Hunan province, where I saw how diligent the Chinese people were, as if they never feel exhausted. After then, I realized that hard-working Chinese people holds the key to China's rapid development. In addition, I found that most Chinese people attach great importance to education. Chinese parents sacrifice a lot to send their children to a better university. The products "Made in China" such as high-speed train, mobile phones, and televisions have turned the world looking China with admiration. China is doing better than any other country in terms of improving people's living standards. In China, it is convenient to do online shopping, buy tickets, order food, pay the bill, hail cars, book a hotel, order take-away food and rent a house. The most amazing thing is that all of these things can be done on a phone, and now I can't even remember the last time I bought something in cash.

Another thing to mention is the shared bikes. You can ride the bike by scanning the QR code on it, which is very convenient. The shared bike riders you see all over the roads look very happy and relaxed because they don't need to worry about their bikes being stolen. Once I was hurried to class, I will be late either on more than ten-minute walk or six-to-seven-minute trot. However, shared bike made sure I arrived on time.

Recently, I participated in the third Silk Road Youth Touring Program. Together with my classmates and overseas students from various universities in Nanjing, I visited Jiangsu Province and many companies and factories there, and saw "Made in China" with my own eyes. I found that China has graduated its products from "Made in China" to "Created in China" , and promoted its

发展如此迅速的秘密武器是勤劳的中国人民。另外，我发现大部分的中国人都非常重视教育，中国父母为了让孩子上更好的大学都付出了很多，这也是中国的一代又一代，能在各方面都逐渐领先的主要原因。"中国制造"让整个世界对中国刮目相看，比如高铁、手机、电视，等等。中国在提高人民生活水平这一方面做得比任何国家都好。在中国，网购、买票、点餐、结账、打车、订酒店、点外卖、找房子等都很方便。最神奇的是，这些事情都可以用一个手机解决，现在我都想不起来我最后一次用现金买东西是什么时候了。

还有一个不得不提的是最近比较火的共享单车。现在路上随处所见的共享单车骑行者看上去都非常欢快，扫个码就能骑走，真方便！骑行共享单车的人往往心情放松自在，因为不用担心自己的单车被偷。就拿我自己来说吧，有一次我赶着去上课，还差几分钟就要迟到了，正常步行要十来分钟，小跑过去也要六七分钟吧，反正步行和小跑都会迟到，正发愁不知如何是好时，突然眼睛一亮，看到了楼下的共享单车，然后

南京理工大学提供

南京理工大学提供

high-speed train, QR code payment, shared bikes and online shopping across the world. This is also a way of interpreting the Belt and Road Initiative. Projects are implemented one by one; natural moat changes into thoroughfare; tidal flat becomes bustling ports; factories shoot up; deserts show vitality. No other initiative in the world has brought such great changes, and also new opportunities and challenges to China's economic development.

In a word, living in a constantly developing environment encourages me to make unremitting efforts, find problems, know myself, and figure out in which direction I should make progress. China is a great country and I'm glad I chose to come to China and spend the best years of my life here.

骑上车很快就到了，也避免了迟到。

最近我参加了第三届丝绸青年行，我跟同学和南京各个学校的留学生一起游览了江苏，参观了好多公司与工厂，亲眼看到了中国制造。我发现中国已经从"中国制造"变成了"中国创造"，并把高铁、扫码支付、共享单车和网购向世界传递。这也是"一带一路"的一种方式吧。一个个项目落地，天堑变通途，滩涂成良港，工厂拔地起，荒漠现生机。世界版图上，没有哪个倡议像"一带一路"这样，带来如此巨大的改变，也为中国经济发展带来新的机遇和挑战。

总而言之，生活在不断发展的环境里激励我不断去努力，不断发现问题，不断认识自己，不断明确方向，从而能不断进步。中国是个伟大的国度，我庆幸自己选择来到中国，我庆幸自己一生中最美好的岁月在中国度过。

没有不历经艰辛就得到的宝藏
Treasures Succeed Hardships

［伊朗］ 贾维德 中央民族大学

[Iran] Javad Yaghout, Minzu University of China

Five years ago, I was preparing for my first journey to China. In order to form a relatively clear picture about my life in China, I asked one of my friends who had been China before to make a brief introduction about the transportation, banks and shopping there. However, "three years ago, I was in China, but it was three years ago. So, what I told you must be totally different from that of today's China, " he said. His words confused me. Since in my country, there will not be any big changes even in ten year's time.

When I first came to China in 2013, there was no ofo sharing bike, Wechat pay, or Alipay. However not long after that, I went to a store and found that people did not use cash anymore and everyone used mobile phones to pay. More and more people prefer shopping online than offline. After a while, I found that there were sharing bikes everywhere on the street, and many people have already started riding them. In a blink of an eye, the era I know is over, and I have entered a new world. I wonder if I am on another planet, or I traveled to the future. Soon after returning to Iran in summer holidays, I was still estranged every time I had to pay for something with cash in supermarket.

　　五年前，在我正准备第一次来中国的时候，我请了一个曾经去过中国的伊朗朋友给我介绍一下中国的情况，以便我对中国的交通、路线、银行、购物等情况有一个初步的了解。但朋友跟我说："我三年前在中国，我说什么也都是三年前的中国，跟现在肯定不一样。"那时候我无法理解朋友的话，因为对于我的国家来说，就连十年内也一般不会发生太大的变化。

　　2013年我刚来中国的时候，还没有小黄车，没有微信和支付宝付款方式。但有一天，我去了商店，发现人们已经不用现金了，大家都用手机支付，而且越来越多的人喜欢在网上买东西，去实体店买东西的人变少了。再过了一段时间，我发现街上到处都是公用自行车，而且有好多人已经开始骑这些自行车了。一眨眼间，我认识的时代就结束了，而我已经进入了一个新的世界。心里想是我到了另一个星球，还是坐着时间汽车旅行到了未来？因此我的生活方式也完全改变了，每年暑假回国要用现金到超市买东西的时候我还感觉有点不习惯！

　　中国近年来的发展使得中国文化在世界上受到了更加广泛的关注。几年前我们国家的人对中国没有太多的了解，但现在很多伊朗人开始喜

Owning to China's development in recent years, Chinese culture has also caught wide attention from all over the world. Several years ago, people in my country did not know much about China, while now many Iranians are showing great interest in Chinese. Chinese food and Chinese Kungfu are also very popular in Iran. With an increasing number of Iranian students going to China for further study, the communication between China and Iran is at its best. Chinese culture has now gained followers. By "Chinese culture" , I do not only mean the language but also Chinese medicine, Taichi, and Chinese food culture.

In many Iranians' eyes, China is a mysterious country embodied with profound history and diverse culture. In ancient times, people lacked the correct communication mechanism to pass on important events, therefore in countries like China and Iran, people made many legends based on the real stories, coloring these old countries with mystery. I still remember when I first stepped on the Great Wall. Right there and then a thought came to me that the development of today's China was actually based on its culture and history, and the Great Wall, which was not only a remarkable achievement but a monument of Chinese culture, has safeguarded China and her people for thousands of years. The Great Wall threads through the mountains like a huge dragon, and dragon is also a symbol of Chinese culture. Like a military general, I think it deserves a bravery medal.

In my view, what contributes to the mystery of China is not only its profound history and culture but also the modern development and transformation of it. Many Iranians, affected by Chinese movies, believed that Chinese people are embodied with some superpower. And when I came to China, I realized that this kind of "superpower" did in fact exist, albeit in different form. Chinese people

中央民族大学 / 郭文忠摄

欢学习汉语，喜欢吃中国菜，而且中国的武术在伊朗也非常受欢迎。近年来，越来越多的伊朗人到中国留学，让中国人和伊朗人互相之间有了更加深刻的了解。中国文化在世界上的传播不仅限于汉语，像中医、太极拳、中国的饮食文化等也在世界上拥有许多的爱好者。

在很多伊朗人的印象中，中国是一个非常神秘的国家。中国有着悠久的历史和文化。像中国和伊朗这样古老的国家，因为历史非常悠久，很早以前没有记录事情的文字，国家的历史与传说结合在一起，使得这些古老国家变得特别神秘。记得我第一次去长城的时候，心里想，中国今天的发展都是在中国的历史和文化的基础上建立的，而长城又是这个文化的一个高峰点，它是中国文化的一个伟大的纪念碑，这个纪念碑在过去很多年里保护了中国和中国人民。长城蜿蜒在重山之间，像一条躺在山上的大龙，而龙也是中国文化的象征。我觉得可以跟嘉奖一个军事将领一样给长城颁发一个英勇勋章。

have done unbelievable work in a very short period of time, transforming China from a poor country into one of the largest economies that is equipped with highly advanced technologies. What surprises me most are China's express delivery and the high-speed train. For example, if you make a purchase on line, the parcel is received the next day in many big cities, and with the high-speed train, you can enjoy a time-saving and convenient trip.

Today we are experiencing these changes but still cannot understand how they have come to be, while many years later, when researchers study the development of China, they might be more unlikely to give an explanation about such fast development. They are full of mysteries, which are just like the pyramids of Egypt and the Great Wall. And scientists now are still trying to find out what tools the ancient people used to create such splendid buildings. In the future, scientists then will also wonder how China, in a short period of time, could make such great progress and development since the reform and opening-up policy implemented in 1978. The reform and opening-up not only brought out changes in China, but also greatly influenced the rest of the world. Like an envoy, the products made in China deliver the great news of reform and opening-up to the world. As a student from Iran, I feel so lucky to have had the opportunity to study in China, witnessing and even taking part in China's development. I hope in the following years there will be more Iranians with this aspiration at heart. China's success today is actually the reward of arduous work made by Chinese people during the past thousands of years. Their perseverance and hard-working spirit are examples to be taken into account. I would like to end my article with a saying by Iranian poet Sadi: "Treasures succeed hardships. Success ultimately comes out of arduous work. "

其实我认为中国的神秘不仅是因为它深厚的历史和文化，而且也是因为中国当代的发展与演变。许多伊朗人受到中国电影的影响，觉得中国人有超越人类的力量。来到中国以后我发现中国人确实有一些超越人类的力量，因为他们让中国在非常短暂的时间内取得了不可思议的发展，让中国从一个比较贫穷的国家成为世界上经济和科技最发达的国家之一。最让我佩服的是中国的快递和高铁，今天网上买的东西，第二天就可以收到，而高铁呢，既快捷又方便。

现在我们看这些变化，尚且无法完全理解它们的奇异，以后人们去研究中国的发展，可能更无法解释这种超级快速的发展。就像伟大的金字塔和中国的长城一样，科学家还在研究那时候的人们是如何用最基本的工具建造了那些宏伟的建筑。以后的科学家也一定会问，中国是如何在改革开放以后短暂的时间内取得了那么好的成绩和发展。改革开放不仅改变了中国，而且还影响到了世界上的其他国家。中国制造的产品像一个大使，把中国这个伟大的改革的消息传播到了全世界。作为一个伊朗学生，我有机会在中国留学，亲自去体会甚至成为这发展中的一部分，觉得自己非常幸运。希望以后能够让更多的伊朗人了解到中国的奇迹。中国人今天取得的成功是因为几千年的努力，这份意志和努力值得我们所有人学习。我以伊朗诗人萨迪的一句话作为我文章的结尾："没有不历经艰辛就得到的宝藏，只有通过努力才能得到成功。"

我的中国心
My Chinese Heart

［俄罗斯］ 李飒 中央财经大学

[Russia] Elizaveta Kleimenova, Central University of Finance and Economics

Five years ago, I was only a fifteen-year-old student who had just finished junior school life. With the curiosity and yearnings for the learning life in a foreign country, I got on the green train to China, carrying the 100-yuan notes that were bought from Russian note brokers at the Suifenhe Port. 48 hours later, I finally arrived at my first learning destination, Bo Hai Middle School in Qinhuangdao. On that journey, I felt the hospitality of the people in Northeast China, who taught me how to say "nihao" (hi) and "xiexie" (thank you) with a strong northeastern accent. Until now, some of my Chinese friends still ask me: "Why do you speak Chinese with a northeastern accent?"

Five years later, I have become a sophomore at the Central University of Finance and Economics, majoring in international economics and trade. It seems that Chinese has now become my first language. When Didi drivers come to pick me up, they always ask me in surprise: "Is that you who called me? You sound totally like a native speaker." Hearing that, I always reply with a joke: "I am Chinese, but Chinese with Russian nationality. " I can use Chinese to make PPT, write papers and do my homework, and I know many new cyber words and can sing several Cantonese songs. Therefore, many

　　五年前，我只有十五岁，初中刚毕业。怀着对异国学习生活的好奇和向往，一个人怀揣着在绥芬河口岸跟俄罗斯"倒爷"老乡换的百元人民币大钞，站了两天两夜的绿皮火车，来到了中国学习的第一站：秦皇岛渤海中学。火车上热情的东北大爷、大婶教会了我带有大糙子味儿的"你好""谢谢"，以至于直到今天还有中国朋友问我："你的普通话怎么有点儿东北味儿？"

　　五年过去了，我现在是一名中央财经大学国经贸专业二年级的学生，在专业领域中文已经俨然成了我的母语，滴滴司机总是惊讶地问："刚才是你叫车吗？一点儿听不出你是外国人。"每每遇到这样的情况，我都会淡定地说："中国人，中国人，俄罗斯族的。"除了会用汉语做 PPT 和写论文、作业之外，我还会不少最新的网络词汇，甚至还会唱几首粤语歌，所以很多人都说我是一个假的俄罗斯人。中国人形容那些长着一副东方人面孔，但从小生活在西方国家的人为"香蕉人"，我觉得我自己就是一个"甜瓜人"，外面是白的，里面是黄的！我有一颗中国心。

　　常言道：通向一个人的心的捷径是抓住他的胃。中国菜在抓住别人的胃方面优势巨大，我一个俄罗斯人就心甘情愿变成俄罗斯族了。我一

friends of mine say that I am a fake Russian. In China, oriental people who grow up in western countries are called "bananas" while I consider myself as a "melon" that is white outside and yellow inside. I have a Chinese heart.

As a Chinese saying goes, the shortcut to capture one's heart is to capture his stomach. Chinese food does have the advantage in capturing people's stomach. Take myself for example, because of the fancy food, I am now most willing to be a Chinese with Russian nationality. For a long time, I had thought my favorite food was Sichuan cuisine such as the Boiled Fish with Pickled Cabbage and Chili, and the Numb Spicy Hot. But as I came to Guangzhou, I changed my mind. I cannot give the name of the dishes I like, because all the foods there are delicious. I have been to Guangzhou with my family and classmates for several times. I accompanied them there to attend trade meetings, working as an interpreter while putting the theories I learned in school into practice. But for me, the more important thing in Guangzhou was that I could eat plenty of fancy foods, for example, roasted goose, assorted spiced meat, steamed vermicelli roll and wonton. Just thinking about these foods makes me feel hungry. A friend of mine, who came from Beijing, once asked me whether I dared eat Asian swamp eel, a kind of fish that looks like snakes. I told him that I had eaten many snakes in different flavors: spicy ones, salty ones, braised ones, and slices for hot pot and that the eel dishes in Guangzhou were served as a whole one, which were of higher nutritional value. I also said that I had once eaten the bamboo worms, a kind of insect that grow in bamboos. The fried worms tasted good. If eaten with beers, the worms are even more delicious. Hearing my words, he was so surprised, asking me "Are you a foreigner?" I replied: "No, I am not. I am a Chinese with a Russian face."

On the bank of the Huangpu River sits the prosperous Lujiazui financial district, and in western China are snow-capped mountains and widespread

直以为我最爱吃川菜，例如酸菜鱼和麻辣烫。直到我去了广州，在广州就没有名菜，因为每道菜都那么好吃。有好几次我陪同学和家里人去广州参加交易会，当翻译的同时也尝试使用了一下专业知识。更重要的是，可以去广州吃很多很多好吃的东西：烧鹅、卤味、肠粉、馄饨，想起来都让人流口水。有一次，一个北京朋友问我敢不敢吃黄鳝，一种长得像蛇一样的东西。我说连蛇我都吃过不少，椒盐的、红焖的、切片打火锅的，而且我在广州吃的黄鳝都是整条的，据说这样吃营养价值高。我说我还吃过竹虫，一种长在竹子里的爬虫，炒了以后很香，配啤酒特别好吃。那个北京朋友瞪大眼睛张大了嘴说："你还是外国人吗？"我说："不是，我是一个披着洋皮的中国人。"

中国有黄埔江畔陆家嘴金融区的繁华，也有着西部山区雪山草地、大江大河的壮丽风光。当我行驶在西部 318、319 国道，看着阳光把高耸入云的雪峰染成金灿灿的，我深深地爱上了这个美丽的国度。而当我来到汶川、北川，看到了地震的遗址，又看到了在短短几年间重新建设起来的现代化家园，我更是对这个国家的人民充满由衷的钦佩和赞叹！

中国和俄罗斯有着相似的历史和意识形态，可如今中国的发展却远远地把俄罗斯甩在了后面。总是有刚认识的朋友知道我来自俄罗斯的符拉迪沃斯托克，喜欢问我一个问题："你知道这个地方原来属于中国，叫海参崴吗？你们什么时候把这个地方还给中国？"面对这样尖锐的问题，我一般这

grassland. In this land, we can fully admire the splendid sceneries of great rivers. As I drove along the 318 and 319 national roads in Western China, I saw the snow peaks colored by golden sunlight. At that moment, I fell in love with this beautiful country. When I came to Wenchuan and Beichuan counties, I visited the earthquake ruins. But as I saw the modern buildings that were newly established in recent few years, I was filled with deep admiration for Chinese people.

China and Russia have the similar histories and ideologies, but today's China has left Russia far behind. When knowing that I come from Vladivostok, friends who have just met me always ask me: "Do you know your hometown belonged to China before and used to be called 'Haishenwai' ? And jokingly say: 'Do you plan to give it back to China?'" For such acute questions, I often reply: "Today, the number of Chinese people in Haishenwai is almost the same as that of Russians. Many of my classmates and friends are studying or working in China now. In this era of the global village, it may be a question whether our grandparents live there or not decades of years later. Do you think arguing about which side it belongs to makes any sense?" Another question I was often asked was why the Russian girls, who are so beautiful in their teens and twenties, turn into fat women when they reach 30. Well, that is what I want to know too. So I could only tell them that maybe Chinese food was helpful for weight loss. Haha!

As a Russian who has spent the best part of his life in China, I have a Chinese heart. I will go all out to put the theories that I have learned in China into practice, and devote myself into deepening the friendship between the two peoples of China and Russia and making contributions to the implementation of the Belt and Road Initiative. I sincerely hope that the friendship between China and Russia will last from generation to generation.

中央财经大学提供

样回答："现在海参崴的中国人跟俄罗斯人数量上已经差不多了，我也有很多同学、朋友目前在中国工作或学习，在这个地球村的时代，再过几十年可能就是爷爷奶奶、外公外婆住这边还是住那边的关系了，再去纠结这个地方是谁的有意义吗？"然后大家听完都哈哈大笑，说"对对对，大家都是亲戚"。还常有人问我："为什么俄罗斯女孩十几、二十岁的时候都很漂亮，一到三十岁左右怎么就突然变成胖大婶了呢？"这个问题我也想知道，大概是中国菜能减肥吧，哈哈哈！

作为一个人生最美好时光都在中国度过的俄罗斯人，我有一颗中国心。我将竭尽全力，运用好在中国学习到的专业知识，为加深中俄两国人民友谊，落实"一带一路"倡议做出自己的贡献。我发自内心地祈盼：中俄两国世代友好，人民友谊源远流长！

漂洋过海来看你
Traveling Far Across Oceans to See You

[尼日利亚] 王明 北京理工大学

[Nigeria] Daramola Adedolapo Ademola, Beijing Institute of Technology

It is always a pleasure to greet a friend from afar.

Last year, I obtained a Confucius Institute scholarship after fierce competition, and my dream of studying in China finally came true. I chose Beijing as the destination of my study in China, because it is a well-developed city where sit the best universities of China, and here I can find a platform for my talents.

At 2:15 pm, on September 12th last year when the plane landed in Beijing, I let out a sigh of relief as I finally stepped off the plane, onto a place that I had dreamed for thousands of times. The entry formalities done, I got on the school bus with the volunteers who met us at the airport. Outside the bus window were the beautiful sceneries of the city. Trees were in line, numerous buildings stood everywhere, cars were in a stream, and so were the bicycles. "Why are there so many bicycles?" I wondered. Later, I found that those were not private but sharing bikes. They cost little to use and are very convenient, which has now become a necessity for people going out. Today, I am already a "native Beijing resident". Wherever I go, I always ride a sharing bike, unless the place is too far.

有朋自远方来，不亦乐乎

通过激烈的竞争，去年我获得了孔子学院奖学金，如愿来到中国学习。我之所以选择北京是因为北京是一个发达的大城市，有中国最好的大学，北京能够给我一个展示才能的平台。

去年9月12日下午2点15分，飞机降落了。我松了一口气，终于来到了梦到过成千上万次的北京。入境手续办完后，我跟接机的志愿者上了大巴。透过车窗，我看到了外面美丽的风景。一棵又一棵树，高楼林立，汽车如流水，自行车也如流水。"北京人怎么有这么多自行车呢？为什么都停在了路上？"我想。后来才发现那些自行车是共享单车，而非私有。共享单车不仅方便而且便宜，实在是出门在外之必备品。现在我已经"北京化"了，去哪儿都会骑自行车，除非我要去一个特别远的地方。

没课的时候，大家会经常看到我骑着共享单车溜达，跟北京人一样，时不时来一句："朋友，上哪儿去？"嘿嘿，我已经成了北京人的好朋友。

In my spare time, people often see me riding round on a sharing bike, occasionally greeting my friends: "Hey, where are you going?" I do this just like a native Beijing resident, and I have become a friend of Beijing.

One who fails to reach the Great Wall is not a hero.

When I was in Nigeria, I had seen a lot of pictures of the Great Wall. Since then I started dreaming of going there. Not more than two weeks after I arrived in Beijing, I invited several of my friends to the Great Wall with me. My dream, going to the Great Wall, then became a reality, and I became my own "hero". Haha! I sent many photos we took that day to my family and friends, and they all liked them. Stroking the wall, I felt so close to the ancient Chinese people who had struggled those days and the scene that they were building the Great Wall was vividly spreading in front of my eyes.

The three savings of Taobao: Trouble—saving, Money—saving and Time—saving.

I had never enjoyed so convenient online-shopping services before I came to China. When I first arrived, I had to buy some daily necessities and clothes, so a friend recommended me a shopping APP called Taobao. After downloading it, I made a brief tour on the app. Seeing that the stuff there were at good prices, I decided to have a try. To my surprise, in the afternoon of the next day I received a message telling me that the clothes had arrived. I could not believe the delivery could be so fast, and the clothes were also of good quality. Since then I have started my shopping routine on Taobao. Taobao supports sales return, so whenever the goods did not satisfy me, I could just return them. On November

北京理工大学提供

不到长城非好汉

在国内时我会常常看到万里长城的照片，我随之有了个爬长城的梦想。到了北京不到两个星期我就请了几个朋友带我去长城。我实现了我小小的梦想，爬上了长城，成了一位"好汉"。哈哈哈！我那天拍了好多照片，给亲朋好友发了，他们给我点了很多赞。我那天和古代老百姓的苦战进行了近距离的接触，抚摸着古老的城墙，仿佛看到了古代人修建万里长城的场景。

淘宝三省：省事、省钱、省时间

我从来没享受过这么方便的网购服务，刚到北京的时候我需要买一些日用品和衣裳。有朋友推荐淘宝，我下载了后，看淘宝的货物很实惠，我决定试试。第二天下午，我就收到了短信，我的衣服已经到了。我觉得太神奇了，送货这么快，衣服质量也不错。从此，我迷上了淘宝购物。虽然有时候会遇到质量不好的东西，但可以退货，所以不是很大的问题。

11th, I bought a lot of stuff on Taobao. I really want to express my gratitude for this app! Thank you for bringing the "three savings" to me.

In Beijing, there is always a platform for you.

I am a Nigerian boy who likes to debate with others. "No", "you are wrong", "it is nonsense" and "think about it", I always say. But, I can only debate with my friends in English or my mother tongue, Yoruba. Therefore, I have for a long time looked forward to joining a Chinese debate. The 2018 Chinese Debate Invitational Competition for College Foreign Students was held in Beijing, and the Beijing Institute of Technology was on the invitation list. Thankfully, I became a candidate for the competition. When we had the debate with Beijing Language and Culture University, defending champion, I got the title of "the best debater" in the first round, which I considered as the best prize. Finally, our university held the third place. I was so proud of my team!

Looking forward to a healthier and more beautiful Beijing.

Beijing, my old friend! Before I came to you, I had known that you were ill and polluted, so people had to wear masks when they went out. Fortunately, effective measures have been taken by the government, as a result, the environment is getting better and the blue sky is even more attractive. Beijing, my friend, I love you so much, and I hope one day you will become an even healthier and more beautiful place.

双十一的时候，我买了很多东西，嘻嘻。淘宝给了我"三省"，谢谢你哦！

在北京，总有适合你的舞台

我是个喜欢跟朋友争辩的尼日利亚帅哥。但一般只能用英语或我的母语"约罗巴语"跟朋友争论。"不是""你说错了""你说得没有道理""再仔细思考吧"……我一般会跟朋友说这些。哈哈！我一直期待着有机会用汉语辩论。北京市举办了 2018 年高校外国留学生汉语辩论邀请赛，北京理工大学应邀参加，我很荣幸地成为一名辩手。和卫冕冠军北京语言大学辩论的第一场我拿到了"最佳辩手"，这是我最大的荣幸。现在我们北京理工大学辩论队取得了辩论赛的季军，我为我们骄傲！

美丽的你，快恢复身体吧！

北京，我的老朋友，我来之前在电视上看到你不舒服，有污染。有时候人们非得戴口罩。但是，政府已经在行动，污染渐渐缓解了，你的蔚蓝天空日渐醉人。虽说我们相爱了，但还有一条漫长的路要走呢，我希望我们可以一起牵着手走到最后。

北京——我的初恋
Beijing — My First Love

[津巴布韦] 史凯 北京理工大学

[Zimbabwe] Mushonga Keith Zvikomborero, Beijing Institute of Technology

Before I came to China, Beijing, in my mind, had been an ancient city that embraced profound history and was full of mysteries. There would be a lot of quadrangle courtyards and big trees; the melody of Beijing Opera floating sky above; and people practicing Kung Fu everywhere. However, when I arrived, I found that Beijing was totally different from what I had thought. She is both ancient and modern. Beijing is just like a flower. As I smell its fragrance, feel its beautiful petals and listen to its sweet words, my spirits are pepped up and I really want stay in this "garden" forever. I'm deeply fond of her.

I love Beijing. I love the food here. I have many hobbies, the biggest being to enjoy delicacies. I have been to many restaurants in Beijing, while my all time favorite is Beijing special—Beijing Roast Duck. One day, I ordered a roast duck in a small restaurant. As the waiter put it on the table, I was shocked. A golden roast duck lying on a huge fancy white plate— I had never expected it to be so delicate. I tasted it slowly, enjoying its mellow flavor. Both my friend and I were satisfied with the dish. There is no wonder that Beijing roast duck is the special!

I love you, Beijing. I love your beautiful snow scenery. When I first arrived

　　来中国以前我觉得北京是一个有着悠久历史，神秘而又古老的城市。四合院、大树、京剧的旋律飘扬在城市上空，到处都是练功夫的人。可是，当我到北京时才发现，跟我想象中的完全不一样，她不仅是一座古都，同时也是一个充满了现代气息的大城市。北京就像一朵美丽芬芳的花朵，我嗅着她的芬芳，触摸着她那美丽的花瓣，聆听着她的甜言蜜语，觉得自己的精神一下子振奋起来，我多想永远在这个花园领略你的魅力！北京——我爱你！

　　我爱你北京，我爱你的美食。我有很多爱好，其中最大的爱好就是品尝美味佳肴。我和朋友一起去过各种各样的北京饭馆，但最让我垂涎的还是北京特色菜——北京烤鸭。有一天，我在一个饭馆点了烤鸭，当烤鸭被服务员端上来的时候，我惊呆了。在一个巨大的白色盘子里躺着一只金灿灿的烤鸭。看到这么精美的包装，我都不忍心吃了，我慢慢地咀嚼着，品尝着那醇厚的滋味。我们都满足地伸出了大拇指，烤鸭真不愧是北京特色菜，好吃，太好吃了！

　　我爱你北京，我爱你美丽的雪景。刚来北京理工大学的时候，常常听到中国人说："唉，今年没有下雪！"我听出了他们的遗憾，自己也觉

北京理工大学提供

in Beijing Institute of Technology, I often heard people say "Alas, there has not been any snow this year!" I felt their pity, and also thought it a pity for myself. For some people, snow is nothing new, but for people like me who had never seen it before, it is the single biggest spectacle. I still remember the delight I felt when I saw the snow. One morning, as I was checking the Moments in WeChat, I saw some photos of snow. Dubious about that, I came to the window, drew the curtain aside and was surprised to find that it was snowing outside! The large snowflakes were slowly falling down on the ground, each of them shining with gentle lights. It was so beautiful. I rushed out with my roommates, and we took many photos. The only thing that made us feel regretful was that the snow melted too fast as the temperature outside was not cold enough, and only retaining its state on trees and the top of cars. However, considering that we

得非常可惜！雪，对有的人来说习以为常，但是对从未见过的人来说简直是世界美景之最。还记得，一天早上我打开手机，看到微信朋友圈里的照片，惊喜地发现下雪了！我半信半疑地拉开了窗帘，竟然真的下雪了！大朵的白色雪花飘落下来，每一朵都反射了柔和的光线，就像童话故事一样美丽。我赶紧跟同屋跑下楼，去合影留念。唯一美中不足的是，温度比较高，雪很快就融化了，只有树上、车上还可以看到雪的身影。但是，没关系，因为我们已经拍到了最漂亮的照片，也亲眼看到了雪的六瓣形状。

我爱你，北京，我爱你带来的便利生活。在北京，我最离不开的就是手机了。我买了一个新的华为手机，它是一把探索北京的钥匙。一个手机怎么能让我探索北京呢？答案在于一款巧妙的软件——微信。微信是我迄今为止见到的最灵活的 APP，你不仅可以跟朋友聊天儿，而且能用微信解锁自行车。任何时候我都可以扫码解锁一辆共享单车。我骑着车子左看右看，看路上匆匆忙忙的人，看周围五颜六色的广告。这是我在北京最喜欢的休闲活动之一。

除了骑车以外，我还能用微信买东西。我记得刚来北理工的时候，跟朋友购物进到一个商店，拿了枕头、被子等，我紧张地跟在朋友身后，只见他拿出手机，打开微信，"滴"的一声就完成了支付。我站在柜台旁边目瞪口呆。接下来就到我付款了，"一百五十四块。"售货员说。我学着他的样子拿出了手机，扫描了售货员的二维码，输入了总额和密码。一秒以后收到了一条"成功"的信息。这实在太厉害了，太方便了，以后出门再也不用带钱包了，只要有手机随时随地就可以买东西。

北京，我爱你！我和你有个爱情故事。在不久的将来我可能要离开你回国。哦，我真的不想离开你！我突然想起汪峰的一首歌："我们在这儿迷惘，我们在这儿寻找也在这儿失去，北京，北京。"我回国以后，

had already taken the most beautiful photos and saw the six-petal snowflakes, we felt satisfied.

I love you, Beijing. I love the convenient life here. The most indispensable tool for me is my Huawei phone which is key to exploring Beijing. But how can a phone help me explore Beijing? It lies in a smart APP called WeChat. I have never seen such functional app like WeChat before, with which you can not only talk with your friends but unlock the sharing bike at any given time. And one of my favorite activities in Beijing is to ride a sharing bike, watching the bustling crowds and colorful advertisements.

Besides, WeChat also supports online shopping. I remember when I first came to BIT, I came to a store to buy a pillow and a quilt with my friend. As I was waiting nervously to pay the bill, my friend who stood in front of me took out his phone and opened WeChat. With only a "di", the payment was done. I stood there, shocked. Then, it was my turn. "A hundred and fifty-four yuan," said the cashier. I copied what my friend did, taking out my phone, scanning the QR code, then typing the sum and pass code. Instantly, I received a message telling me the payment had been finished. It is so powerful and convenient that I can buy anything anywhere at the tip of my fingers with my phone.

Beijing, I love you. Between you and me there is a love story. But we will have to part ways soon. Oh! I really do not want to depart from you! It reminds me of a song of Wang Feng, and the lyrics go like this: "we have been wandering here, we have been seeking something here and we also lost something here. Beijing, Beijing. " As I come back home, I will miss you. The first love will always be in our memory, emitting a faint scent. Beijing—my first love, I will always cherish you in my memory.

北京理工大学提供

我永远等着，想着你。初恋就是这样的，仿佛永远陪着我们，白头偕老，但一瞬间就又消失了。然而，它永远在我们的记忆里飘着清香，北京——我的初恋情人，你会永远留在我的记忆里。

透过车窗望北京
Observing Beijing Through Bus Windows

［英国］ 冯语旭　北京师范大学
[United Kingdom] Joseph Coningsby, Beijing Normal University

I was woken up this morning by birdsong. Being half awake, I could not help smiling as I listened to the warble. Somehow as time went by, the twitter and tweet turned louder and louder. I found it strange that a quiet morning birdsong had suddenly become a loud and annoying noise. When I opened my eyes in my dim room, I realized that the sound was not from the birds but my alarm clock. It was 5:47 am and time to get up! I lived in a community that was far away from my campus, so I had to take a bus to school and get up early every day, which made me pretty upset. Through the bus window, I had observed the hot summer turning into the cool autumn, the short autumn period suddenly into grey winter days, the long winter days slowly into the warm spring, and finally the spring fleetingly into a new summer.

The advantages far outweighed the disadvantages in terms of living in a community outside the campus rather than a dormitory, as I could personally experience the community culture in China. In this way, not only could I have a better understanding of Chinese people's way of thinking, but also a greater sense of security. My life here is comfortable and stable. Every morning, I had a routine of my own: first I

今天早晨，嘤嘤成韵的鸟鸣声把我吵醒了。我半梦半醒地听着它们的表演禁不住微笑。不知为什么，随着时间的流逝，鸟鸣的声音越来越大。我觉得很奇怪，原本安静的晨歌突然变成又嘈杂又惊人的一团糟。我在漆黑的房间里睁开眼睛时，才发现那个声音不是鸟鸣而是我的闹钟。5点47分，起床喽！我住在一个离校园比较远的小区里，因此不得不坐公交车去上课，所以每天起床早得让我想哭。我透过公共汽车的窗户，看着酷热的夏天变成凉爽的秋天，分外短的秋天突然变成灰暗的冬天，悠悠的冬天慢慢地融入温暖的春天，最后看到春天飞驰而去又变成一个新的夏天。

住在一个校外小区而不是学校宿舍利远大于弊，因为我能亲身经历中国的小区文化。那不但能让我更清楚地理解中国人的想法，而且它给我很大的安全感，让我的生活又舒服又稳定。每天早晨我有个自己的程序：首先我坐拥挤的电梯下27楼，然后我去大楼下的小超市买早餐，一边用微信付款，一边很困地跟超市的阿姨打招呼，最后我直奔小区东门等候带我去学校的620路公交车。

620路的特点就是它很难预料。有时候我很容易就找到一个在二层的座位，如果那样，我就会打开窗户，享受微风拂过我的脸的感觉，让自己沐浴

would take a crowded lift down to the 1st floor (I was on the 27th floor), and then go to the store to buy breakfast through WeChat payment. I would greet the cashier. Finally, I would go directly to the east gate of my community, to wait for bus 620.

The characteristic of bus 620, a double decker, was its unpredictability. Sometimes it was easy for me to find a seat on the second floor, and then I would open the window to let the breeze touch my face and bathe myself in the warm morning sunlight. Nothing was better than the quiet morning when I was half asleep, but the passengers on bus 620 often interacted with me, which I did not mind. For example, if I opened a Chinese book on the bus, it would always attract people's attention. They would come to me and ask me questions such as "How long have you learned Chinese?" , "How long have you lived in Beijing?" , and "Where are you from?" I was not used to such interactions when I first came to Beijing, probably because British people rarely talk to strangers. Therefore, to avoid questions from others and maintain personal space, I always put on headphones and pretended to listen to music.

However on a steamy August morning, I met two interesting ladies as I stood on the crowded bus. There were so many passengers that day, and I had to stand on the stairs between the first and second floors. Next to me were two ladies who had been looking at me on the sly. When we arrived at Aoti Dongmen Station, I turned to the two ladies' direction to see if there were any seats available on the second floor. When they saw my face, one lady said to her friend, "Wow! He has beautiful eyes!" They took it for granted that I did not know Chinese, but I was complacent. I said with smile, "Thank you. "

When arriving at Beitucheng Station, many passengers would disembark, and I would finally find a seat. On the second floor, a small TV was placed in

在温暖的朝晖中。虽然早晨半睡半醒时，没有什么比寂静更好，但是620路的乘客常常给我的生活带来许多有意思又热闹的交际互动。比如说，坐公共汽车时，如果我打开一本中文的书，这总会吸引别人的注意，他们会过来问我"学习中文多久了""住在北京多久啦""你是哪国人"之类的问题。我刚来到北京时之所以不习惯这样的交流，可能是因为在英国人们很少会跟陌生人交谈。因此，为了避免别人问问题，更是为了保持个人的空间，我在中国时每每会戴上耳机假装自己在听音乐。

有一天，当我站在闷热的八月某个早上的拥挤不堪的公共汽车上时，我碰到了两个很有意思的女士。因为那天乘客分外多，所以我不得不站在一层和二层之间的楼梯上。在我旁边有两位女士一直偷偷地看我。我们到了奥体东门站时，我向这两位女士的方向转了头看看在二层有没有空的座位。她们看见我的面孔时，一位女士对她的朋友说："哇！他的眼睛很好看！"我知道她们以为我听不懂汉语，我心里暗暗得意，于是笑

北京师范大学提供

the front of the bus with a variety of news and programs broadcasting on the screen: Brexit, two celebrities advocating "no leftovers" to the public, one lady teaching audiences how to bake a cake, and a cartoon girl in Hanfu explaining the connotation of the Chinese dream. As the TV reran what I had already seen, I turned my head to the boulevard and was lost in thought, wondering what my year in China would be like.

I had learned some Mandarin when I studied in a Hong Kong high school. So when I first arrived in Beijing, I was only familiar with traditional Chinese characters and never spoke "Zheli" (meaning "here") with the unfamiliar sound "r" (denoting rhotic accent). Once when I got to Beitaipingqiao Nan Station, I stood up quickly and got ready to get off the bus in advance. As I got off, my mind wandered as I watched the college I was about to enter.

As the year nears its end I can understand taxi drivers. Moreover, I can talk to strangers without any concern. I understand that such interactions, far from being a nuisance, are a good opportunity to understand Chinese people's thinking. Over time, I come to regard Chinese people's curiosity as a positive and enthusiastic expression, and that means I have adapted to China's customs and practices.

Unfortunately, I have to say goodbye to you, Beijing.

着对她们说："谢谢。"

我们到了北土城站时，乘客突然减少了许多，我终于找到了一个座位。在公共汽车二层的前面有一台小电视，在屏幕上出现了各式各样的新闻和节目：英国准备脱欧，两位明星嘱咐老百姓"不剩饭，不剩菜"，另一位女士教观众怎么烘蛋糕，一个穿汉服的卡通女孩儿给我们解释中国梦的思想内容。当小电视开始重播我已经看过的视频时，我转头望向下面的林荫大道，陷入了沉思之中，仔细想着我生活在中国的这一年会怎样。

我最初接触普通话是我在香港上高中的时候。所以我初来乍到时，我还是用繁体字，说"这里"时也从不用"儿"这个很生疏的字。到了北太平桥南时，我麻利地站起来提前做好下车的准备。下车时，望着我即将要进入的大学，我不由得浮想联翩。

将近一年的时间不知不觉地匆匆而去了，一切的一切都改变了：我听得懂甚至可以说精通的士司机的话语了。还有，我在中国跟陌生人交谈也没有什么问题了。我明白这样的行为，非但不是一个需要为此烦恼的事，反而不失为一个能理解中国人想法的好机会。随着时间的推移，我渐渐地把中国人的好奇心看作一个很积极热情的表现，也就是说，我适应了当地的风土人情。

不幸的是，现在我得告辞了啊，北京。

给未来女儿的一封信
A Letter to My Future Daughter

[巴基斯坦] 方晗兮　中国地质大学（武汉）

[Pakistan] Tariq Farheen, China University of Geosciences (Wuhan)

My dear daughter,

Hi there!

Hope you are living a happy life.

Keeping learning is one of the most important lessons life teaches us. I know that I have always been very strict with you. But please do not think of your mother as a harsh person. That is because, when I was a kid, most of the Pakistani girls' goal was just to be a housewife, and the same is true in our home. And now I want to tell you a different story.

When I was in middle school, I read a book about a developing country, China, and about the story of Chinese people and bicycles. In that story, I saw not only the hard-working Chinese people, but also a country full of hope. Since then, I have had a dream: to go to China and study there, a dream that goes against the majority in our reality.

When I shared my dreams with those girls, they all thought I was unrealistic. I have been waiting for the opportunity, anxious and sad both. But at that time, my mother told me that opportunities are everywhere, and the

我亲爱的女儿：

　　你好！

　　希望你正过着幸福的生活。

　　别让学习停下来，这是生活教会我们最重要的一个道理。我知道，一直以来我对你的要求都很高。你不要觉得妈妈太严厉，这是因为，在我小的时候，大部分巴基斯坦女生的目标只是成为一个家庭主妇，在我们的家也是这样。而我，现在想跟你讲一个不一样的故事。

　　中学的时候，我读过一本书，书里介绍了一个正在发展的国家——中国，也讲了中国人和自行车的故事，在这个故事里，我不仅看到了勤劳努力的中国人民，也看到了一个充满希望之光的国度。从那以后，我心里有了一个跟其他女孩子不一样的梦想——去中国，去中国学习。

　　当我跟她们分享我的梦想时，身边的朋友们觉得我不切实际。我一直都等不到机会，又着急又难过。可是那时候，你的外婆告诉我："机会无处不在，关键是我们要有一双善于发现的眼睛。"这句话点醒了我，我开始四处留意中国的各种信息。

　　终于有一天，机会来了！巴基斯坦政府有了一个送学生到中国学习

key is that we should have discerning eyes. Those words woke me up and I began to pay attention to all sorts of information on China.

Finally, the opportunity arose! The Pakistani government had a program to send students to China to learn its language and culture. I signed up for the exam without hesitation, and I eventually had a chance to experience Chinese history and culture.

When I first came to China, I was very uncertain. Having had a problem with my luggage, I had to go to the airport to get it back. But I could not speak a word of Chinese, let alone understand the road signs. However, with the constant help of my teachers and friends, I successfully retrieved it. I also wanted to learn Chinese and adapt to life in China.

I live in Wuhan now, a city in central China. Unlike home, people organize their routines meticulously here. I also gradually feel the development pace of a modern city. Life in China is very convenient. Who says money can't buy all the happiness? Those who believe so must never have experienced Chinese online shopping! It's so convenient to shop in China, and products on Taobao are good and cheap.

I have never forgotten the story of the bicycle, and in this era, China has a new kind of bike. When I first came to Wuhan, I saw rows of yellow bicycles on the street, and my Chinese friends told me they were "sharing bikes". I couldn't ride a bike before I came to China, but I have come to learn. I like the feeling of opening the bike with a "ding" of my mobile phone, and I prefer to ride a shared bike around the city. One day, I met a Chinese friend while riding one. I saw him looking for a bike, so I gave him mine. After expressing his thanks, he first helped me lock the bike, and then took out his phone to open again. How can

语言和文化的项目，我毫不犹豫地报名参加了考试。最终，我真的获得了体验中国历史和文化殿堂的门票。

刚来中国的时候，我特别伤心。因为我的行李箱出了问题，我要去机场取回它。而我，一句汉语也不会说，更别提看懂汉字，认识路

中国地质大学（武汉）提供

牌了。可是，在周围的中国老师和朋友的帮助下，我顺利地拿回了行李，由此也开始想要学会汉语，一点点去了解中国的生活。

我生活在武汉，这是中国中部的一个城市。不同于在家的日子，这里的每一天人们都安排得满满当当，我也逐渐感受到了一个现代化都市的发展节奏。中国的生活很便利，谁说钱不能买下所有的幸福？那他肯定从来没体验过中国的网上购物！在中国买东西太方便了，淘宝网上的东西又好又便宜。

我始终没有忘记中国自行车的故事，而在这个时代，中国有了一种新的自行车。初到武汉，我看街头巷尾都有一排排黄色的自行车，我的中国朋友告诉我它叫"共享单车"。来中国以前，我不会骑自行车，可是在这儿，我学会了！我爱上了用手机"嘀"一下就打开车的感觉，更喜欢骑着共享单车走遍城市的角角落落。有一次，我骑着共享单车碰到了一个中国朋友，看他在找自行车，我就把我的车让给了他。谢过我之后，只见他先帮我锁上了车，然后再拿出手机来扫一扫打开。这样一个

such an orderly country achieve poor development?

I have learned a lot during my study in China. Experiences in China enable me to insist on doing everything. I believe that success is waiting for me ahead.

My dear daughter, whether you are studying now or competing in an athletic competition, you have to prepare with your best efforts, and I hope you always have confidence in yourself. You may be under a lot of pressure, but learn to turn it into motivation. Please don't view your mother as a wordy person. There is a Chinese idiom "wish your child to become a dragon", which means that all parents want their children to become talented in the future. They bear great hopes on their children and are willing to devote time and energy on them, and so do I. I hope you can grow up healthily and become a useful person, just as the Chinese spirit taught me.

In the end, mommy wants to tell you to let your dream fly freely, and your future will be different!

Yours truly,

Mother

中国地质大学（武汉）提供

遵守秩序、井井有条的国家，怎么会发展不好呢？

在中国学习期间，我明白了不少道理。这些经历也让我能够一直坚持做每一件事情，我相信，成功就在前方等着我。

女儿，此刻不管你在学习，还是在参加运动比赛，你都要努力准备，也希望你一直对自己有信心。可能你正面临着很大的压力，但要学会把它变成动力。你不要觉得妈妈啰唆，中国有个成语叫"望子成龙"，意思是父母都希望自己的孩子将来能成为人才。他们在孩子身上寄托了很大的希望，并愿意为之付出自己的时间和精力。我也是这样。希望你能像我所感悟到的中国精神一样，健康成长，做一个有用的人。

最后，妈妈想告诉你，试着给你的梦想插上一双翅膀，未来一定会不一样！

你的母亲

我的 C.H.I.N.A(中国)
My C.H.I.N.A

[美国]　林默　东北师范大学
[The United States of America] Amaryah Hannah Robinson, Northeast Normal University

I believe that many people have come to China for the study and exploration of the mysterious Orient. My reason was probably the same. However the beginning of my journey was met with endless hiccups, which also served as experiences that would later open doors. What does China mean to me? China means creating, hope, inspiring, nurturing and achieving the impossible.

First, it comes to creating. I grew up in a mountainous area in Alaska, the United States. Although my hometown is attractive and breathtaking in its wildness, it is not inhabitable. I had always been a hardworking student, but my mother fell ill when I was 8 years old. So I started my first job. I pursued my academic study while taking on work, and graduated with honors. At first, while studying, I had to do three jobs at the same time. Unfortunately, one day I injured my back severely in an accident while working. Three fractures brought to an end of my labor and sent me to the operation table. Fast forwarding many years, it was my mother's idea that I came to China to study. I had never thought about leaving the United States, but opportunities missed cannot be

　　我相信很多人来到中国是为了研究或探索神秘的东方，但你会发现我的故事是一系列的"失误"。这些所谓的"失误"导致我打开这扇意外之门，来到中国。中国对我而言意味着什么？中国是 Creating（创造），Hope（希望），Inspiring（鼓舞人心），Nurturing（培育）以及 Achieving the Impossible（创造奇迹）。

　　Creating（创造）　我在美国阿拉斯加的山区长大，虽然这是一个充满野性魅力、美丽得让人震撼的地方，但不是一个适合居住的地方。我一直是一个很好的学生，但由于我的母亲生病了，8 岁的时候我就开始工作。工作的同时，继续我的学业，并且获得荣誉学位。一开始在美国大学学习时，我不得不同时做三份工作。在做其中一份工作时，由于一次意外我受了很严重的伤，脊柱三处骨折，我不得不停止这样的工作同时接受脊柱治疗。事实上，是我的母亲发现了可以来中国学习的这个机会。我以前从来没想过我会离开美国，但机会往往是一生只有一次的。我打包行囊，冒险来到中国。是中国为我创造了学习的机会和时间，让我在伤痛中得以恢复。中国"创造"了一个机会让我对未来有了新的希望。我利用自己的时间研究语言，但不仅仅局限于汉语。我总会细心观察生活中的人。老人们

regained. Therefore, I packed my luggage and started my exciting adventure in China, where I was offered the opportunity and time to study and relieved my pain. As for me, China "created" an opportunity to hope for the future. I made use of my time to study languages, not just Chinese. And I always made careful observations on Chinese people. The senior citizens often sat against the sunlight and played Chinese chess, poker and other games. While middle-aged women would gather together, talking about their families, neighbors, and children. This was how I learned Chinese.

Then it comes to hope. I have always studied hard. But as far as I know, we pay little attention to secondary education in the United States. To cover expensive tuition fees for higher education, we either take out a loan or have a rich family to rely on. I came from a single-parent family, and my mother had to take care of four children. So it seemed like an impossible dream for me. However, China brought me the hope of realizing my dream. For the first-year study in Northeast Normal University, I got good grades on my exams and could apply for scholarships. And it was a great honor to be offered a full scholarship by China Scholarship Council. That was the first time, since I was 8 years old, that I did not have to worry about tuition fees and cost of living. In this way, China has given me hope and opportunity.

Next is inspiration that brings new vitality to me. The pursuit of higher education is my dream, and inspiration makes it achievable. China has brought me infinite possibilities, so I am inspired to motivate others as much as possible. I often served as a volunteer inside and outside the campus to help others with my own strength. And I would keep on teaching in rural areas. It was my duty because China promised me a better future. Thus these people could be

总是坐在阳光下玩中国象棋、扑克和其他游戏。而妇女们会聚在一起谈论着她们的家庭、邻居和孩子。我通过观察周围的人来学习汉语。

Hope（希望） 我一直是一名好学生，但是在美国我们不大重视中等教育，这是我的个人意见。为了实现更昂贵的高等教育，你要么埋在债务里，要么来自一个富裕家庭。我来自一个单亲家庭，妈妈要抚养四个孩子。因此，接受高等教育看起来像一个很遥远的梦想，但中国带给了我实现梦想的希望。我学习的第一年，就取得了良好的成绩并且被告知可以申请奖学金，我荣幸地被授予了中国留学基金委的全额奖学金。这是我 8 岁以来第一次不用担心我的学费和生活费。这希望和机会都是中国给予我的。

Inspiration（灵感） 使我充满了新的活力。实现高等教育是我的梦想，这灵感使我的梦想更大。我在计划做更多的事情，中国为我带来了无限的可能，它也启发我要尽可能地寻找机会去激发其他人。我经常在校内或者校外做志愿者，用我可以的力量来帮助其他人。我一直在做并会继续做农村教学工作。因为我觉得中国给了我一个美好的未来，我应该回报，这样可以鼓舞大家，去敢于实现他们想做的事情。

Nurturing（培育） 东北师范大学老师们的教育方式使我更向往

inspired and brave enough to realize their dreams.

Nurturing is the next word. The way professors at Northeast Normal University teach makes study more attractive. The professors are always willing to help me solve any problem. I ran into trouble when I first learned Chinese, and suffered from many language tests. But the professors encouraged and helped me from the very beginning. I thought that Northeast Normal University was like fertile black soil in China's northeastern areas, providing good environment and essential nutrients for students. They nurtured students, making them achievers of infinite possibilities. Last year, not only did I pass all the exams, but was also awarded the "2017 Outstanding International Student" prize.

Finally, achieving. I have achieved my dream of receiving higher education in China. Moreover, I have obtained a deeper understanding of the world and realized many more dreams. I once had a dream when I was 5 years old, i. e. to learn another language. I could not find the words to express my passion and gratitude for China. My mother always said, "Fortune equals effort plus opportunity. " China created an opportunity for me and I kept on working. I will not waste this time, this hope, this inspiration, this nurturing, and I will achieve my dreams.

China has offered me so many opportunities and continued bringing forward new challenges and chances. China has given me hope and inspired me to realize my potential. Therefore, I have achieved my distant dreams in the past and future. This is my China.

学习。学校的老师们总是愿意帮助我解决任何问题。刚开始学习汉语时我遇到了很多困难，各种语言考试也让我头疼。是学校的老师不断地鼓励和帮助我。我觉得东北师大很像东北肥沃的黑土地，为学生提供良好的环境和上进的营养。他们培育我们成长为令人惊叹的人。去年我不仅通过了所有考试，还被评为学校"2017年优秀国际学生"。

Achieving（实现）　在中国实现我的梦想。我实现了接受高等教育的梦想。我实现了更深入地了解世界的梦想，并且我将继续实现我的更多梦想。我学会了英语之外的另一门语言，这是我5岁时就有的梦想。我对中国的热爱和感激之情无以言表。我的母亲总是说："运气，就是当努力遇到机遇的时候。"中国为我造了机会，我会继续努力，我不会浪费这个时机，这希望，这灵感，这培育。我要实现我的梦想。

C.H.I.N.A，中国给予了我这么多的机会，并继续在创造新的挑战和机会。中国给了我希望，实现了我从未想过能完成的梦想，启发我开启各种潜力，实现我过去和未来的梦。这就是我的中国。

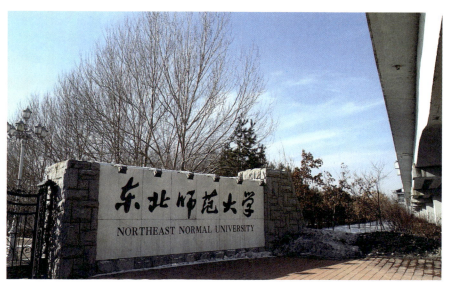

东北师范大学提供

[意大利]　康云龙　北京外国语大学
[Italy] Lorenzo Giammei, Beijing Foreign Studies University

Although I started learning Chinese four years ago, I can't remember when I began to yearn for China. I can only say that I have always loved China.

I love traditional Chinese culture. Because the traditional culture has gone through the test of time, people of different eras have bestowed different forms upon it, many of which are still familiar to people today. We can see varied and colorful Chinese characters, tea art and calligraphy throughout Chinese history. The time-honored Chinese traditional culture, like the history of Roman Empire, deeply attracted me.

I love a yellow China. Chinese characters have recorded five thousand years of Chinese civilization. Ancient and time-honored words are a kind of magic and interesting line art. The ever-changing characters express different meanings through the changes of strokes. The most wonderful part of Chinese characters is polyphonic words. The same Chinese character can make various sounds, which can be combined into an interesting sentence. For example, I have ever seen a pair of couplets. The upper line reads "long, long, long, long, long", the second line reads "long, long, long, long, long", and the horizontal

虽然我四年前才开始学习汉语，但是从什么时候开始萌生出对中国的向往我已经记不起来了。我只能说，长久以来我都爱着中国。

我热爱中国的传统文化。因为它经过几千年的洗礼一路走来，不同时代的人们赋予了它不同的形式，有许多至今为人们所熟知。翻开中国历史这幅长长的画卷，映入眼帘的是汉字的多姿、茶艺的多彩、书法的多变……拥有悠久的历史的中国传统文化和罗马帝国的历史一样深深地吸引着我。

我爱黄色的中国。汉字记载了中华上下五千年文明史。这古老而又悠久的文字，是一种神奇而又有趣的线条艺术。汉字千变万化，通过笔画的变化，表达出不同的字义。最奇特的是汉字还有多音字，同一个汉字可以发出多种读音，组合在一起竟然是一句有意思的话。比如，有一副对联是这样写的，上联"长长长长长长长"，下联"长长长长长长长"，横批"长长长长"。这样深奥但有趣的语言，我怎么能不被吸引呢？汉字书写的句子还常常表达人们的情感，比如我最喜欢的中国诗句："人生自古谁无死，留取丹心照汗青。"短短十四个汉字，体现了诗人希望为国尽忠，希望死得有意义的热血情怀！

line bears "long, long, long" . Sentences written in Chinese characters also express people's emotions, like my favorite Chinese verse, "Death comes to all men, but a loyal heart can live forever. " Only 14 Chinese characters, but all reflect the poet's belief that sacrifice for the country is death in a meaningful way.

I love a green China. Tea leaves can descend its delicate fragrance into a glass of water, and such fragrance can directly diffuse in our hearts. The tea art expresses our feelings and shows classic demeanor. Accompanied with a long history, tea leaves, tea fragrance and tea art have become symbols of China. At the Tianfu Tea House in Beijing, I stepped into the world of tea with the guidance of my Chinese teacher. I knew about Lu Yu and his *Book of Tea*, learned about the classification of tea and watched the process of tea processing. In the end, I learned the knowledge of tea art and tea ceremony from the tea art master. I also made a pot of white tea, and served a cup of tea for my teacher to express my gratitude. At that moment, I really understood the meaning of tea and relationships.

I love a black China. I love Chinese calligraphy. I prefer not only the brush, ink, paper and ink stones, but also the structure, shape and artistic conception of calligraphy. From oracle, bronze inscription, small seal script, large seal script, regular script... it expresses the character, life and spirit of a calligrapher. Chinese say that calligraphy is unlettered poetry, soundless music and uncharted pictures. In the future, I also want to be like the Chinese people to spread the rice paper, pick up the writing brush, dip in the ink, and write my life.

I love a red China. Since the reform and opening-up, China has become world-renowned thanks to the innovation of numerous Chinese entrepreneurs.

康云龙在北京城中心点

　　我爱绿色的中国。一片茶叶，落入水中，染香一杯清泉；一盏茶香，飘香四溢，扑进人们心里；一席茶艺，述说心声，尽展古典风范。茶叶、茶香、茶艺伴随着悠久的历史，成为中国的一种象征。在北京天福茗茶馆，我跟随我的汉语老师走进茶的世界。我知道了陆羽和《茶经》，我了解了茶叶的分类，观看了茶叶的加工流程。最后，我跟随茶艺师学习茶礼、茶道知识，还亲手泡了一壶白茶，向老师敬上了一杯谢师茶！那一刻，我明白了一杯茶、一份情的含义。

　　我爱黑色的中国。我热爱中国的书法，不仅爱书法的笔墨纸砚，还爱书法的结构、外形、意境。从甲骨文、金文、小篆、大篆、楷书……它表现的是书写人的性格、人生和精神。中国人说书法是无言的诗歌、无声的音乐、无图的画面。未来我也想像中国人一样铺上宣纸，拿起毛笔，蘸起研好的墨，书写自己与中国的人生。

　　我爱红色的中国。改革开放后，无数中国企业家敢试敢闯敢创新，最终让中国闻名于世界。随着中国经济的发展，人民的生活水平逐步提高，中国社会的变迁也是随处可见。城市立交桥纵横交错，道路变得更

北京外国语大学提供

With the development of China's economy, people's living standards have been gradually improved, and the changes in Chinese society are on full display. As urban overpasses intertwine, roads have become wider and the public transportation more convenient. Electronic technology is widely applied in our daily lives. Online shopping and express delivery have changed people's shopping methods. I Pass, Alipay, WeChat and other payment methods greatly facilitate people's lives. Sharing bikes and high-speed train make travel easier. In fact, more and more Chinese companies have gone out to the world. China is facing the world with a brand-new look. We are truly amazed at the achievements of China's 40 years of reform and opening-up.

Although I have only learned Chinese for four years, I love China. I love China because it is full of passion, vitality and diversity.

北京外国语大学提供

宽，公共交通也越来越便捷。电子科技广泛运用于生活，网购和快递改变了人们的购物方式。一卡通、支付宝、微信等支付方式，大大方便了人们的生活。共享单车、高铁的出现让出行变得更加轻松。事实上，越来越多的中国企业已经走向世界。中国正以崭新的面貌面对世界，中国改革开放 40 年的成果不禁让我们这些老外惊叹。

　　虽然我学习汉语才四年，但是我爱中国，因为它充满激情，因为它富有生命力，因为它多姿多彩。

世纪的奇迹
——中国交通的现代化
Miracle of Century
—Modern Transportation in China

[日本] 宫川晓人 北京语言大学

[Japan] Asato Miyagawa, Beijing Language and Culture University

In September of 1985, I came to China to study Chinese at the Beijing Language Institute (Currently known as Beijing Language and Culture University). Since my graduation, I have been working on business communications between China and Japan, involving banking business, education, IOT consultation and so on, which allows me to have the opportunity to visit many cities on China's mainland.

Public transportation: from fuel–driven to electric buses, metros extending in all directions.

In 1985, the main public vehicles in Beijing were buses and tramcars. At that time, the passengers, when taking a bus, had to buy their bus tickets from the steward. The steward often repeated it loudly with a strong Beijing accent : "Mei piao er de mai piao er" (those without a ticket hurry up and buy one). Since at that time my Chinese language skill was at its infancy, I could not understand what was being said exactly. Therefore, when he looked at me, I wondered why

我是 1985 年 9 月到中国留学的日本人，那时在北京语言学院（现北京语言大学）读的是汉语专业。从毕业后到现在，我一直在从事中日两国之间的商务交流业务，比如银行业、教育、IOT 咨询业等。所以我有很多机会游历中国的城市。

公共交通：柴油车变为电动车，地铁四通八达

1985 年的时候，北京市内的公共交通工具主要是柴油公交车和有轨电车。当时公交车还是有人售票的，乘客需要向车上的乘务员买票。乘务员同志用着北京话儿化音大声地连喊"没票儿的买票儿"。刚刚开始学汉语的我听不懂乘务员说的。我以为他说"买票儿，买票儿"。我说"我已经买了票"，为什么他还是看着我说买票？

最近两年我去了杭州、大连、无锡等城市。现在杭州的城市公交车都变成了电动化的车辆，电动车没有以前的柴油引擎公交车产生的乌黑的排气。我觉得电动车很安静很干净，在日本没有体验过电动车，所以我很开

he asked me to buy the ticket though I had already paid him.

In the past two years, I have been to cities such as Hangzhou, Dalian, and Wuxi. Now, in Hangzhou all diesel-driven buses have been replaced with electric buses. These buses are cleaner and quieter than the old ones, and there is no more black exhaust. I have never seen such electric buses in Japan, so the experience in Hangzhou made me happy. I often introduce my Japanese friends the advantages of electric buses, and every time I do this, I feel a little bit proud. As for metros, there are well-developed metro networks in many big cities as Beijing and Shanghai. Even in cities like Hangzhou, Dalian and Wuxi, there are also brand-new subways that are very comfortable. Over 30 cities in China are covered by metro lines. Both electric buses and metros are environment-friendly tools, and I am looking forward to the new achievement made in these transportation tools.

The high speed: high–speed train surpasses Shinkansen.

In 1985, it took 17 hours from Beijing to Shanghai by train, therefore flying was more time-saving. By contrast, it only takes four and a half hours by high-speed train now. Beside the ever increasing speeds in railway technology, the efficiency of transportation services has also been improved. In the past, we had to buy tickets at the city's ticket offices. Now, I can book the ticket online even when I'm in Japan. It is of great convenience. Today, whenever I have a business trip to China, I take the high-speed train, where a punctual journey is the norm, and it comes with beautiful views and fancy food. There are many railway fans in Japan who do not know the joy and comfort by taking the high-speed train in China. If they know the charm of China's high-speed train, there will be more Japanese tourists to China. In my opinion, China's high-speed train has already surpassed the Shinkansen.

心，甚至有点儿自豪的感觉。我经常向日本朋友宣传中国电动车的优点。

看地铁的话，北京、上海这样的大城市都有大型地铁网，而且已经四通八达非常方便。甚至连杭州、大连、无锡，也都有地铁而且都是最新的车辆，很舒服。据统计现在中国国内有 30 多个城市有地铁。

电动车和地铁都是环保的交通工具，我会继续期待中国电动车和地铁的发展。

高速化："高铁"超越"新干线"

1985 年的时候，从北京到上海坐火车要 17 小时，所以飞机会比较方便。现在，坐高铁从北京到上海只需要 4 个半小时，很快。除速度的高速化以外列车服务也实现高速的提升。以前买车票有非常多的困难，我们必须到市内的售票处买火车票。现在，虽然我在日本，但是也可以通过网络订票，方便得不得了。如果有中国国内商务出差，我会选择高铁作为出行工具。舒服的座位，准确的时间，怡人的风景，而且列车上餐饮质量也提高了。在日本有很多铁路迷，他们还不知道乘坐中国高铁的快乐和舒服。如果日本铁路迷知道中国高铁的魅力的话，来中国的日本旅客肯定会增加。我认为"高铁"已经超越日本"新干线"。

不变的乘客的爱心

1985 年的时候，当时的公交车经常发生故障，比如突然停车。可能是因为当时的公交车柴油引擎有问

1986 年 2 月，北京语言学院安排去成都旅行，在成都陈麻婆豆腐老店前

2018 年 9 月在日本东京站新干线前

The unchanged loving and caring heart.

In 1985, maybe due to problems regarding diesel engine, vehicle failures, such as a sudden shutdown, often happened. Every time the bus suddenly broke down, all the passengers would get off to push the car forward together. At that moment, I was amazed at the cooperation spirit of Chinese people. Without any words, they made their efforts together, and then the bus started running again. Today, as diesel-driven buses are made obsolete, engine failure is a thing of the past. However, the loving heart and the cooperation spirit of the passengers have never changed. For example, when passengers, especially the young such as high school or junior students, come across a senior, they offer their seat with no hesitation. In my eyes, such kind upbringing is very common in China, and the young generation has already made it a habit. I think such behaviors are the achievements of both China's school education and its public moral education. I'm looking forward to new progress in the modernization of China's public transportation. From the changes I saw from 1985 to now in China, the development of public transportation can be said to be "the miracle of the century". While what I value most is the unchanged loving heart of Chinese passengers.

北京语言大学（原北京语言学院）提供

题。有时我乘坐的公交车突然因为发生故障停车，然后所有的乘客二话不说马上下车，开始推车。当时我觉得中国人在紧急时配合的精神很不错。我吃惊他们无言地配合推车后，公交车又恢复了正常的行驶。

现在，由于电动车替代了柴油引擎车，就再也没有发生以前的故障，但是乘客的爱心和配合的精神仍然是不变的。比如在地铁上有老人乘车，乘客们会马上站起来给老人让座，特别是年轻乘客，比如高中生、初中生等。我觉得中国年轻人这样的行为都已经习惯化了。我相信这是中国学校教育的成果，中国的公共道德教育的成果。

1985 年到现在我看中国的变化，公共交通的发展可以说是"世纪的奇迹"。我将继续期待中国公共交通的现代化，但是我最爱的是不变的乘客的爱心。

我的美好中国回忆
My Beautiful Memories of China

［意大利］ 王小龙 华东师范大学

[Italy] Dragonetti Carlo, East China Normal University

Studying in China has completely changed my life!

When I applied for the scholarship, I had no idea I would grow up like today. I first came to China in 2013, and could barely speak Chinese back then, but now I can write an article in Chinese!

After coming to China, I experience different things every day, which helps me grow and makes me a "China hand". I just realized that my past life was a complete waste. As a native Italian, if I had not come to China, I would not have known that it is not good to wear green hats or give your girlfriend shoes as gifts in China. These are not simple cultural phenomena, but real factors that urge me to change my mind-set, my habits and myself. There are plenty of examples proving that I have blended into China. For example, I get used to drinking plain water, I learn to pass my card with both hands, I always offer my seat to the elder, and I eat with chopsticks skillfully. How can I be the same as I was when I lived in Italy?

I only experienced certain aspects of China in Shanghai, while other parts of China also deeply attract me. In the past 10 years, China has improved its infrastructure. I'm so lucky to travel to more different provinces by convenient

在中国的留学生活彻底改变了我的人生轨迹！

当初我在申请奖学金的时候，完全没想到自己会有这番成长。2013年，我第一次来到中国，当时我的中文水平非常不好，但是看看现在的我，都可以用中文写一篇文章了！

来到中国以后，每一天都可以经历不同的事情，帮助我成长，也让我成为一个中国通，因此我才发现之前的生活就是在浪费生命。作为土生土长的意大利人，我要是没来中国的话，我怎么会了解到在中国不要戴绿色的帽子，也不要送女朋友鞋子作为礼物这种有趣的说法呢？这些不仅仅只是微小的文化现象，而是真正地改变我思维，改变我自身，改变我习惯的因素，又比如说，我开始习惯喝白开水，学会用双手递给别人名片，乐于给老人让座，熟练地用筷子吃饭等，我入乡随俗的例子不胜枚举。而现在的我，又怎么会和当初在离中国 9000 公里远的意大利生活的我一样呢？

在上海的生活让我只体验到中国的某些方面，而中国的其他地方也都深深地吸引着我。中国在过去 10 年完善了不少基础建设，通过四通八达的交通网络，我有幸能到更多不同的省份旅行。从辽宁到云南，再从甘肃到香港，包括四川、台湾等很多地方我都去过。诸多经历中，最

public transportation. I have been to many places including Liaoning, Yunnan, Gansu, Hong Kong, Sichuan, and Taiwan. I will never forget when I worked as a volunteer teacher in Wuyuan, Jiangxi Province.

Back then, the school organized us to work as volunteer teachers in Jiangxi. Several international students and I got to know thousands of Chinese primary students through this opportunity. I'm honored to be a part of the activity where we helped children broaden their horizons and helped them cultivate a more open mind. Can you imagine how happy children were when they played and studied with us? In fact, I have to admit that I was happier than they were. Although I have participated in many volunteer activities, the volunteer teaching was the most meaningful thing I have ever done in my life. As the slogan of our volunteer teaching said, "Love is boundless" , our goal was to bring love and care to those innocent kids. But we found that we felt more love in them. Chinese kids are brilliant! I taught them geography. The reason why I chose geography was that when I was a kid, China seems so distant on the map, but now I am in this beautiful country. China's reform and opening-up and globalization have made all parts of the world more connected, and we are full of hope for the future.

I'm grateful for what I have seen and done. I would like to thank the Chinese government for providing us with scholarships and East China Normal University for nurturing me. What I admire most is that they have won the trust of the young generation around the world, which is hard to achieve even in western countries. We are the leaders of the next era. We will not forget the quality education and warm memories China has given us. If you get to know China, it will be hard for you to leave her and forget the memories of being here. China is home to me. I love China.

让我刻骨铭心的一次经历是在江西婺源的支教活动。

那年，学校组织我们到江西支教，我和其他几位国际学生通过这个机会认识了几千名中国小学生。我很荣幸能够参与到这个活动中来，我们开拓孩子们的眼界，也给他们带去了更开放的观念。你能想象孩子们在与我们这些"老外"一同玩耍、一同学习时会有多开心吗？但事实上，不得不承认，当时的我比他们还要开心。虽然我也参加过不少的志愿者活动，但我真心觉得这是我一生做过的最有意义的一件事。就像我们当时去江西支教的标语所说的："大爱无疆"，我们的目标就是给那些孩子带去爱和关怀，但是我们发现，我们在那些天真无邪的孩子身上感受到了更多的爱，中国的孩子简直太棒了！我在支教中给孩子们上了地理课，把我所知道的一些地理知识教给他们。为什么选择地理课呢？因为在我小的时候，在地图上看

华东师范大学提供

到的中国是那么遥远，而如今我已经置身于这个美丽的国度。中国的改革开放和全球化进程让世界各地的联系都更紧密，让我们对未来充满了希望。

我对自己所经历的这一切心存感激。感谢为我们提供奖学金的中国政府，感谢培育我的华东师范大学。让我更加敬佩的是他们赢得了世界各地青年一代的信任，而这是在当今西方国家都很难做到的事情。我们就是下一个时代的主导者，那时的我们不会忘记当年中国所给予我们的优质教育和温暖回忆。当你真正了解了中国之后，你很难离开她，很难忘记你在这里的回忆，因为她就像家一样，我爱中国。

日新月异的中国
Fast Changing China

［越南］ 希氏红绒　华东师范大学

[Vietnam] Hy Thi Hong Nhung, East China Normal University

I came to East China Normal University(ECNU) to pursue my master's degree in the autumn of 2008. On the enrollment day, I was impressed by bicycles packed around the playground, dormitories and canteens. I bought one as well for convenience. When riding on the new bicycle, I was overwhelmed with excitement. Back then, as our dormitory did not have access to the internet, I had to head to the nearest Internet cafe in order to chat with my parents. Even today, I can still recall the loneliness and homesickness I felt those times.

In the autumn of 2014, I came back to ECNU to pursue my doctor's degree. With the help of my classmates, I set up my WeChat game and consequently all contact between teachers, family and classmates themselves improved tenfold. I have over ten active chat groups currently, some of which are "doctor candidates of ECNU enrolled in 2014", "fans of South Korean stars", "students of old Wu" , "Vietnamese students in China" , among others. Before, most messages were sent to students by emails, but now our working efficiency has been significantly improved for it only takes seconds for us to get informed via WeChat messages. My parents also have WeChat installed on their phones, and

2008 年秋天，我来到华东师范大学攻读硕士学位。令我印象深刻的是，报到那天，操场上、宿舍楼下、食堂附近都停满了各式各样的自行车。为了方便校园生活，我也买了一辆，骑着崭新的自行车，我欣喜激动。当时由于无法申请宽带，宿舍里无法上网，只能去网吧跟父母聊天，那时的思乡之情还记忆犹新。

2014 年秋天，我又回到母校攻读博士学位。班里的同学帮我安装了微信，从此，我和老师、同学、家人的联系方式发生了巨大的变化。微信里至少有十多个常用群：2014 年华师博士、韩门姐妹花、老吴桃李芬芳、越南学子群……之前要发邮件通知每个学生的事情，现在只要几秒钟的时间就可以完成，我们办事的效率提高了几百倍。在家里的爸妈也跟着我安装了微信，这样随时随地都可以和我网上视频。

博士三年级时由于课题要求，我要回国做实验研究，时隔一年后重返华师大。跟往常一样，某天中午我跑到楼下取当当网上购买的书。我很自信地报了一下货号，快递小哥看到我手里拿着一张一百块钱后竟然对我说："我没带零钱啊，现在没人付现金了。"原来我以前所熟悉的"货到付款"方式也发生了天翻地覆的变化。现在我出去玩儿要买个零食或

now they can have a video call with me whenever and wherever they want.

In my third year of pursuing my doctorate, I returned to Vietnam to do some research and survey, and came back to ECNU a year later. One day, I went downstairs to pick up pay-on-delivery books ordered online. As before, I told the courier my package number and was ready to pay in cash. But when the courier saw the one hundred yuan note in my hand, he told me, "Sorry, I don't have small change with me. Few people pay in cash now. " I suddenly realized that the pay-on-delivery method I was familiar with had also changed. Now whenever I need to buy a drink or snacks, I can easily pay for them with my phone.

Once I tried to take a taxi from the campus to a bus station, but was unable to do so. A few taxis stopped, but other people beat me to it. Half an hour had passed, and it was beyond me why I had failed in such a trivial task. Fortunately, a kind Chinese student told me I should use Didi app to catch a taxi. I suddenly realized that other people had this APP on their phones for convenience.

There is no doubt that many foreign students in China would be deeply impressed by the rapid technological development just as I am.

China has made remarkable achievements since its reform and opening-up, all of which have promoted prosperity for Chinese people and made their lives and work much easier. It has also brought more benefits and expanded development space for enterprises and businesses. Besides, thousands of international students in China have also seen the tangible benefits achieved under reform and opening-up. Though greater difficulties come with unprecedented opportunities, we believe that the Chinese people can face either present or future challenges with bravery and wisdom. We will have a brighter future.

饮料也不用现金了，一个手机就全搞定了。

某天上午想在校门口搭乘出租车去车站，许多空车擦肩而过就是不肯停下来，偶尔停下来的车也都让旁边的人捷足先登了。大概过了半小时都没打到车，我百思不得其解。这时一个热心的中国同学提醒我要"滴滴打车"才行。我恍然大悟，原来旁边的人手机里都安装了"滴滴打车"的APP。

相信许多外国同学都会跟我一样经常感叹：中国科技发展得太快了，那些日新月异的变化都在推着我们与时俱进，每日更新。

中国改革开放以来这些举世瞩目的成就不仅让中国人民富裕起来，方便了老百姓的工作和生活，给企业和商家带来了更多的利润和发展空间，也让成千上万的来华留学生切实感受到了改革开放带来的好处。中国面临的机遇前所未有，面对的挑战也是前所未有的，但我们相信目前和未来的挑战都难不倒勇敢无畏的中国人，期待并相信我们共同的明天会更好！

华东师范大学提供

拾忆我的留学时光
Reminiscence of My Overseas Study

[韩国]　申在原　浙江大学
[Republic of Korea] Shin Jae Won, Zhejiang University

There is a self-deprecating saying in Zhejiang University that people who do not do well in the college entrance examination come to Zhejiang University, but when the graduation season comes, the pride of "I am from Zhejiang University" is all over the WeChat Moments. The spirit of the people from the province's universities originated from Zhu Kezhen's two questions: what do you want to do in Zhejiang University? And who will you be after graduation? Those two questions accompany us for the four years on campus and it may take us a lifetime to answer those two questions. The spirit is the other shore that we are struggling to reach as well as the origin that we have to be back after seeing all the flourishing.

When I was a freshman, I just laughed the two questions off. Study can be neglected while entertainment is indispensable. During my freshman year, I participated in nearly ten club activities and spent my time eating and drinking. As a foreign student, I had very low requirements for myself. I just hoped not to fail any exam, and a passing score was fine. In the first year, although I had participated in many activities, I did not have more expectations for Zhejiang

　　虽说浙大坊间流传着"考败来浙"的自黑说法，但每逢毕业季，满满的"我是浙大人"之自豪感总是刷屏朋友圈。浙大人之精神，起源于竺老两问："诸位在校，有两个问题应该自己问问，第一，到浙大来做什么？第二，将来毕业后做什么样的人？"这两问，伴随我们走过大学四年，也将伴随我们走过余生，甚至，需要我们用一生去作答。它是我们奋力拼搏后才能抵达的彼岸，也是我们繁华看尽后需要回到的原点。

　　大一新生时，对于这两问只是一笑了之。学业，可以荒废；娱乐，不可缺席。大一期间，参加近乎十个社团活动，在混吃混喝中慢慢度过。作为一名留学生，对于自己的要求极其低，不挂科、低分飘过即可。大一一年，虽然参加的活动不少，但是并未对浙大拥有更多的期望。或者说，对于自己的未来尚未确定，不知如何发展。

　　升至大二，看着大一新生入学不禁感叹岁月如梭，多了一分紧迫感。阴错阳差之下，选择了国际政治作为我的专业。我们学院的院训是"以天下为己任，以真理为依归"。"天下为己任"是感性，"以真理为依归"是理性，院训告诉我们感性永远不能缺乏理性的支持，成功需要理性地思考、合理地安排未来计划。基于大一参加社团活动的基础，我积极参

University. In other words, I was not sure about my future and I did not know how to develop myself.

When I transitioned to sophomore, I sighed over how time had flown and had a sense of urgency on seeing the freshmen. I accidentally chose international politics as my major. The motto of our faculty is "take the world as one's own duty, and take the truth as the basis" . "Take the world as one's own duty" is of sensibility and "take the truth as the basis" is of rationality. The motto tells us that sensibility can never lack rational support and that success requires rational thinking and reasonable arrangement of future plans. On the basis of participating in club activities in my freshman year, I actively participated in model United Nations activities, English debate activities and other competitions on behalf of the university and won many awards. During the summer vacation, I had the honor to attend a program to study in the United Nations. Since then, I had a clear plan for the future and a deeper understanding of "Tianxia" (the world) in our motto. Meanwhile, teachers paid much attention to our study. Previously, one of my articles on politics of China and the Republic of Korea(ROK) posted on WeChat was lucky to be seen by my teacher and finally published in a paper under the teacher's recommendation. Later, I started to work as a part-time independent writer. As of today, I have published five articles as a foreign student of Zhejiang University.

During my junior year, I had the honor to take an internship at a Chinese think tank by virtue of previous accumulation, and my main direction was China-ROK relations. At that time, China-ROK relations had stalled due to the THAAD system. During the internship, my major task was to improve the relations between the two countries through public diplomacy and people-

加模拟联合国活动、英语辩论活动等，多次代表学校团队外出参赛，荣获多个奖项。在暑假期间，有幸参加外院项目到联合国学习，对于未来有了一个清晰的规划，对于"天下"有了更深层次的理解。与此同时，学业上一直有老师们的悉心照料，在学业上一直为我们护航。先前，写过一篇关于中韩政治的相关文章至微信平台，有幸被老师看到。在老师的推荐下投稿至澎湃新闻，成功刊登。而后，就开始了兼职独立撰稿人之路。截至今日，作为浙江大学留学生成功在澎湃新闻发表 5 篇文章。

大三期间，通过先前的积累，有幸在中国的智库实习，主要方向为中韩关系。此时，正值"萨德"事件高峰时期，中韩关系极度冷淡。实习期间的主要任务是研究如何通过公共外交、民间外交促进两国关系，从另一个角度为两国做贡献。每当有疑问，便询问学校老师，虽然这不是和课程相关的内容，但是老师们也悉心给予指导，让我收获颇多，结合理论与实践成功完成了一系列任务。

大四期间，学院推荐我到台湾大学交流半年，让我对两岸关系有了更深层次的认知。由于有先前的积累，我有幸被邀请参加台湾省对外交流部门的活动，接待韩国来宾；以台湾大学的学生身份参加京都大学的

申在原（左）在澳门大学举办的东亚模拟联合国大会比赛中获奖

to-people diplomacy and make contributions to two countries from another perspective. When in doubt, I asked the university teachers. Although those questions were not related to the curriculum, the teachers still gave me earnest guidance, which made me gain a lot. I successfully completed a series of tasks by combining theory with practice.

During my senior year, the school recommended me to Taiwan University as an exchange student for half a year, which gave me a profound understanding of cross-strait relations. Due to my previous accumulation, I was honored to be invited to participate in the activities of the external exchange department of Taiwan to receive the ROK guests and attend the Kyoto University seminar as a student of Taiwan University. As a student of Zhejiang University, I introduced Zhejiang University to students in Taiwan University and welcomed them to apply for exchange programs. When I was back in Zhejiang, I took the initiative to apply for an entrepreneurship project to help overseas students in China understand Chinese laws and popularize the laws for foreign students in multiple languages. This project was successfully established with the support of the school. In just one semester, it helped overseas students in China get acquainted with laws.

If I compare the four-year university life to four seasons, fresh year was the wanton spring; sophomore the vigorous summer; junior the accumulated autumn; senior year the sedimentary winter. If I compare myself to a tree, then I am glad that I was seeded at Zhejiang University. The free, deep and rich soil of Zhejiang University has provided precious nutrition for my life and allowed me to thrive and further see the world from a higher perspective.

浙江大学提供

研讨会；作为浙大学子，向台湾大学学生介绍浙江大学，欢迎他们申请交换。回到浙大，我主动申请创业项目，帮助在华留学生了解中国法律，以公益的方式用多国语言为外籍学生普及法律。这一项目在学院的支持下成功立项，短短一个学期内帮助在华留学生普及多项法律，并为他们减少损失十万元。

大学四年，倘若以四季喻之，那么大一，是肆意烂漫的阳春；大二，是蓬勃生长的骄夏；大三，是厚积薄发的深秋；大四，则是温素沉淀的晚冬。若将自己喻为一棵树，那么我很庆幸，自己被播种在了浙大园。浙大自由、深厚、丰美的土壤，为我的人生提供了宝贵的营养，也让我得以茁壮生长，看到了更高、更远的世界。

我与李太白的二三事
My Stories with Chinese Poet Li Bai

[韩国] 申昊澈 北京大学
[Republic of Korea] Shin Hochul, Peking University

Li Bai is a household Chinese name in Republic of Korea, while in my memory, Li Taibai (Li Bai's courtesy name) is more famous. In Korean nursery rhymes, we also sing a song about Li Taibai. Although I may know his name in the song, I did not know who he was and what he did during childhood until I went to college.

I had studied the Chinese major at Gachon University in Republic of Korea for two years as an undergraduate when I got to know Li Bai.

"Abed, I see a sliver light, I wonder if it is frost aground. " "Do you not see the Yellow River come from the sky, rushing into the sea and ne'er come back?" "A time will come to ride the wind and cleave the waves, I will set my cloudlike sail to cross the sea which raves. " After I crammed these poems appeared on my final exam, I realized that Li Taibai was an acclaimed poet in the Tang dynasty. A year later, when I almost memorized his poems, I began to serve in the army.

After a two-year full military life, I cannot see my own future. I returned to the school, chose a course named "Chinese Poetry Analysis" and met my "bro" Li Taibai again. At that time, we were asked to choose one of our favorite

在韩国，一直以来最有名的中国人就是李白了，不过我的记忆里，李太白比李白更有名，韩国的童谣中我们也唱过：달아달아밝은달아이태백이놀던달아（大意是：月亮很明亮，跟李太白一起玩的月亮）。虽然唱过他，但是儿时的我并不知道李太白是谁，做了什么，直到上了大学。

我在韩国嘉泉大学读过两年本科，中文系，从那以后才真的认识了李白。

"床前明月光，疑是地上霜""君不见，黄河之水天上来，奔流到海不复回""长风破浪会有时，直挂云帆济沧海"这些诗词，开始变成了我的期末考试，我死记硬背地考完试了，也终于知道，李太白是个诗人，很会写诗的唐朝诗人。一年后，等到我把他的诗都背得差不多的时候，就去当兵了。

两年的军队生活很充实，以至于快结束的时候，我对未来迷茫了。走出军营回到学校以后，刚好选了一门课——《中国诗歌解析》，和李太白大哥又见面了。当时那门课期中考试的内容是，选一个自己最喜欢的诗歌做报告，我选了《行路难》。确切地说，服完两年兵役是一个很重要的契机，心里开始盘算如何追求自己想要的人生。嗯，世界这么大，

poems and deliver a report for mid-term exam. I chose Li Bai's poem Hard is the *Way of the World*. To be exact, serving two years in the military was an important turning point, and since then I was beginning to figure out how to pursue my ideal life. Well, the world is waiting for me to see. What Li Bai wrote such as "ride the wind and cleave the waves" and "set the cloudlike sail" paved the way for my life in China.

I wanted to drop out.

Hearing such a "surprise", parents who were in their fifties could do everything but accept my self-willed decision, but they did not beat me together for the sake of blood ties.

"You have been studying for two years. Now the most urgent thing is to find a job. Go to China to re-study at university? It is a waste of time and you may miss the opportunity. Your mom and I cannot understand it. "

"I think there are more choices in the early 20s. There is no point in staying on the seemingly right path. It is more important to see the outside world rather than working without a purpose. If I did nothing in my age, I would regret

北京大学 / 李香花摄

我想去看看。太白的"长风破浪""直挂云帆"推开了我通往中国的大门。

我要退学。

听到这种"惊喜"，年过半百的父母当然无法接受，不过考虑亲情的前提下，他们没有对我"混合双打"。

"你已经读了两年大学，现在最重要的是赶紧毕业找工作，到中国重新读大学这种想法，浪费时间又可能错过时机，我和你妈妈无法理解。"

"我觉得二十出头的年纪可以有更多的选择，不应该一成不变地走看似正确的道路，看外面的世界比盲目地就业更重要，如果错过了这个年纪，我老了会后悔的。"

"好吧，如果你坚持，那我给你一年时间。你可以在这一年内做自己想做的，但是不能退学。一年之后再给我答复。"

就这样，带着一纸机票和满腔热血的申昊澈到了北京，目的地——北京大学。

一年的预科学习比想象中困难得多，在北京大学——旁边的小教室里，我开始了真正的汉语学习，翻来覆去的小测验、背诵、考试和巨大的压力没有浇灭我的热情，"济沧海"的李太白始终还在。

北京大学 / 王天天摄

it when I get old. "

"Well, if you insist, then I will give you one year. You can do what you want in this year, but you cannot drop out of school. Tell me what you do after one year. "

The plane took me, Shenhaoche (Shin Hochul), a motivated young guy, came to Beijing, to my destination — Peking University.

One year of preparatory study was much more difficult than I imagined. In Peking University — actually in the small classroom next to Peking University, I started the real Chinese learning. The endless quizzes, memorization, exams and tremendous pressures did not dampen my enthusiasm. Li Taibai and his poems still accompanied me.

In 2015, Shenhaoche (Shin Hochul), the monitor of the "Preparatory Class 6", who had eaten for a year's Kung Pao Chicken and gained 22 *jins* weight, finally won the admission letter from Peking University. My desired life as an exchange student in China has begun.

Coming to Beijing, to Peking University, is a decision that I would never regret. At Peking University, all kinds of experiences different from Korean undergraduate life make me deeply understand the "inclusiveness" of Peking University. Since I majored in international relations at Peking University, on the course we often discuss the current political affairs, the relations between countries, and what happens in the international community. However, teachers on the platform and students in the class do not rigidly adhere to their identities. Their standpoints are always objective and convincing. I can feel the atmosphere of intellectual earnestness everywhere on campus. There are students learning in the study room, in the library, by the Weiming lake, and on the lawn of Jing Garden, immersing themselves in knowledge. A variety

北京大学提供

2015 年，"预科六班"的班长——申昊澈，在吃了一年的"宫保鸡丁"，胖了二十斤之后，终于拿到了北京大学录取通知书。向往的留华生活开始了。

来北京，来北大，是我不会后悔的决定。在北大的生活，种种不同于韩国本科生活的经历让我深深地体会到了北大的"兼容并包"。由于在北大的专业是国际关系，课程中常常要讨论到当下的时政，各国的关系，国际舞台的林林总总，但是讲台上的老师们，课堂上的同学们并没有拘泥于自己是中国人或其他各国人的身份，大家的立场总是客观的，让人信服的。校园里随处可见的自习氛围也让我觉得不可思议，自习室、图书馆、未名湖畔、静园草坪上到处都有学习的身影，课程内外的知识让每个人沉浸在其中。更让我耳目一新的是课堂"辩论赛""模拟联合国大会"这种

of discussion forms including debating contests in the class and MUN (Model United Nations) is a breath of fresh air for me. My Participation in the intense discussion has given me more to think about.

However, the colorful campus life does not let me forget my dream of seeing the world. The authentic Beijing culture is also what I want to know and understand. When I first arrived, I was struggled to understand the locals' "R-ending Retro-flexion" accent. I deeply felt that my efforts on the Chinese course were to no avail. I could not understand the taxi driver when I was taking a taxi. Likewise, he might not understand me. Later when I thought that I had learned the essence of Beijing accent, I went to the restaurant and clumsily shouted, "Waiter-er, Kung Pao Chicken-er", leaving the waiters around laughing ...

The fun of living in Beijing is more than that. It is a warm and inclusive city that cannot be described between the lines. Still I want to talk about Beijing, a city where ancient customs and modern style coexist. I have long known that ancient Beijing has hutongs and quadrangles. I have long known that modern Beijing has CBD and neon lights. But when I really come here, the harmonious existence of modernization and historical heritage stunned me. I see a city that carried its history making great strides in technological and scientific as well as economic development.

Last year, a friend from South Korea came to Beijing. Before his departure, he told me that what struck him most was e-commerce platform such as WeChat, Alipay, vending machine, car-hailing app except for the scenic spots. He cannot help but admire the rapid development of China's science and technology.

In conclusion, in ancient times there was Li Bai who wrote 100 poems after drinking white spirits. Today, there is Haoche who gains much weight after coming to China. This article is dedicated to Li Taibai. He lives in my heart.

讨论形式，论点的激烈交锋让参与其中的我有了更多的思考。

不过丰富的校园生活并没有让我忘记"我想去看看"的初心，地道的"北京儿"也是我想深入了解和体会的。初来乍到的时候，老北京的儿化音让我感到绝望，深深觉得课堂上的汉语可能白学了，打车时听不懂出租车司机的话，当然他可能也听不懂我的；后来自以为懂得了儿化音的我，餐厅吃饭的时候笨拙地喊着"服务员儿，宫保鸡丁儿"，留下周围狂笑的"服务员儿"们……

显然在北京生活的趣事不止于此，字里行间写不下的是温暖包容的北京城。可我还是想再絮叨一下古老和现代交融的北京。我早就知道古老的北京有胡同儿，有四合院，也早就知道现代的北京有 CBD，有霓虹灯。但是当我真的来了，站在马路上，望着一条马路的两边可以共存的"古老和现代"时，还是被震惊到了，眼前的北京是科技经济突飞猛进的北京，可是一回头也是饱含历史和情怀的京城。

去年韩国的朋友来了北京，临走前他对我说，除了景点带来的震撼之外，印象最深刻的是四处可见的电子支付平台，微信、支付宝、自动贩卖机、手机打车等，方便之余不禁佩服中国科技发展之迅速。

最后的最后，古有"李白斗酒诗百篇"，今有"昊澈来华胖三圈"，谨以此纪念我心中永远的李太白。

一个印度人的中国印象：
玄奘、改革和担当
An Indian's Impression about China: Xuanzang, Reform and Readiness to Take Responsibilities

［印度］　冠秀杰　西北大学

[India] Ajay Krishna, Northwest University

Born in the 80s, I have witnessed reform and opening-up in India and experienced the slow change happening in the country. In some fields, the changes are significant, while in others, the changes are unnoticeable. Before I went to college in 2006, I knew little about foreign countries. I was admitted into Banaras Hindu University in Uttar Pradesh and studied in the Department of Foreign Languages. When I started to learn about foreign countries, it was China that left me the deepest impression. So I began to admire Chinese culture and was especially interested in traditional Chinese culture. I got the Chinese government scholarship in 2011, and came to China the first time to pursue my master's degree at Shenyang Normal University. From then on, I have not only benefited a lot both in my study and life experience, but also had further learning about China and a deep impression about its all-round reform.

In the past six years of staying in China, I have obtained a master's degree in Linguistics and Applied Linguistics, and have proceeded to the doctor's

（左一为作者）

作为 80 后的印度人，我是印度自身改革开放的见证者，感受着印度本身的缓慢的变化，这些变化在某些领域比较明显，某些领域却完全没有发生。没进大学之前我对别国的情况一无所知，直到 2006 年考入北方邦的瓦拉纳西印度大学外文系，才第一次对别的国家有了初步的认识，其中对我影响最深的就是中国了。从那时起，我就逐渐成为中国文化的倾慕者，特别是对中国传统文化产生了浓厚的兴趣。2011 年拿到中国政府奖学金后，我第一次来到中国，在沈阳师范大学攻读硕士学位。迄今为止的六年里，我对中国有了进一步的认识与了解，在学业及人生经验方面，收获甚多；在中国的全面改革方面，印象颇深。

在这六年光阴里，我获得了语言学及应用语言学的硕士学位，正在攻读佛学博士学位，主要研究方向是玄奘法师的精神。诚然，在中国上下五千年的历史里有很多具有影响力的人物，可在我看来，能代表中国博大精深的传统文化的典型人物就是玄奘法师。作为南亚国家的成员，印度人最爱慕和敬佩的就是玄奘法师。历史上到过印度的民族很多，可

degree in Buddhism with the study of eminent monk Xuanzang's spirit and commitment to Buddhism as focus. Indeed, there are many influential figures in Chinese history, but Xuanzang is the representative of China's extensive and profound traditional culture in my eyes. With India being a Southeast Asian country, Xuanzang is most admired by Indian people. Among all kinds of people from different nations who came to India in history, it was the Chinese noble and virtuous monks who made the most profound influence on India. Their manners and experience of practicing Buddhism have greatly elevated the level of exchanges between the two countries from a spiritual perspective. During my stay in China, I can keenly feel the extensive spiritual exchanges between our nations.

As people all know, China has experienced tremendous changes since its reform and opening-up. As an Indian, I pay more attention to China's rapid progress from the perspective of culture exchanges and mutual learning between the two countries. Among various similarities shared by India and China, the most significant one is their population. Yet facing huge population, they hold different ideas about managing it. For one thing, Chinese government provides people with basic education, career opportunities, medical facilities and good living conditions. Moreover, it gives people the most desired dignity and confidence, making them enthusiastic and hopeful about the future. The experience of China's development can be used for reference in India, and I hope India can carry out the experiment of social economy at home and make achievements in reform.

But beyond all these, what touches me most is China's readiness to take responsibilities. China not only holds itself to high standard, but also

对印度影响最深远的就是这些来自中国的高僧大德，他们的言行举止和修行经历从精神层面大大提升了两国的交流境界。我在中国的这段时间里，能深深地感受到两国之间流动着博大精深的精神气息。

中国自改革开放以来经历了翻天覆地的变化，我作为印度人则站在文化交流与互鉴的角度上，加倍关注中国日新月异的进步与发展。印度跟中国有很多共同点，最大的共同点就是两国的人口数量。这两个国家面对巨大的人口数量，却在管理理念上有着显著的不同。中国一方面给予了中国人民基础教育、事业机会、健康设施，良好生活条件等，一方面更给予了中国人最渴望的自尊和自信，使人们面对未来充满了热心及希望。中国的发展道路和经验对印度来讲非常具有借鉴价值，希望印度在自己国家内能实施中国的社会经济试验，取得改革成就。

除此之外，中国给我感触最深的就是不止于独善其身，而是要兼济

西北大学提供

contributes to the well-being of the world. As an ancient civilization, China has never left its responsibilities to human civilization behind. It makes efforts to develop and improve Chinese people's livelihoods, and at the same time, it also contributes to improving the livelihoods of people in its neighbor countries. The profoundness of Chinese culture is well displayed in China's position and actions it takes in international affairs. One of the models demonstrating Chinese wisdom in dealing with global issues is the Belt and Road Initiative. The readiness to take responsibilities is more than advancing the well-being of Chinese people, but making efforts to improve the well-being of the world, and it is the just cause of pursuing to save countless people from suffering.

西北大学提供

天下的担当精神。中国作为文明古国从未忘掉自己对人类文明的责任，在努力改善自身、改善本国民生的同时，也积极谋求改善周边国家的民生生活。中国文化的博大精深明显体现在对国际问题的立场和处理方式上，"一带一路"倡议的提出就是为全球问题提供中国智慧的典型例证。这种担当精神不仅是为本国民生谋福，更是为改善世界民生的整体状况而努力，力求拯救无数人民命运的大道精神。

北京爱情故事
Beijing Love Story

[俄罗斯] 安娜 北京理工大学
[Russia] Ivanchenko Anna, Beijing Institute of Technology

Beijing is a matchmaker between me and China. Our love story begins here.

Two years ago, I came to China for the first time and found Beijing to be my dream city. Surrounded by hospitable residents and roaming all kinds of food streets, I feel like every moment of my life in Beijing has been a fairy tale. I often communicate with local friends in daily life with some newly-learned Chinese words. Although I have made some stupid mistakes during the learning, I am thrilled to be challenged and to achieve.

I find that every season in Beijing has its unique smell: the autumn in Beijing has the aroma of watermelon and small bun; in winter, the smell of hot pot and milk tea permeate the air; now it is spring in Beijing, and the sweet scent of flowers is everywhere. Wherever I go, I can smell their fragrance: jasmine or rose? Sometimes I take a wild guess: will it be pineapple flower, orange flower, or cucumber flower? What will next summer smell like in Beijing? I will see as it comes.

I also find that every season paints Beijing in different colors. I came to

我与中国的缘分，是从北京开始的。这个城市于我而言，就像月老一样，牵住了我和中国的红线。

两年以前，我第一次来中国。在北京生活的每一分每一秒，都让我仿佛置身于童话中一般，热情好客的北京人、琳琅满目的美食街，这就是我梦想中的世界啊！我常常把刚刚学到的汉语词汇运用到生活中，跟当地朋友们交流，虽然在这个过程中闹了不少笑话，但是我特别喜欢这种充满挑战又能获得成就的新鲜感。

我发现每个季节的北京都有独特的气味：秋天有西瓜和小甜面包的香味；冬天则到处充斥着火锅和奶茶的气味；现在是北京的春天，随处可闻的是特别甜的花香味。不管我走到哪里，都能闻到各种不同的花香，我常常猜测这些香味的来源：茉莉花？玫瑰花？有时候我会天马行空地想象：菠萝花？橘子花？黄瓜花？北京的夏天闻起来是什么味道呢？到时候我就知道了。

我还发现每个季节都把北京染成了不同的颜色。我来北京的时候，秋天刚到，那时的北京仿佛一个盛满水果的篮子，有杧果颜色的黄树叶，有各种葡萄颜色的树叶，有西瓜色、橙子色的草地。冬天来了以后，北

Beijing in early autumn. At that time, Beijing was like a basket full of fruits, with yellow leaves in the color of mango, leaves in the color of various grapes and meadow in the color of watermelon and orange. When winter comes, Beijing morphs into beef in a frying pan, turning from red to dark brown. Now, spring dresses Beijing in lush greenery. Changing from verdancy to dark green, the whole city is like a fresh cucumber, tender and crisp, exuding an attractive charm.

If Beijing is the matchmaker, then the Summer Palace connects me and China. In Beijing, I fell deeply in love with the Summer Palace. To tell you the truth, I have been to the Summer Palace seven or eight times. Vast as the Summer Palace is, you could always find a quiet place to rest and think even when it is packed with visitors. I often enjoy my time with the Summer Palace alone. The Seventeen-Arch Bridge and Hanxu Island are my must-visit locales every time I go to the Summer Palace. On each arch of the Seventeen-Arch Bridge, there is a different statue of a lioness and two cubs. One arch has little lions sleeping under their mother's belly, and the other has little lions playing with their mother's paws. Every time I go to the Seventeen-Arch Bridge, I kiss the lioness on her nose. It is my tradition.

Some people say that a capital cannot represent the whole country. But for me, Beijing epitomizes China. Beijing has many developed urban areas like those in Shanghai and Guangzhou, for example Xidan shopping street. The China Central Television (CCTV) headquarters building is also in Beijing. Surrounded by green mountains and rivers, Beijing is also covered by high-rise buildings, hutongs and courtyards. Filled with all kinds of sounds, Beijing is awakened by the automobile horn and the bicycle bell in the morning. When

京好像煎锅里的牛肉，慢慢从红色变成了深棕色。现在是北京的春天，到处都是绿色，从青绿到深绿，好像一根新鲜的黄瓜，嫩嫩的，脆脆的，散发着诱人的魅力。

若说北京是我与中国的月老，那么颐和园便是红线那头牵住的地方。在北京，我爱上了颐和园，深深地爱上了。实不相瞒，我已经去过七八次颐和园了。颐和园非常大，大到即使游人如织，也能找到一个安静的属于自己的地方，休息、思考。我常常在颐和园享受只属于"我们俩"的时光。园内的十七孔桥和涵虚岛是我每次必去的地方。十七孔桥的每个孔上面都有一座不同的母狮子和它的两个小狮子的雕像。一个孔有小狮子在妈妈的肚子下睡觉，另一个孔有小狮子跟妈妈的爪子玩耍。每逢到了十七孔桥，我都去跟母狮子用鼻子"接吻"。这已经成为我到颐和园的惯例了。

北京理工大学 / 柴运春摄

people arrive at the office, the city becomes quiet and you can only hear the sound of elder people exercising, chatting and strolling. At noon, Beijing is again buzzing with people hurrying along the roads and packing lunch. After a while, the streets sink into peace again when you could only hear the grandpas and grandmas bring their grandchildren out to play. At night, Beijing seems to have changed its garment. The whole city is filled with neon colors and loud music. This is a time for square dancing, bars and restaurants.

I used to think that people here lives a fast pace of life. They would be busy working, taking care of their children and exercising. However, to my surprise, I often see people strolling, enjoying delicious food, appreciating the beauty of flowers and plants, or standing on the street watching others dancing and singing. The different looks of Beijing draw me to explore.

I love Beijing, and I think Beijing loves me, too. I have a hunch that I can realize all my dreams here!

有人说，首都不能代表全国。但对我来说，北京就是全中国的缩影。这里有很发达的市区，好像上海或者广州，例如西单商业街，还有中央电视台总部大楼。此外，北京还有很多青山绿水、高楼大厦、胡同四合院等。北京整天都充满着各种各样的声音：汽车的鸣笛声、自行车车铃声开启了北京的一天，等人们到了单位以后，安静成为主旋律，只有老人们运动、聊天、散步的声音。中午的北京又变得热闹非凡，路上的行人们神色匆匆，打包午饭的声音不绝于耳。不一会儿，街道又静了下来，除了老人聊天的声音外，还有小孩儿的声音。这是爷爷奶奶带孙子孙女儿出来玩儿了。到了夜晚，北京仿佛换了一身衣裳，充满了霓虹的色彩，还有吵闹的音乐，这是属于广场舞、酒吧和饭馆的时间。

我曾经以为，居住在北京的人应该天天忙着工作、照顾孩子、运动健身等，他们的生活节奏应该很快。但是，不一定！我经常看到人们悠闲地散步、享受美食、欣赏花草的美丽，站在街上看别人跳舞、唱歌。我想，这就是这个城市的双面性吧，不管哪一面，都吸引着我去探索更多。

我爱北京，我觉得北京也爱我，我有预感，我将在这里实现我所有的梦想！

我的第二个故乡——青岛
My Second Hometown—Qingdao

[韩国]　朴贤珍　中国海洋大学
[Republic of Korea] Park Hyunjin, Ocean University of China

I think many people associate Qingdao with red tiles, green trees, blue sea and azure sky. In Qingdao, you can feel the sea wind softly breezing over the Zhanqiao Bridge, enjoy the falling leaves in Badaguan (Eight Great Passes), roam the artistic Daxue Lu (College Street) with other literary youth, explore the bustling and hustling eastern part and appreciate the beautiful scenery in the famous Laoshan Mountain.

I have been in this beautiful city for ten years, enough time to transform a person's character and bring dramatic changes to a city.

Ten years ago, I came to Qingdao for the first time as a young and innocent girl. The city was then grey and alien to me with strangers all around. I remember that when I got off the plane and was about to go to my relative's house, I found the airport gate in a mess and the taxi filled with weird and smelly smoke. I did not know how many cigarettes the driver had smoked prior to my boarding, and could not also count how many he had along the way. When we finally reached the destination, I got off the taxi and took a deep breath as if being liberated from captivity. Ten years later, I had another

红瓦绿树，碧海蓝天，我想很多人想起青岛就能想到这两个词。有栈桥的海风、八大关的落叶、文青游荡的大学路、繁华拥堵的东部，还有海上名山之一崂山。

我来到这个美丽的城市也有十年了。对个人而言，十年完全可以改变一个人的性格；对于一座城市，十年足以翻天覆地。

十年前刚来到青岛，对于一个年少不懂事的我来说，这座城市是灰色的。陌生的城市，陌生的人，下了飞机去亲戚家。在杂乱无章的门口，我们搭上了车，刚一上车，我就被从未闻到过的烟熏味冲到了鼻子，一路上不知道师傅抽了多少根烟，终于到了目的地，一下车我就像被解放了一样深吸了一口气；而十年后的青岛，同样是刚下了飞机回家，到了指定的出租车等候区，出租车井然有序地在指定的位置等待，没有人抢也没有人闹。轮到了我，师傅很热心地帮我抬行李，上了车有一股淡淡的花香，在路上也会问我"热不热，要不要开空调啊……"一路上和师傅聊着天，也看看窗外美景，到了目的地师傅也很礼貌地说一声"慢一点哈"。

十年前刚来到青岛，对于一个充满好奇心的我来说，想和朋友去景点的时候，要先在家查好先坐几路车到哪一站再倒几路车。公交车上总

experience when going home from the airport in Qingdao, but my impression of this city had deeply changed. When getting off the plane, I went to the designated taxi waiting area, where taxis waited for their turns in an orderly manner. All the people waited in a queue and no one vied with each other in getting a taxi. When it was my turn, the driver helped me with my luggage willingly. The taxi had a trace of flowery fragrance inside. The driver was very considerate and asked me if I was hot and whether he should turn on the air conditioner. Along the way, I was chatting with him while enjoying the beautiful scenery out of the window. When I arrived at the destination, the driver politely said goodbye to me and reminded me to be careful on the way home.

In my beginnings here, I was curious about everything. But whenever I wanted to go to any scenic spot with my friends, I had to check the bus route in advance to find out which bus to take and be aware of transfer hubs. The bus was always full of people. You must have your change ready and the conductor will ask where you will get off. Being afraid of getting pushed over by others, I would hold the bus handrail along the way and kept my head down nervously, feeling eager to get to the destination. Ten years later, however, with the opening of metro line 2, line 3 and line 11, traffic congestion has been alleviated in Qingdao and people have been enjoying more convenience in commuting. My journey time from home to school was cut from one hour and a half to less than 40 minutes.

When I first came to Qingdao ten years ago, as a lazy girl, I would choose to take a bus or a taxi to go to the supermarket, which was a 30-minute walk from home because it was still a little too far on foot and would cost no more than the basic charge by a taxi. Ten years later, however, on the streets of

是人山人海，有收钱的阿姨问你到哪一站。你一定要准备好零钱，一路上扶着扶手，紧张得低着头，就怕会被人挤倒。一心想着快一点到目的地；而十年后的青岛随着地铁 2 号线、3 号线到 11 号轻轨的陆续开通，不仅减轻了交通拥堵而且也给人们带来了很多便利。以前从家到学校要坐一个半小时的公交车，现在不到 40 分钟就能到学校门口。在宽敞的地铁上看着外面的风景，不知不觉就到目的地了。

十年前刚来到青岛，对于一个懒惰的我来说，去离家 30 分钟的超市，都会选择坐公交车或者是打个车，想走过去感觉还是有点远，打个车也就是起步费；而十年后的青岛，走在大马路上，你就可以看到蓝色、黄色、橙色的共享单车，用手机扫一下码就可以骑走，你想骑到哪里就骑到哪里。自从有了共享单车，之前很少能看见骑车的青岛，也陆陆续续有很多人在上下班或者是在市场上骑着单车了。

青岛这十年的变化，不仅仅是体现青岛的交通发达，也体现了人们

Qingdao, you can always see blue, yellow and orange shared bikes wherever you go. Scan the QR code on a bike with your mobile phone, and you can ride it to anywhere you want. It was a rare scene to see people riding bikes in Qingdao before, but since the advent of shared bikes, more and more people ride bikes to go to work, go home after work or go to market.

The changes of Qingdao in the past decade not only demonstrate how full-fledged the transportation system has become, but also reflect people's cognitive changes, the improvement in citizens' qualities, the development of the economy and the advancement of science and technology. When I think of the dramatic and ever-present changes in Qingdao, I realize I only saw a fraction of them. China is developing rapidly as a whole. Most people say that China, a rising star, is well-positioned to be a new superpower just like a giant dragon flying high in the sky. I hope this dragon can fly even higher!

认知的变化、素质的提高、经济的发达、科技的发展。我看着青岛日新月异的变化，想着我只是看到了微乎其微的部分。整个中国都在飞一般地发展，都说中国这条巨龙已经雄起腾飞，我希望它能够飞得更高！

土库曼斯坦人在中国
Turkmenistan Man in China

［土库曼斯坦］ 拉蒙德　北京工业大学

[Turkmenistan] Rahmedov Resul, Beijing University of Technology

I am Lamengde (Rahmedov Resul) from Turkmenistan, a sophomore majoring in Applied Chemistry in Beijing University of Technology. Including a year of language learning in northeast China, I have been in the country for three years.

It is hard to see three years as a short time.

In the first few months of learning Chinese, I found it particularly difficult to learn as it was quite different from the languages I had known before. In spite of difficulties, I often went to a different shop to buy stuff and talked to the local people. Constant dripping wears away a stone and many a little makes a mickle. Gradually I knew how to chat with them and make a bargain. Sometimes I was even praised for my oral Chinese. During that time, I found that the use of Wechat and Alipay was so common in China. QR codes for payment were present in every store, no matter its size, even at food stalls of grilled cold noodles. There are various functions on Wechat, including communication, comments, payment, recreation, and so on. Alipay focuses on the payment function. It also offers financial management. But it is such a pity that without a Chinese identity card, Yu'ebao,

　　我叫拉蒙德，来自土库曼斯坦，是北京工业大学应用化学专业大二的一名学生。加上在东北学习语言的一年，我来到中国已经三年了。

　　三年说短不短。

　　在学习汉语最初的几个月，我觉得汉语特别难学，它和我接触过的语言都不一样。不过我经常去不同的商店买东西，和当地人交流，滴水穿石，聚沙成塔，渐渐地我学会了和他们聊天儿、砍价，不时还会被夸赞中文说得不错。在这个过程中，我发现微信和支付宝的使用在中国太普遍了，几乎每个商店，无论大小，甚至路边的烤冷面摊都贴着微信和支付宝收款码。微信功能很丰富，交友、朋友圈分享、支付、娱乐……支付宝注重支付功能，还能理财，可惜我没有中国身份证，不能使用余额宝，希望支付宝可以早日增加用护照注册余额宝的功能。我刚来中国就注册了微信和支付宝，要不然真是寸步难行。最近我在网上看到一个台湾男生在大陆挑战72小时无现金生活的视频，我觉得在中国72小时只用现金生活才是真的挑战呢，看了网友的评论，原来大家和我想的一样。在中国待久了，我习惯了只拿手机就出门，一旦回国，常常因为不带现金，好几次都付不出钱，特别尴尬。

one of its functional services, is not available. I signed up for Wechat and Alipay upon coming to China; otherwise it would be too inconvenient. Recently I saw a video about a guy from Taiwan who challenged to live without cash for 72 hours in mainland China. In my view, only using cash on the mainland for 72 hours would actually be a challenge. I saw the comments of other netizens. It turned out that everyone thought the same way. Having been in China for a long time, I am used to going out only with my mobile phone. Once I came back to Turkmenistan, it was so embarrassing that it happened a lot when I could not make payment because I did not have cash on me.

Studying in Beijing, I realize the advance and inclusiveness of this international metropolis. The shared bikes spread over Beijing, the birthplace of shared bikes. Outside every metro station stand bikes in yellow, orange, and some in white, green, and different colors. With the sound of a beep, the bike gets unlocked. I ride it to explore local and foreign things, from streets to lanes, which is very cool. In this city, I can eat food and meet people from all over the world, including my compatriots. When I miss home, I can get a familiar taste in a Turkish restaurant or a Xinjiang restaurant.

During my vacations, I stay for a while at my friends' in other cities to experience different urban lifestyle. What impressed me the most during one of these visits was an online shopping experience in Nanjing! Sometimes I visit Taobao, and often see many stores offer free mailing to Jiangsu, Zhejiang and Shanghai. While staying at my friend's house in Nanjing, I bought something delivered from Shanghai and submitted the order late at night. The next morning, I received the express call! In Jiangsu, Zhejiang and Shanghai, the express service of Taobao is not only free but also fast in delivery. It would have

　　来到北京学习后，我体会到了这个国际大都市的先进与包容。作为发源地，北京的共享单车遍地都是，每个地铁站外都有小黄和小橙，有时还有小白、小绿、小彩……"嘀嘀"几声，"啪嗒"开锁，骑着它们接触当地的、外来的事物，从大街浪到小巷，很拉风。在这个城市，我可以吃到世界各地的食物，见到世界各地的人，还有很多同胞。想家的时候去土耳其餐厅或新疆餐厅可以吃到熟悉的味道。

　　当然，我在假期也会到中国其他城市的朋友家逗留一段时间，体会不同的城市风格。最让我印象深刻的是在南京的一次网购体验！我平时逛淘宝经常看到江浙沪包邮，于是我在南京的朋友家下单购买了上海发货的商品，深夜提交订单，第二天上午竟然接到了快递电话！在江浙沪，快递不但包邮，速度也飞快，一晚上就到货，真是不可思议。

　　微信、支付宝、共享单车、网购这些东西正如柴米油盐酱醋茶，看

北京工业大学提供

been hard to fathom such convenience before I came to China.

Things like Wechat, Alipay, shared bikes and online shopping are just like daily necessities—fuel, rice, oil, salt, sauce, vinegar and tea. They seem inconspicuous and nothing magnificent, but are the most powerful and influential things for social life. Although they are not necessary for everyone, once you use them, you cannot do without them. They do bring a lot of convenience.

It is hard to see three years as a long time.

Though I have travelled to a lot of places by high-speed train, China is of such a large territory that there are still many places worthy of my footsteps. Though the area of the city is fixed, there are new technologies and ideas changing our lives. Though there has not been much change in my campus, the knowledge changes with each passing day and it is impossible to finish learning. With so many things waiting for my exploration, five or even ten years may not be enough.

After studying some relevant courses in school, I know that many of China's achievements today are the results of 40 years of reform and opening-up. The policy has proven itself. I like the way everyone works and lives. I enjoy the positive atmosphere full of competition. I want to integrate into this kind of convenient, quick, efficient, and beautiful life. I also want to introduce this lifestyle and bring those attitudes toward life to my country, let the people of my country know more about a modern China, and unveil the mystery about this major oriental country.

似不起眼，与高大上无关，却是最具传播力和影响力的东西，虽不是人人必需，却让人用了就不想离开，更带来了不少便捷。

三年说长也不长。

虽然我坐着高铁去了很多地方，但中国这么大，还有很多值得我去踏足；虽然城市的面积固定不变，但每时每刻都有新的科技和创意在更新我们的生活；虽然学校的样子没有太大变化，但知识日新月异，我怎么学都学不完。这么多事等我去探索，别说三年，五年、十年都不够。

经过学校相关课程的学习，我知道今天中国的成就很多都是 40 年来改革开放的成果。改革开放真是太棒了，我喜欢这里人人都认真努力生活的样子，我享受充满竞争的积极氛围，我想要融入这方便、快捷、高效、美好的生活，更想要将这种生活以及生活态度带到我们国家，让我们国家的人更多地了解现代的中国，揭开神秘的东方大国的面纱。

中国纳我　我望中国

China Welcomes Me and I Hold Expectations on It

［孟加拉国］　拉比　山东大学

[Bangladesh] Rasheduzzaman MD, Shandong University

Deng Xiaoping, the chief designer of China's reform and opening-up, holding the belief "I am the son of the Chinese people, and I love my motherland and people deeply", led the Chinese people onto the path of reform and opening-up with his extraordinary wisdom and strong will. Since he spoke these words, China has developed from the stage of restoring national strength and rebuilding the economic system, the stage of deepening reform, to the stage of accelerating development to pursing a better life for its citizens. China's politics and economy have developed rapidly, at the same time, Chinese culture strode forward greatly during the time. Under the guidance of the thought that "building roads is the first step to becoming rich", China has not only built its roads at home, but also built them abroad. China leads the world in science and technology, such as high-speed train, Alipay, WeChat, and sharing bikes, and has achieved international connectivity and integration with these technologies.

As an old Chinese saying goes, a king who wins hearts by compassion is the attracting force behind his subjects, and for a king whose virtue is never

　　"我是中国人民的儿子，我深情地爱着我的祖国和人民"，改革开放的总设计师邓小平正是本着这种精神，并以其非凡的智慧和坚强的意志带领中国人民走上了改革开放之路。四十年以十年为一个节点，从恢复重建、深化改革、加快发展到美好生活。中国的政治经济迅猛推进的四十年同时也是中国文化大步向前的几十年。"要想富，先修路"，中国不仅建好了自己的路还把路修到了国外。高铁、支付宝、微信、共享单车……中国的科技领先世界，用这些技术实现了国际间的互通共融。

　　"未之见而亲焉，可以往矣；久而不忘焉，可以来矣。"习近平主席倡导共建"一带一路"，加速了沿线领域的合作发展，实现互利共赢。

　　我来自孟加拉国，2012年11月底，我第一次来到中国，也算是搭上了"一带一路"的顺风车。我要去的地方是西安，当时我除了勇气一无所有。唯一清醒的是我将要在中国度过四年的时光还要攻克语言和食物两大难关。时光荏苒，白驹过隙，慢慢地，那种异国他乡的陌生感消失了，我更感觉自己像西安本地人。坐公交、找商店甚至是砍价对我而言都没任何问题。

　　本科学习结束后，为能让自己的汉语水平再上一个台阶，阴差阳错

forgotten, support from the people follows. President Xi Jinping's proposal of jointly building the Belt and Road Initiative accelerates the cooperation and development of countries along the road and achieves mutual benefit and win-win results.

Riding along the initiative, I came to China for the first time from Bangladesh at the end of November, 2012. I was going to Xi'an, but I had nothing but courage. The only thing I knew was that I would spend the next four years in China, and I would have to overcome the difficulties of learning the language and adapting the local food there. Gradually, the sense of strangeness of living in a foreign country disappeared as time passed. I felt more like a Xi'an native, and it was no longer a problem for me to take a bus, look for a store, and even to bargain.

After my undergraduate study, I went to Hohhot, the Windy City, to improve my Chinese to a higher level. Everything was completely new for me in Hohhot, including the environment and climate. Despite of a number of inconveniences upon arrival, I established a very friendly relationship with my friends and even with the city as I had more friends and more knowledge of new things, culture and language. I had a completely different experience in Hohhot from that in Xi'an, and I had gained a lot there.

After a year's advanced study, Shandong University offered me an opportunity for postgraduate education. Then I went east for Shandong with just a backpack. Nurtured by the Confucian culture, Shandong people are very hospitable, and they always do their best to help when I am in need. "It is always a pleasure to welcome friends coming from afar." To them, I am an international friend who shares the same values with them. From writing my

2016 年，登上陕西华山

在内蒙古师范大学的迎新
晚会上表演

和朋友一起参加山东大学
留学生文化节

山东大学提供

paper to doing my job, I could not make such improvements without their encouragement and help. Now, I am busy leading my ideal life in my own way.

In the future, China certainly will play an important part in this multi-polar world. China is experiencing political, economic and cultural development in an integrated and coordinated way. As an international student from a country along the maritime road under the Belt and Road Initiative, I deeply feel the impact and collision between cultures. In the future, I believe that China, under the leadership of a vibrant and effective social mechanism, will realize its dream.

的我又与"风之城"呼和浩特结缘。不一样的环境，不一样的气候，一切都是全新的，初来乍到虽有诸多不适应，但是随着朋友圈一天天壮大，随着新事物、文化和语言的累积，我和朋友们乃至这个城市间建立了一种非常友好的关系。相隔十几小时车程的距离，给我完全不一样的体验。也正是在这种环境下我收获颇丰。

一年的进修结束后，山东大学给了我研究生学习的机会，一个行李箱一个背包，就这样简简单单地向东前往山东。受孔夫子文化熏陶的山东人热情好客，他们在我不明白的时候尽可能地帮助我。"有朋自远方来，不亦乐乎？"我是一名志同道合的国际友人啊！从论文到工作，我的进步都离不开大家的鼓励和帮助。现在我正忙着以自己的方式过自己理想的生活。

中国的未来必定会是世界多极中的一极。现在中国的政治、经济、文化都在整合协调的发展中。作为"一带一路"中海路国家的一名留学生，我深感文化间的冲击与碰撞。未来中国在富有活力、有效的社会机制的带领下将抵达理想的彼岸。

求知，哪怕远在中国
Seeking Knowledge unto China

[埃及] 诺莱丁 北京理工大学

[Egypt] Noureldin Mohamed Abdelaal Ahmed Mohamed, Beijing Institute of Technology

In my memory, China has been a distant yet familiar place. Far away is China on the other side of the world, 8, 000 kilometers away from Egypt; where my father had been on frequent business trips after which he would bring back a few but memorable presents that would also shape my childhood and accompany my growth. China has always seemed like a movie with a changing scene to me. And I dream of one day taking up a big role in this movie.

Finally, there came the opportunity! In 2015, I won the World Mathematical Olympiad and a computer programming competition, therefore being admitted to the University of Cambridge as a master's and doctoral student. But at that time, I was uncertain where to study for my bachelor degree. My father saw what had been bothering me, and one day suddenly asked me: "China is a great country. Do you want to study there?" "Really? I must be dreaming!" I asked in surprise. Never before had I expected my dream to come true!

The Koran says, "Seek knowledge, even unto China. " I began to study computer programming on my own at the age of 4, and dreamed that I could go to Beijing Institute of Technology to study computer science. This was a completely

　　在我的记忆中，"中国"是个既遥远又熟悉的地方。遥远的是中国在地球的另一边，离埃及8000公里外的地方；熟悉的是爸爸经常来中国出差，每次都会给我带很多有意思的小东西，这些小东西填满了我的童年，陪伴着我的成长。因此，中国在我的印象中好像一部电影，在慢慢变化着。而我对这部"电影"也越来越感兴趣，总是梦想着有一天自己也能成为电影里的一个主角，演着属于我们自己的故事。

　　终于，机会来了！2015年，我获得世界奥林匹克数学竞赛和计算机编程竞赛冠军，并被剑桥大学录取为硕士、博士研究生。但那时，去哪儿读本科是让我最头疼的问题，因为有很多选择，我无法决定。爸爸好像看出了我的烦恼，有一天他突然问我："中国这么棒，想不想去那儿看看？""真的吗？我不是在做梦吧？"我吃惊地问，没想到我真的梦想成真了！

　　古兰经中提道："求知，哪怕远在中国。"我4岁就开始自学计算机编程，一直梦想着可以去北京理工大学学习计算机科学专业，这简直是从天而降的幸运。另一方面，埃及拥有独特的地理优势，是"一带一路"西端交汇地，塞西总统更是"一带一路"建设的重要支持者和参与者，

在北京理工大学国际文化节（良乡校区）

stroke of luck. On the other hand, Egypt has a unique geographical advantage—the western end of the Belt and Road. Moreover, President Abdel Fattah al-Sisi is an important supporter and participant in the construction of the Belt and Road Initiative. It is he who encourages us to go to China for broader horizons.

As soon as I arrived in Beijing, I felt the strong Chinese culture that my father used to talk about. Instead of strangeness, there was a kind of joy. More amazingly, I took a high-speed train in China, used Alipay, shopped online, and rode sharing bikes. Such inventions are completely new to me and provide a lot of convenience to my life. I cannot help but wonder how innovative the Chinese are.

After a year of learning Chinese, I have found it increasingly difficult to leave. China keeps surprising and touching me. My teachers have not only helped me with my study, but also cared for me like my family. This is my second home where teachers are like my parents and classmates are like my brothers and sisters. Although we come from different countries, we love China and each other.

In addition, the experience of learning Chinese also enables me to see the world from different perspectives, and at the same time, draws me closer to the Chinese people and to understand their lives. I still remember my listening to Peking Opera for the first time. This kind of art had been so mysterious to me — the characters were elegantly dressed and their voices were as beautiful as those

他鼓励我们去中国开阔眼界。

刚到北京，我就感受到了爸爸口中浓厚的中国文化，没有陌生感，反而有一种和老朋友约会的欣喜。更神奇的是，我真的体验到了中国的高铁、支付宝、网购、共享单车等。每一个发明都是我以前没见过的，每一个发明都为我的生活提供了很多便利，每一个发明都让我不禁感叹：中国人真的是太伟大了！

经过一年的汉语学习，我发现我已经离不开这个地方了，因为她给了我太多惊喜和感动。特别是我的老师们，他们不仅在专业上帮助我，而且在生活中还给了我像家人一样的关心和照顾。这里就是我的第二个家，老师们就像我的爸爸妈妈，同学们就像我的兄弟姐妹，虽然我们来自不同的国家，但是我们有着相同的感情。

除此之外，学习汉语的经历还可以使我从不同的视角看世界，同时，也可以让我离中国人近一点，再近一点儿，从而能了解他们的生活。记

在湖南凤凰古城

诺莱丁在天津

of the birds in the woods. I could not take my eyes off any of their expressions and movements. In addition, Laoshe Tea House also showed me the quiet, peaceful and "down-to-earth" lifestyle of the Chinese people. Friends get together and chat, drink a cup of scented tea and see a drama. They leave the troubles and pressures in life behind just for the ease and happiness of that moment.

These elements of Chinese culture have had a profound impact on me, not only affecting my way of thinking, but also making my life in Beijing more interesting. I have been seizing every minute to see this city and this country.

From one ancient civilization to another, from the pyramids to the Great Wall, from the Nile to the Yangtze River and Yellow River, I am not lonely at all but full of positive energy during my "traveling east" days. I love China, I love her ancient culture, I love her long history, I love her kind people, and I love the surprises brought by her rapid development. Now, I have really become a character in this "movie" and connected with this country in many aspects. I hope our movie will be a pleasing comedy without ending.

北京理工大学提供

得第一次听京剧，这种艺术对我来说是如此神秘，人物的装扮精致华丽，声音像树林里的鸟儿一样动听，每一个表情每一个动作都牵动着我的视线。另外，去老舍茶馆也让我感受到了中国人安静、祥和、接地气的生活方式。朋友们聚会聊天，喝一杯花茶，看一出戏曲，忘了生活中的烦恼与压力，只享受那一刻的轻松与快乐。

这些中国文化元素对我产生了很深的影响，不仅影响了我的思维方式，而且还让我在北京的生活更加有趣，恨不得每时每刻都瞪大眼睛、竖起耳朵努力感受这个国家、这个城市的无穷魅力。

从一个文明古国到另一个文明古国，从金字塔到万里长城，从尼罗河到长江黄河，"东游"的日子里，我没有感到丝毫孤独，而是满满的正能量。我爱中国，爱她古老的文化，爱她悠久的历史，爱她善良的人民，更爱她快速发展带给我的惊喜。现在，我真的成为这部"电影"里的一个人物，也和中国发生了千丝万缕的联系，希望我们的电影永远没有 Ending，也希望我们的电影会是一部令人欣慰的喜剧。

遇见更好的自己
Finding a Better Self

[卢旺达] 甘达 北方工业大学

[Rwanda] Sinigenga Daniel, North China University of Technology

Time is fleeting, and I have lived in Beijing, a beautiful city rich in culture, for nearly two years, years unforgettable to me. Deeply impressed by Beijing, I would like to share what I have experienced and learned with you.

First, what I want to mention is the "speed" of Beijing. As the capital of China, Beijing enjoys rapid economic growth and advanced technologies. As such, its "speed" as a cosmopolis is embodied in many aspects including subways extended to all directions, high-speed trains, as well as widely used WeChat and Alipay. However, our lives in Africa are relatively slower-paced due to the lack of transportation infrastructure, let alone, high-speed trains, and we have to take cash with us when shopping. But I believe it will not be long before Africa also develops world-class technologies to guarantee its people sophisticated and cosy lives just like what Beijing offers.

Second, I want to talk about the "buildings" in Beijing. From what I have learned in my college as an architecture student, I find that Beijing is home to many ancient buildings boasting profound historical heritages and demonstrating its time-honored history, namely, royal gardens of the Ming

时间匆匆流逝，不知不觉我已经在北京这座美丽、富有文化内涵的城市生活了快两年的时间，度过了一段回忆满满的日子。北京给我留下的印象非常深刻，现在我要把我所看到的、学到的、感受到的跟大家分享一下。

首先，我想说说北京的速度。北京是中国的首都，经济发展十分迅速，各方面的技术也非常先进，不管是四通八达的地铁，朝发夕至的高铁，还是微信和支付宝，无处不体现着一座国际化大都市的速度。与北京相比，在非洲我们现在要慢很多，我们没有高铁，出门购物必须要带现金，等等。但是，我相信用不了很久，我们的非洲也能像北京一样，拥有一流的技术，拥有先进、舒适的生活方式。

其次，我想说说北京的建筑。从我学习的建筑学专业来看，在北京有很多古老的建筑物，历史底蕴十分深厚。不管是明清时代的皇家园林，还是传统的胡同、四合院，无不彰显着北京悠久的历史。同时，鸟巢、水立方、国家大剧院、中央电视台、望京SOHO等一些现代建筑设计独特、造型各异，似乎又在告诉我们北京是一座现代化大都市。大学的老师经常安排我们去参观一些有代表性的建筑，拍照、研习，

dynasty and the Qing dynasty, traditional hutongs, and quadrangle dwellings. Meanwhile, Beijing's image as a metropolis is also presented by some buildings with unique designs and various structures such as National Stadium—Bird's Nest, Water Cube, National Centre for the Performaning Arts, CCTV and Wangjing SOHO. Teachers in my college often arrange for us to visit some prototypical buildings where we can take some pictures, and do some on-spot study. After that, we go back to our college and exchange ideas about these buildings with our Chinese peers. These experiences turn out to be very interesting. So it even dawns on me that I can also make more contributions to my country by designing such buildings.

Third, I would like to talk about Beijing's "flavor" . There are many well-known foods in Beijing. You can taste nearly all kinds of foods from across China here, my favorite being Beijing roast duck and hot pot. I still remember tasting nothing but some western food such as hamburgers and pizza in Shanghai. At that time, Chinese food did not impress me that much. However, when I came to Beijing, after tasting many delicious local foods with my friends, I have gradually changed my views, and even tend to love Chinese food bit by bit now.

Last but not least, I want to talk about my friends in Beijing. I have made a lot of friends from different countries, including many easy-going and lovely Chinese friends. We get along well by learning from and helping each other. Even though I am far away from my homeland, I still feel at home and so warm because of their friendliness and hospitality. My Chinese was poor at first, but it has been greatly improved since I started my study here. Additionally, I even become more active in helping those new international students in Beijing.

All in all, I am honored to work on the major I like in this lovely university,

北方工业大学提供

回来和中国同学交流、学习，这些都是非常有意思的。我觉得毕业以后我也可以试着在我的国家设计一些这样的建筑物，并且为我的国家做更多的贡献。

再次，我来说说北京的味道。北京有很多美食，基本上全国各地的美食都可以品尝到，我最喜欢的有北京烤鸭、火锅等。我还记得以前在上海的时候我只尝试过汉堡、比萨等西方的食物，当时我觉得中国的食物很难吃，可是来北京后，我跟我的朋友一起尝试，渐渐觉得中国的食物不但没有我想象得那么难吃，而且有的很有特色，味道也很不错。我慢慢喜欢上了北京的味道。

最后，我想说说我北京的朋友。我在北京认识了很多朋友，来自不同的国家，也有很多美丽大方的中国朋友，我们互相学习，相互帮助，相处得十分融洽。这让身处异国他乡的我感受到了无比的亲切和温暖，我感受到了到中国朋友的友好、热情。以前我的中文不是很好，

北方工业大学提供

and I have made so many good friends here over the past two years. In the upcoming two years, I hope I can find a better self by acquiring more knowledge, and I will never stop my hard work just like the way the sun and moon never cease rising in the sky, and rivers never stop running through high mountains. Here I want to thank my dear teachers and classmates. I love you all and I love Beijing!

北方工业大学提供

在北京这段时间的学习，我觉得我的中文水平有了很大提升，而且现在我也退去了生涩，开始主动帮助一些刚刚来到中国、来到北京的留学生。

总之，在过去的两年，我很荣幸能在北京一所我非常喜欢的大学里学习，学习我喜欢的专业，认识这么多好朋友。在未来的两年时间，我希望能学到更多的东西，让我遇见更好的自己。日月恒升，山高水长。在此感谢我的老师和同学们，谢谢你们，我爱你们，我爱北京！

我在北京的留学生活
My Study Life in Beijing

[加蓬] 西德尼　北方工业大学

[Gabon] Sydney Cletrick NSAH ALLOGO,North China University of Technology

"If given the chance, I will tell you my story. "

This is a free and easy line from a Chinese film I have seen named *The Continent*, and its connotation is so lingering and unfinished for me. I am Xideni (Sydney Cletrick NSAH ALLOGO) from Gabon. Currently, I am majoring in architecture at the North China University of Technology. As for my reason for being here and studying architecture in Beijing, the answer is but one: my curiosity to see this country thorough.

When I first arrived in Beijing, I felt everything was so unfamiliar to me. Back then, I could not speak Chinese, and did not have any Chinese friends. I did not know how to order food in a restaurant, or buy anything in a shop, nor did I know how to take a bus or the subway. So many "I don't know" kept isolating me in my classrooms and dormitory. However, it was these hardships that have made me determined to work hard in learning Chinese. So I spent six months learning the basic Chinese vocabulary and became gradually more confident to go around and intentionally find more Chinese people to chat and converse with.

"有机会，我把我的故事讲给你听。"

这句话是我看过的一部中国电影《后会无期》里一句洒脱的台词，听来意犹未尽。我叫西德尼，来自加蓬，目前在北方工业大学学习建筑学专业。至于当初为什么选择来中国，来北京学习建筑学，答案只有一个：那就是怀着对东方神秘国度的好奇，我要用自己的眼睛来看看。

初到北京时，两眼一抹黑。不会讲中文，没有中国朋友，导致我在生活上都很困难。我不会点菜，不会买东西，不会坐公交车和地铁，如此多的"不会"直接导致我除了教室和宿舍，去哪里都很艰难。也正是这些艰难促使我下决心必须努力学习中文。于是我用六个月的时间学习了基本的词汇，渐渐地我有信心走出去，并刻意找周围的中国人去沟通和交流。

在公园里我见到了跳广场舞的大爷大妈，还有用毛笔蘸水在石板上练字的大爷，这一切都让我感到新奇；我去了三里屯，那里有来自全世界的时尚的年轻人，在那里我感受到了北京的无比繁华和时尚潮流；我品尝了北京的烤鸭和各式小吃，感受到了和家乡美食不同的味道；慢慢

In parks, I saw old people dance on squares, and seniors use the brush to practice calligraphy on the slab. All of these made me feel fresh and new. I went to Sanlitun, where fashionable young people from all over the world gather. There, I felt the incomparable hustling and bustling as well as the fashion trends of Beijing. I tasted Beijing roast duck and all kinds of snacks, which taste so different from those of my hometown cuisine. As I became more and more familiar with Beijing, I came to love this city even more.

I visited the hutongs in Beijing and they are square courtyards. They were buildings surrounded by symmetrical forms of squares and later I came to know that this building style symbolizes harmony and reunion. I enjoy chatting with residents there. When they talk too fast, I can hardly understand, yet I can still understand what they say through their body language and facial expressions. They tell me about the history and culture of Beijing, and introduce me to the recreation and delicious food here. Their enthusiasm has made me feel that I am not a foreigner at all, and that has enabled me to embrace the warmth and enthusiasm from people in Beijing towards people from other countries.

I also visited the Forbidden City, where the splendor and solemnity astounds me. I have been to the Tian'anmen Square. With a solid and majestic appearance and a beautiful contour, it is not only a splendid masterpiece in the history of ancient Chinese palace architecture, but also a long-standing symbol of Chinese civilization. Above the central gate of the Tian'anmen Square, there is a portrait of Mao Zedong and on both sides are the slogans "Long live the People's Republic of China" and "Long live the great unity of the people of the world". Unfortunately, I have not seen the flag-raising ceremony at the Tian'anmen Square until now. However, if chance permits, I must go to watch

地我对北京越来越熟悉，也越来越爱这座城市。

我去了北京的胡同，胡同里的建筑几乎都是四合院，是四四方方的对称形式围在一起的建筑物，后来我才知道这种建筑象征和谐与团圆。我很喜欢和胡同里的老北京人聊天，虽然他们说快了，我很难听懂，可是通过他们的肢体语言和神情，我大概能理解他们所说的内容，他们和我讲述北京的历史和文化，给我介绍北京的好玩的好吃的，他们的热情让我感觉到我不像是一个外国人，让我感受到来自异国他乡的温暖与热情。

我去参观了紫禁城，那儿金碧辉煌、庄严绚丽，让我叹为观止；我参观了天安门，天安门城楼外观稳健持重，又不失美丽的曲线，它不仅是中国古代宫殿建筑史上辉煌的杰作，也是中华文明悠久历史的象征。天安门城楼正中门洞上方悬挂着毛泽东的画像，两边挂着"中华人民共和国万岁"和"世界人民大团结万岁"的大幅标语，遗憾的是到现在我还没看过天安门广场的升旗仪式，有机会我一定要去感受一下这庄严肃

北方工业大学提供

such a solemn scene in person.

Now, I am slowly integrating into this city. In the previous year, as my Chinese proficiency improved, I have come to know some interesting sites and places for delicious food that even locals are unaware of. I also have a lot of "fellows and buddies" from Beijing and they have always cared and helped me, giving me the much needed warmth in this metropolis. Now, my dream is weaving here, my youth is blooming, and my soul is flying freely here.

If asked to use a color to depict Beijing in my heart, I would certainly choose red. The autumn sun that I saw when I first met with Beijing, the red leaves of Xiangshan, the ancient city gates, the neon lights flashing on the commercial streets, and the lanterns in front of the shops are all red. Beijing always has a strong festive, prosperous, gorgeous, passionate and vigorous atmosphere. Red is also the dominant hue of Beijingers' character in that they are all outgoing, enthusiastic, and full of passion and inclusiveness.

I love Beijing. I love its enthusiasm, long-enduring history and construction achievements. Beijing is like home, I will take an active part in contributing to it. I am Sydney, thank you for listening to my story.

北方工业大学提供

穆的升旗仪式。

我在慢慢融入这个城市，最近一年，随着我中文水平的不断提高，我甚至知道了一些北京当地人都不知道的好玩、好吃的地方。我也拥有了很多北京的"好哥们儿"，他们给我关心和帮助，让我在这个陌生的城市感受到温暖。我的梦想在这里编织，青春在这里绽放，灵魂在这里飞翔。

如果让我用一种色彩来形容我心中的北京，那么我心中的北京一定是红色的。那些我初与北京相识时看到的秋日的艳阳、香山的红叶、古老的城门、商街上闪烁的霓虹灯、商店前的灯笼，个个都红红火火。北京这座城市有着浓烈的喜庆、富贵、华丽、热情和生机。红色，也是北京人性格的主色调，热情奔放，激情四溢，包容四方。

我爱北京，我爱它的热情似火，爱它的历史悠久，爱它的建设成就。未来的几年，在北京，我会以主人翁的精神继续爱它并维护它，我是西德尼，谢谢你们听我的故事。

异域他乡的青春拼图
Puzzle of My Youth in a Foreign Land

[越南]　刘文胜　西北大学
[Vietnam] LƯU VĂN THẮNG, Northwest University

With yearnings and dreams, through the roaring of the plane, I came to China from Vietnam and began my new study life. A year ago, I encountered all the fresh and beautiful things in this ancient city. On this foreign land are memories which formed my youth.

The first piece of the puzzle is my admiration for the development of China's e-economy.

Grasping the trend of fast-developing science and technology is like taking the lead in the future development of the world. Anything can be done on a mobile phone through the convenient cashless payment of WeChat and Alipay. I've been amazed by the development of e-commerce here.

The second piece of the puzzle is Xi'an, the city where I live.

Xi'an is an ancient city. Living here seems as if traveling back in time as I explore millennia-old alleys and ancient buildings that mix with modernity. There is romance and poetry to this ancient city. Strolling along Shuncheng Lane, you hear the quiet, simple and clear moat flowing in an unhurried pace, and the bluestone road by the river tells the history of this imperial capital.

　　带着憧憬与梦想，在飞机的轰鸣降落声中，从越南抵临中国，展开在中国留学的人生新历程。一年前，和一切新鲜和美好相遇，相遇在悠悠古城，一念相遇，在异域他乡，拼起一幅青春人生的回忆拼图。

　　第一块，拼在我对中国电子经济发展的赞叹中。

　　科技的更新发展迅速。在当代，掌握科技的趋势潮流，就好比掌握世界未来发展的先机，微信、支付宝付款带来诸多便利，无现金电子快捷支付，生活大小点滴事，衣食住行等，都可以通过一个手机解决，在中国，电子经济和电子商务的发展，方便着我的生活也同时让我感到赞叹。

　　再一块，拼在我所在的城市——西安。

　　西安是一座古城，走在大街小巷，风格绮丽的建筑中，仿佛走在古装戏剧里。古城的浪漫与诗意，顺城巷的步道，宁静、古朴、清丽，护城河吟唱着古老的歌谣，不紧不慢地流淌着，仿佛在诉说着皇都变迁的历史，漫步在河边青石板路上。斑驳的印记清晰刻在古色古香城墙壁上，一方古城墙，历经风花雪月的繁华，人走茶凉的悲伤，或美或伤，时间锻造出沧桑，望着岁月的痕迹，仿佛听见历史的回声。西安，在春天百

The ancient city wall has witnessed this city's past prosperity and people's routines. Looking at the trace of the times, I can hear the echo of history. Xi'an showcases unparalleled beauty in all four seasons. They endure so as to show unique charm. Xi'an, standing through the vicissitudes, will always be a witness to history.

The third piece of the puzzle is my schoolwork and extracurricular life.

When I first arrived in China, the heat in early autumn had not yet dispersed. I took some time to adapt to the climate and the life here. My new classmates were from all over the world. We came to know each other in the days of learning Chinese together, chatting, playing and experiencing culture together. Learning Chinese was extremely difficult at the beginning. I found it hard to pronounce each *pinyin*, not to mention the Chinese characters that seemed impossible to remember. Thanks to the day-to-day practice and

西北大学提供

花娇艳时绚丽，在盛夏月明星稀中璀璨，在秋日天朗气清中诗情，在隆冬银装素裹中沉淀，古城的春夏秋冬，散发着不同的韵味。一念长安悠久地，寒来暑往千年记。

接着一块，拼在我的课业课余生活中。

初来中国，初秋的天气，暑热还未散去，慢慢适应气候和生活，新来到班级上课，同学来自世界各地，在共同学习中文和聊天嬉闹中，和各种文化碰撞，渐渐从陌生到熟悉。最初学习中文，真的觉得好难，每个拼音的发音都很困难，汉字看起来就更像鬼画符般难以记忆和理解，通过日复一日的练习和记忆，到现在终于可以得心应手地自如交谈。

课后，每天傍晚的羽毛球活动，让我的生活更加丰富多彩。在操场上、体育活动中，和中国人一起打比赛，挥洒汗水，总是可以结识志同道合的朋友。

最后一块，拼在我的爱情里。

memorizing, I today can talk without hassle.

After class, playing badminton in the evenings has added color to my life canvas. Playing sports with people here always brings you friends.

The last piece of the puzzle is my love.

Xi'an in early December is freezing. It seems that the icy wind devours everything. However, my most beautiful encounter with her warmed the whole winter. She is an outgoing, lively and decent Chinese girl who has a charming smile. Her laughter and gentleness warmed my first cold winter in China. It was not long after I began to learn Chinese that I first met her. I had no choice but to smile at her when she spoke too fast and I could not follow. She was really talkative and lovely when she acted like a spoiled child. She has been a great help for me in learning Chinese.

We had lunch together, enjoyed the afternoon in the café, walked and chatted, went to the suburbs for an outing in early spring, watched a movie... When I am with her, I leave all my worries behind to enjoy every minute. We listen to the passing happy times, watch the sun set and pour out our hearts to one another.

I have stayed in China for a year, during which I have learnt new knowledge, experiences a new life, harvested the seed of love and recorded all the beautiful things. I believe there are more puzzles to be added on my studying journey in China.

　　12月初的西安，寒冬的冰封中，冷风凛冽逼人，那冷意似乎可以吞噬一切，但，她的出现，最美丽的邂逅，温暖了整个冬天。她是一个开朗、活泼、大方的中国女孩，爱笑的女孩总是那样迷人，她的笑她的温柔，温暖着我来到中国第一个难熬的寒冷冬天。最初认识她时，我刚学中文不久，她讲话很快的时候，我听不明白，就对她笑笑而已，她真的好健谈，一直一直跟我聊天，撒娇起来的语气，好可爱，也要谢谢她帮我学习中文。

　　我们一起共进午餐，一起在咖啡厅共度午后时光，一起散步聊天，一起去郊外踏青，一起看电影……一起的一切一切，和她相处的时光，可以放下任何多余的情愫，只留下开心就好，聆听幸福时光流动的声音，在静静等着阳光变夕阳时，在有月光倾泻的夜晚里，慢慢慢慢，借着风，轻轻倾诉着。

　　来到中国一年，经历着新鲜有趣的人生新体验，在异域他乡，学习新知，体验生活，播种爱情，将美好书写，纪念，接着书写……相信，留学时光拼起的人生青春拼图，未完待续……

致卡莫的一封信
A Letter to Komol

[乌兹别克斯坦]　周书奇　武汉大学
[Uzbekistan] Zokirov Dilshod, Wuhan University

Dear Komol:

How are you in your hometown? Have you adapted to your new job?

Time flies. Now I have been in Wuhan for two years. Within these two years, my life has undergone dramatic changes, and I have fallen in love with this river city. I hope you can visit this amazing city in person someday. First, I would like to tell you that Wuhan is comprised of three boroughs: Wuchang, Hankou and Hanyang. Although having different historic characteristics and features, they are perfect combination of the past and modern times. Thus, Wuhan is also called "Chicago in the East".

In Wuhan, first time in my life, I was impressed by a bridge. It is the well-known Yangtze River Bridge. Before the new semester, the tutor for foreign students organized us to visit several famous scenic spots in Wuhan. We visited the Yangtze River Bridge for the third stop. We came to the river side of Wuchang at nightfall. With sunset in the sky and river down the bridge, all lights were shining around the bridge. It was such a beautiful scene that I could never forget. At that time, our tutor recited a poem: "A bridge connects north and south, and the trench becomes a

亲爱的卡莫：

你在家乡还好吗？你适应了你的新工作吗？

时间过得可真快，转眼间，我已经在武汉待了两年了。这两年里，我的生活变化了很多，我已经慢慢爱上了这座美丽的江城，我希望有朝一日你也能来亲自感受武汉的魅力。首先我要给你介绍，武汉由武昌、汉口和汉阳这三镇构成，这三个区各有不一样的历史特色和风貌，但是都是历史与现代的完美结合的体现，所以武汉也被誉为"东方芝加哥"。

我来武汉后，生平第一次被一座桥梁所震撼到，那就是闻名天下的长江大桥。记得那时还没开学，我们来华留学生的指导老师组织大家一起去参观武汉的几个著名景点，第三站就定在了长江大桥。我们是在武昌的江滩进行观赏的，那时已到了傍晚，满天红黄相间的晚霞，长江大桥亮起了灯，桥下的长江水慢慢流淌着，这幅美丽景象如画一般，令我终生难忘。那时老师吟诵了一句诗词："一桥飞架南北，天堑变通途。"长江大桥的雄伟气势让我们在场的每个留学生心生敬畏，大家纷纷拿出手机留下那珍贵的画面。在欣赏完如此美景以后，我们去参观了黄鹤楼。后来在中文学习中，我偶然学到了一句李白写的关于黄鹤楼的诗："故人

thoroughfare. " We were all deeply impressed by its majesty and took photos. Then we visited the Yellow Crane Tower. Later when studying Chinese, I learned a Chinese poem about this tower by chance: "At Yellow Crane Tower in the west, my old friend says farewell; in the mist and flowers of spring, he goes down to Yangzhou". It was written by Li Bai, a famous Chinese poet. Once again, I understand how charming the tower is. No wonder it is listed as one of the four great towers in China.

I am also proud of my university, Wuhan University. It is honored as one of the most beautiful universities in China. Our university covers a large area, but most importantly, it is located beside the East Lake, a beautiful 5A tourist attraction in China. Every time when I go out or enter our campus, I can enjoy the green mountains and the blue sky. It is so beautiful. A famous poet in China, Yuan Shuoyou, even wrote a poem about this beautiful scene. Every year, when the cherries are in full blossom, our campus is crowded with visitors.

Within these two years, I have been riding shared bikes and circling around the East Lake. By visiting the Plum Garden and Peony Garden, I learned about the Chinese garden art. Besides, I also visited the ancient buildings at Moshan Hill. They are gorgeous! I took many photos and would send them all to you. You will be amazed for sure. Connecting to the East Lake, the Shuiguohu Lake is adjacent to one of the most bustling commercial street in Wuhan—Han Street. The architecture in Han Street blends perfectly the ancient architectural style with that of the modern times. You can fully enjoy yourself there, and I love going shopping there. One of my favorite food shops is located there, selling egg puffs. When I first tried it, I was amazed to know that eggs can be made into such delicious and creative food. Later, I tried every flavor of egg puffs sold there, and they are all so delicious!

The transportation in Wuhan is very convenient, especially the subway. I love

西辞黄鹤楼，烟花三月下扬州"，我又一次感慨黄鹤楼从古至今的无限魅力，真不愧是中国四大名楼之一啊！

　　我所在的武汉大学也是我引以为傲的，它被誉为中国最美的大学之一。武汉大学面积大，占地广，更重要的是它坐落在武汉美丽的 5A 级东湖风景区旁，每次我从大学门口出去就能欣赏到赏心悦目的风光，碧绿的山水与蓝色天际相接，让人心旷神怡，真就如中国伟大诗人袁说友所写的"野木迢迢遮去雁，渔舟点点映飞鸟"的景象。每年到了樱花季，我们大学里的游客都络绎不绝。

　　这两年里，我曾经无数次骑着便捷的共享单车环游整个东湖风景区，参观梅园和牡丹园，从中见识了中国的园林艺术。我还走进了磨山上的古老建筑，它们的美令我流连忘返。我拍了很多照片留念呢，我会逐一发给你的，你看了后一定会感叹的！与东湖相接的还有一个水果湖，在那里有武汉数一数二的繁华街区——汉街，汉街的建筑风格是集传统与

taking subway by myself on weekends and visiting different places in Wuhan. For example, I went to Zhongshan Park in Hankou and tried an interesting activity with a kind grandpa. It is called "lashing large gyroscopes". Let me introduce it. The player needs to hold a long and heavy whip and lash the large gyroscope, so that it can spin for a long time. I was not good at it. It is actually quite difficult, and it takes a long time to practice and master the required skill. The grandpa told me that practicing this can relieve pain in waist, shoulder and back, so it is good for the elder.

Another impressive activity I took part in is going to a trampoline park. I watched some videos about trampoline online, but I never tried it by myself. I have been curious about it for a long time. Finally, I had the chance to visit a trampoline park with a Chinese friend and had great fun there. Although as a primary player, I bounced on the trampoline with many children, I still learned several difficult moves. By the way, I met a tutor who is also from Uzbekistan. How wonderful fate is! Of course, my whole body ached on the second day, and I could barely leave my bed. However, I do not regret it, because I experienced the rich lives of Chinese students after classes. That's really enviable.

That is my wonderful life in Wuhan, and I want to share it with you. If you have enough time or a good opportunity, I hope you can see me in Wuhan. I will wait for you here!

Hope everything goes on well for you. I look forward to hearing from you.

Yours,

Zokirov Dilshod

July 2, 2018

Luojia Hill

现代于一身，在这里吃喝玩乐的东西应有尽有，我每次购物都会来这里。而且这儿有我最喜欢的一个小吃店，专卖鸡蛋仔。第一次吃它的时候，我才知道用鸡蛋可以做出这么美味又有创意的美食，此后我品尝了他们家所有味道的鸡蛋仔，每种都好吃！

武汉的地铁交通很方便，周末时我经常独自一人乘地铁去武汉的各种地方。比如我去了汉口的中山公园，跟着一位和蔼的老爷爷尝试了一项有趣的运动——抽打大型陀螺。我来给你讲解一下：操作者的手里需要拿一根又长又重的鞭子，手臂和背部要同时用力，抽打大陀螺，让它尽可能长时间地转动。我玩得非常吃力，因为这个运动其实很难，需要技巧与长时间练习。老爷爷告诉我，这个运动有助于缓解腰肩背的疼痛，很适合中老年人。

还有一次让我记忆深刻的体验是和我的一位中国朋友去蹦床体验馆。以前我只在网上看过很多人玩蹦床的视频，我从来没试过，但一直很好奇向往。终于有了机会和一位中国朋友去蹦床空气工厂，我在那里跳得很尽兴。虽然只是初级体验者，而且是和很多小孩子一起跳，但我还是学会了几个有难度的动作。值得一提的是，我碰到了一个和我来自一个国家的教练，缘分真是奇妙啊！玩完蹦床的第二天，我浑身酸痛，几乎下不了床，但我一点也不后悔，我体会到了中国年轻人课余的丰富生活，真令人羡慕。

这就是我在武汉的精彩生活，我想把这些感觉也分享给你，希望你有机会、有时间就过来探望你的老朋友吧！我在武汉等你！

祝你工作一帆风顺，期待你的回信。

你的好友：周书奇

2018 年 7 月 2 日于珞珈山

命运中的邂逅
Destined Encounter

［巴基斯坦］ 沈若祎　中国地质大学（武汉）

[Pakistan] Naeem Shamraza, China University of Geosciences (Wuhan)

How wonderful destiny is.

I had never thought that I would have the chance to study in China. Maybe, it is destiny that sent me here.

I have been told by a mass of articles, books, news and the Internet that China was one of the most vigorous forces in the world. Every time when I read those sentences, I try to imagine what China looks like. Why is it so prosperous? What is its secret to stand on its own feet among all nations of the world?

I did not know if I am looking at a real China When I saw Chinese movies. Neither can I rely alone on books or the Internet to know a country. Therefore, I started my journey to China.

If one does not try and discover by himself, he cannot get close to the reality. During my stay in China, I have gained a clear picture of a major country from every aspect. Now, I came to understand why this country is so successful.

The Chinese government has been serving the people wholeheartedly, providing convenience to the people, and making their lives better. During my one-year stay in Wuhan, I experienced a variety of convenient lifestyles. The

命运真是一个非常神奇的东西。

我从没想过自己会有机会来中国留学，也许，是命运，把我送到了这里。

以前，我在书本里、新闻里、互联网上，读到过各种文章和信息，它们都告诉我，中国是世界上最有生命力的国家之一。每当我读到这些句子时，我都会试图去想象，中国到底是个什么样的国家呢？为什么中国这么发达？中国屹立于世界民族之林的成功秘诀是什么？

看中国的电影，我不知道是不是真实的面貌。而读书、上网看中国的样子，我也觉得还不够全面。于是，我踏上了来中国的旅途。

如果一个人不亲自去尝试，去发现，他就无法接近现实。在中国的这一年，我从方方面面看到了一个真实的大国的样子。而现在，我也慢慢了解到，为什么这个国家如此成功。

中国政府一直全心全意地服务人民。生活中，不断为人民提供便利，竭尽所能让人民的生活变得更美好。在武汉生活的这一年，我体验到了各种便利的生活方式，看到了武汉一条又一条的地铁线、大马路，一座又一座美观、全面的商业广场。这让我的出行方式变得轻松有趣，平日

metro lines and roads have been sprawling, and many beautiful and all-in-one commercial plazas have risen from the ground. Traveling has become easy and amusing and the ways of entertainment are also increased.

In China, every person lives a busy life, be it student or merchant. They have a fixed work plan and also know how to enjoy life. No matter how busy they are, they will squeeze out some time to accompany their families and friends when on holiday. They love sports and can be seen everywhere running, walking, doing yoga, playing table tennis, playing basketball especially at night.

For me, what I most appreciate is Chinese people's friendliness, honesty, devotion and diligence. Whether working in a big company or a small restaurant, they, be it the elderly or ladies, treat every job equally. Meanwhile, they will not lose their courage for life no matter what they are doing for living. When I first came to China, I was so surprised when I saw a female driver on a bus. China is a country where women are given equal rights to work. The Chinese society gives its people equal opportunities without gender discrimination and a safe working environment.

I am also inspired by little things I saw in daily life. As an international student from Pakistan, I also hope to bring what I have seen and learned back to my country so that the people of my country can feel the unique charm of China. Thank the destiny for bringing me here and I will march on with the energy that China endows me!

中国地质大学（武汉）提供

里的娱乐也不断丰富起来。

中国人民也一样。在中国，不管是学生还是商人，每个职业的人，都过着忙碌的生活。他们往往有着合理的计划，也会享受生活。即使工作再忙碌，也会在节假日挤出时间陪伴自己的家人和朋友。他们热爱运动，特别是在晚上，跑步、散步、瑜伽、舞蹈、乒乓球、篮球等。到处都有他们挥洒汗水的身影。

对我而言，我最欣赏的就是中国人友好、诚实、奉献和努力工作的样子。他们平等地对待每一份工作。无论是大公司，还是小餐馆，无论是老年人，还是妇女，他们都有自己的一份工作。同时，他们也不会因为工作的大小而失掉生活的勇气。刚来中国时，当我在一辆公交车上看到一位女司机时，我很吃惊。这是一个给予女性平等工作权利的国家，在这里，男女的能力没有绝对的区别，而社会也会给他们平等的机会和良好安全的工作环境。

经历着生活的点滴小事，我也很受启发。作为巴基斯坦政府派来的留学生，我也希望把我的这些所见所学带回自己的国家，让我的国家也感受一下中国的独特魅力。感谢命运，把我带到这里，让我带着中国赋予我的能量，继续走下去！

第一次坐高铁
My First Trip by High-speed Train

［柬埔寨］ 雷观帖　同济大学
[Cambodia] Luy Kunthea, Tongji University

I am Leiguantie (Luy Kunthea) from Cambodia, an undergraduate enrolled in 2016 by the International School of Tongji University.

Thanks to the Belt and Road Initiative, a Confucius Institute has been set up in Cambodia, from which I have received a scholarship and come to study in China. I was excited when I received the admission letter from Tongji University, because I found that my long-cherished dream was about to come true. I was also worried because as a girl off to a foreign country for the first time, might encounter difficulties. However, my curiosity for China encouraged me to go.

Before I came to China, my previous Chinese learning experience was like observing the moon and the stars through clouds. China is a beautiful but distant country. By coming to China, I started my journey to the outside world, and opened the door to all my expectations. Guess what, the Chinese word that I most frequently use is "Wa". "Wa! What tall buildings! What busy streets!" "Wa! What dazzling goods! What beautiful colors!" "Wa! Is it the China I imaged?"

After settling down at Tongji University, my friends and I could not wait to see the well-known Bund and Pudong Financial Center. The magnificent

我叫雷观帖，来自柬埔寨，是国际文化交流学院 2016 级本科生。

由于中国的"一带一路"倡议，柬埔寨开设了孔子学院，我通过自己的努力，获得了孔子学院奖学金资助来华留学。收到同济大学录取通知书的那一刻，我发觉曾经梦寐以求的愿望突然离自己那么近，我又激动又担心，一个女生第一次出国，在异国他乡难免会遇到困难吧，但是，我对中国的那颗好奇之心，使得我下定决心一定要去中国留学！

来中国之前多年学汉语的经历就像隔着云幕看太空的星星、月亮，中国很美，但也很遥远。到中国留学，则开启了我的宇宙之旅，打开了我所有期盼之门。你们猜得出，我来中国后说得最多的一个汉字是哪一个吗？没猜到吧！是"哇"！"哇！高楼大厦，车水马龙！""哇！琳琅满目，五颜六色！""哇！这是我印象中的中国吗？"

来到同济，安顿下来之后，我就和朋友们一起迫不及待地想见识闻名已久的外滩和浦东金融中心，璀璨耀眼的东方明珠，高耸入云的上海中心，万国建筑荟萃的外滩，繁花似锦、游人如织的南京路步行街，比我在电视和照片上看到的漂亮多了，真是让我大开眼界，激动万分啊！

俗话说，读万卷书，行万里路。除了努力学习之外，我利用业余时

Oriental Pearl Radio & Television Tower, the soaring Shanghai Center, the Bund with a variety of western-style buildings and the prosperous and crowded Nanjing Road Pedestrian Walkway were more beautiful than I had seen on TV and pictures. I was very much impressed and excited to see them.

As a Chinese saying goes, "One needs to read thousands of books and travel thousands of miles." Apart from working hard in my studies, I spend my spare time exploring this amazing country on my own and experiencing the beauty of China's construction and development. Another Chinese saying goes, "Up in heaven, there is paradise; down on earth, there are Suzhou and Hangzhou." My Cambodian friends here and I once traveled to Hangzhou, a paradise for ancient Chinese people, which now takes the lead in modern intelligence development. The world-renowned company Alibaba is based in Hangzhou. The G20 summit was held in Hangzhou not long ago. In recent years, its rapid growth in the animation industry has made her worthy of the reputation as "animation capital".

I took the high-speed train for the first time when I went to Hangzhou. A bus ride from Shanghai to Hangzhou takes at least four hours. However, it took me only an hour by high-speed train. In just an hour, I had a new understanding of the high-speed train. It is extremely fast, and the fare is affordable. You do not need to check in luggage, either. The high-speed train has excellent stability, so I felt more comfortable taking it rather than a conventional plane. Once I saw a video which showed someone turning a coin on the table by the window while the train was moving fast. He managed to keep it from falling down. This demonstrated the great steadiness of the high-speed train and its superiority over other means of transportation. China's high-speed train is

间去亲身探索这个美丽的国度，体验中国的建设发展之美。"上有天堂，下有苏杭"，我跟同胞们去了杭州旅行，杭州不仅是古人心中的天堂，也是现代智能发展的领先之地。举世闻名的阿里巴巴总部就在杭州，杭州刚刚举办了 G20 峰会，近年来杭州动漫产业的迅速增长使得她当之无愧地成为"动漫之都"。

去杭州我第一次乘坐了高铁。上海到杭州坐大巴至少要四个小时，而乘坐高铁我们只花了一个小时就到达了目的地。短短一小时让我对高铁有了新的认知，高铁速度极快，而且票也不算很贵，还不用托运行李。高铁平稳性极佳，乘坐高铁我觉得比坐飞机还舒服呢！前段时间，我看过一段视频，那就是高铁正在行驶的时候，有人在窗边上转动一枚硬币，一直转不倒下，这就说明了高铁的稳定性特别好，不像其他交通工具。高铁技术真了不起！除了高铁，中国的高新技术产业发展得越来越迅速，

在井冈山

awesome! In addition to high-speed train, China's high-tech industry is also developing very fast. More airplanes are made in China. I believe in the future more and more high-tech products will be crowned "Made in China".

Sitting by the window on the train, enjoying the scenery outside and watching the dramatic changes in China's village, I wondered if I could bring these technologies back to Cambodia. Because of the long distance between the capital Phnom Penh and my home, I have to spend 8 hours on the bus when I go to visit my relatives in the capital. It would be great if there were high-speed trains in Cambodia. I believe this dream will come true with China's advancement of the Belt and Road Initiative, from which Cambodia will benefit.

在井冈山（二排左五为作者）

就连飞机现在也有了中国制造呢！我相信在未来会有越来越多的高科技都被冠以中国制造的头衔。

　　坐在高铁上欣赏着窗外的风景，看着中国山乡巨变的面貌，我心里常想要是能把高铁这些技术带回柬埔寨就好了，因为我家离首都金边比较远，每次到首都探亲，在路上坐大巴需要花八小时的时间，如果在柬埔寨也有高铁，那该多好啊！我相信随着"一带一路"建设的推进，柬埔寨搭乘上中国发展的东风，这个梦想很快就会实现的！

[韩国]　申文燮　深圳大学
[Republic of Korea] Shin Moonsub, Shenzhen University

I still remember the moment I got off the plane in Shenzhen in January, 2010.

The first thing which surprised me was the difference in climate. The winter in Republic of Korea is very cold. Shenzhen, however, was wrapped in warm moist air. I thought to myself that how could this be winter. Taking a glance at my first stop, a gloomy and confined airport, I thought I had arrived at the wrong place. On my way to the Daya Bay Nuclear Power Plant where my father worked, everything I saw was in greenery, which is rare in the cold winter in Republic of Korea. The sense of strangeness made me feel Shenzhen was indeed a foreign land.

Since 2010, I have been exploring the city. Habituated myself to the life in this city, I have fit in its community. In this young and vigorous city, I never stop marching forward. I learnt Chinese, and obtained a BA in Chinese language and literature studies, as well as a Master in International Economic Law. I'm currently studying a PhD program in theoretical economics in China Center for Special Economic Zone Research in Shenzhen. I'm growing together with this

我还记得 2010 年 1 月刚下飞机来到深圳的那一刻。

首先让我感受到的是气候的差异。韩国的冬天是非常寒冷的，那深圳呢？一下飞机就有一股暖湿的空气扑面而来，我心里想这哪是冬天啊？再抬眼看看接待我的第一站——暗暗的灯光、破破烂烂不够宽大的深圳机场，我以为我来错了地方。从机场坐车去父亲工作的地方——大亚湾核电站，一路上看到的都是绿色。在韩国寒冷的冬天里是看不到这些树木的，不熟悉的一切，让我感觉到：深圳就是异国他乡！

从 2010 年开始，我一边读书一边开始认识深圳，习惯了深圳的生活，融入了社会。在这个年轻的、充满活力的城市，我也一直在奋斗。我不仅学会了汉语，也完成了汉语言文学的学士学位以及国际经济法的硕士学位，目前我在深圳中国经济特区研究中心攻读理论经济学的博士学位。跟随深圳的发展，我在与深圳一起成长。深圳成了我的第二故乡。

给我印象最深刻的是 2011 年夏天，深圳举办了国际大学生运动会，整个深圳变得特别有活力，并且整个深圳的面貌从此有了巨大的改善，许多低矮的楼房不见了，道路变宽了，人们也变得更文明了。随着科技的发展，尤其是 3G 和 4G 的通信技术的普及，给深圳带来了不少发展空

city. Shenzhen has already become my second hometown.

The summer in 2011 impressed me deeply. The International University Sports Federation was held then in Shenzhen. The entire city took a whole new look. The low-rise buildings receded into the city landscape which was covered by wider roads, and even the citizens are more polite. Benefited from the development of science and technology, such as the popularity of 3G and 4G telecommunication, Shenzhen has seen much more development space and changes. There used to be only two business districts, the East Gate and the Huaqiang North. The Huaqiang North was the dreamland of mobile phone users around the country back then. People joke that you may not know Shenzhen, but you definitely know Huaqiang North. There used to be just one metro line, Line No. 1, named Luobao Xian. If my memory doesn't fail me, most people got off at Lao Jie station or Huaqiang North station at that time.

Time flies. Shenzhen where I have spent eight years of my life is a totally different city now. Surrounding areas including Luohu, Baoan, Longgang, and Huizhou have embarked on the fast lane of development. The former small airport was also replaced by a splendid modern international airport. More metro lines have been put into use, and each district has its shopping malls. All these changes have greatly facilitated transportation and our lives. I don't need to transfer to Hong Kong to go back to my country as now it only takes 20 minutes from Shenzhen University to the airport through metro Line 11.

It is widely known that as the first exemplary innovative city, Shenzhen is regarded as the most Silicon Valley-like city and a gathering place for creators in China. Over the years, the Shenzhen government has taken advantages of the special economic zone to create an innovative and entrepreneurial

间和变化。当年的深圳，只有两个商圈比较繁华——东门和华强北。华强北就是当年在全国最出名的手机天堂！有个笑话：很多人没听说过深圳，但都听说过华强北。那时候的深圳，只有一条地铁线，即一号罗宝线。在我的印象里，大部分人都是在老街或者在华强北站下车的！

时间过得真快，一转眼 8 年过去了。现在的深圳完全不一样了。从罗湖到宝安、龙岗、惠州等，周边区域都开始发展起来了。当年那个不

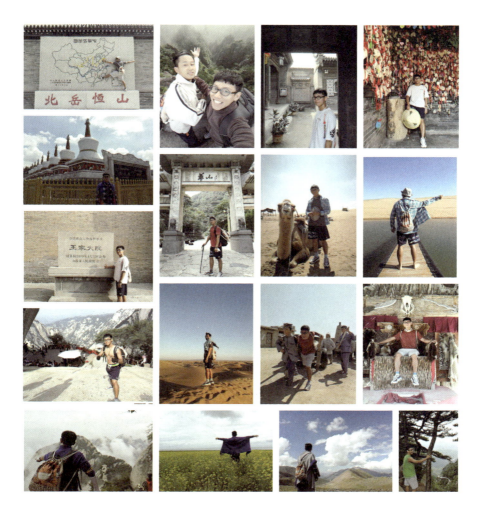

environment characterized by openness, diversity and inclusiveness, providing foreign companies with conditions of maximum freedom for innovation and start-ups in China. In the past, 3G and 4G technologies drove the development of Shenzhen. Recently, 5G telecommunication technologies and AI technologies like AR and VR have also emerged, which would bring Shenzhen an unprecedented lift-off.

My PhD research theme is on China-South Korea Free Trade Agreement and the cooperation between enterprises of China and Republic of Korea. Compared to Republic of Korea, Shenzhen boasts more entrepreneur resources and optimistic atmosphere for innovation and entrepreneurship. I hope that my research can build a bridge for the two sides, provide a broader development platform, and raise the awareness and recognition of more top teams and enterprises in Republic of Korea for Shenzhen.

深圳大学提供

起眼的机场也早就变成了漂亮的现代化的国际机场，地铁线也多了，每个区都有购物中心，交通、生活极其方便。如果从深圳大学坐地铁 11 号线去机场只需要 20 分钟！回国再也不用去香港了。

众所周知，深圳是中国首个创新示范城市，被美国《商业周刊》评价为中国最具硅谷气质的城市和创客之城。多年来深圳市政府利用经济特区优势，努力打造具有开放、多元、包容特点的创新创业环境，为外来企业提供了国内经营自由度最大的创新创业条件。过去 3G 和 4G 的技术使深圳飞速发展起来，如今，已经出现了 5G 通信技术及 AR、VR、AI 科技技术的创新。这将会给深圳带来空前绝后的腾飞！

我博士期间主要的研究课题是中韩自由贸易协定以及与中韩企业合作有关的项目。与韩国相比，深圳有着更多的创业资源以及浓厚的创新创业氛围。我希望，我的研究能成为桥梁与纽带，为更多韩国人提供更广阔的发展平台，让韩国更多的优秀团队和企业认准深圳，加入深圳，融入这美丽的创客之城。

我将梦想融入中国梦
Integrating My Dream into Chinese Dream

［马拉维］ 陶艾德 南京信息工程大学

[Malawi] Tadeyo Edwin Frank, Nanjing University of Information Science & Technology

"There is a dragon in the ancient East and its name is China. There is a group of people in the ancient East and they are all descendants of the dragon." My name is Taoaide (Tadeyo Edwin Frank) from a far-away country Malawi. I am currently studying at Nanjing University of Information Science and Technology and majoring in atmospheric science. I had heard "Descendants of the Dragon" before I came to China. It is this song that has made me long for China. The reform and opening-up has given China a new look and made the ancient China younger. I'm eager to get an opportunity to visit China so that I can see this country with such a rapid economic and cultural development by myself.

There is an old saying in China that "Give a man a fish, and he'll eat for a day. Teach a man how to fish, you will feed him for a lifetime." The Chinese government has provided education assistance to African countries in addition to economic, technical and medical assistance. For instance, China has provided learning materials to African countries and offered scholarships to outstanding students, which come with the opportunity of a sound education in China. I am one of the beneficiaries. In September 2015, my journey in college started. I was

"古老的东方有一条龙，他的名字就叫中国。古老的东方有一群人，他们全都是龙的传人。"我叫陶艾德，来自遥远的马拉维，现在在南京信息工程大学学习大气科学专业。《龙的传人》这首歌是我在来中国之前就听到的歌。正是这首歌让我对中国产生了无比的向往。改革开放使中国旧貌换新颜，使"古老中国变得年轻"。这一切让我渴望能有机会到中国亲眼看看这个经济文化各方面迅速发展的国家。

中国有句古话："授人以鱼不如授人以渔。"中国政府对非洲国家除了提供经济、技术、医疗援助以外，还提供了教育方面的援助。比如，向非洲国家提供学习资料，并向他们的优秀学生提供奖学金，使他们有机会到中国享受良好的教育。我就是其中的受益人之一。2015年9月，我开始了我的大学生涯。中国的大学环境美丽、学习氛围浓厚、各种社团活动丰富，让我觉得又新奇又兴奋。我努力地在大学里学习汉语，汲取各种知识，因为我听中国朋友说"书中自有黄金屋，书中自有颜如玉"。藏书丰富的图书馆也成了我最常去，也是最喜欢的地方。

时光飞逝，如今，我在中国已经三年了。我发现在中国的时间越久，就会越来越深深地爱上这个国家。中国已经成了我第二故乡。在这里，

curious and excited in such a beautiful campus immersed in an atmosphere of intellectual earnestness with various community activities being held. I worked hard to learn Chinese at the university and acquire all kinds of knowledge in that my Chinese friends have told me that one can find gold and beauty in the books. Therefore, the well-stocked library has become my most frequently-visited and favorite place for me.

How time flies! I have been in China for three years. I realized that the longer I have been in China, the more I love this country. China has already become my second hometown. I have not only learned advanced scientific knowledge here, but also met many nice and friendly friends. This is one of the reasons why I love China so much. Just as the old Chinese saying goes, "Isn't it a delight should friends visit from afar?" Whenever I encounter difficulties, there will always be warm-hearted Chinese who offer me help with sincerity. At school, the teachers give us international students the utmost help and spend most of their time tutoring us. Chinese students often help me to understand the knowledge and key points in the classroom. The head teacher teaches us and warms us with love and care as my mother does. I feel like I am home.

Peace and security are other reasons why I love China. Conflict and instability can hinder the development of a country, while peace and security will bring hope to the people longing for development. I have a deep understanding of it in China. As I see, China's public security is top notch and the Chinese government has also given top priority to people's safety. At school, we can often see security guards patrolling on the campus in the early morning to protect teachers and students. In the neighborhood, the police also patrol in the community to safeguard those residents' personal safety and property. In such an environment, the Chinese

我不仅学到了先进的科学知识，还认识了很多善良友好的朋友。这也是我热爱中国的原因之一。中国古话说得好："有朋自远方来，不亦乐乎。"每当我遇到困难的时候，都会有热情的中国人给予我最诚挚的帮助。在学校里，老师们给予我们国际学生足够的帮助，抽出大部分的时间来给我们解释和补习。中国同学们也常常给我解释课堂上难以理解的知识点。班主任老师对我们的谆谆教诲，也给了我们妈妈一样的温暖和关怀。这一切让我丝毫不觉得我是来到了一个完全陌生的国度。

　　和平与安全是我爱中国的另一个原因。冲突和动荡会阻碍一个国家的发展，但和平与安全却会给人民带来发展的希望。这点我在中国深有体会。在我看来，中国的治安情况比世界上任何一个国家都要好，中国政府也把人民的安全放在了非常重要的地位。在学校里，我们经常能看到保安大叔们凌晨还在校园内巡逻，为的是保护学校师生的安全。在小

在南京中山陵

people can be much concentrated and work hard to contribute their due bit to the prosperity and development of the motherland. The Chinese police care about us foreigners. Just as Chinese people, now we often say that whenever you have difficulty, you can turn to the police for help.

As a student, I also have my own dreams. During the three-year life in China, I have gained a deeper understanding of Chinese culture, and I often write poems about Chinese culture and publish them on the WeChat public subscription account of the school. For that, I had the honor of being interviewed by the school's publicity department. I have already felt that my dreams are gradually being integrated into the Chinese Dream. Chinese President Xi Jinping once said, "The realization of the Chinese Dream will not only benefit the Chinese people, but also the people all over the world." I hope that one day my dream can go aboard the enormous ship of the Chinese Dream so that I can build a bridge between my motherland and China to share the fruits of development.

南京信息工程大学提供

区里，警察们也会在社区内巡逻，为的是保障住户们的财产人身安全。在这样的环境里，中国人民得以专心工作，用他们吃苦耐劳的精神，为祖国的繁荣发展贡献自己的力量。中国警察对外国人也格外热心，现在我们也会常说，有困难找警察。

　　作为一名学生，我也有自己的理想和梦想。在中国生活的三年里，我对中国文化有了更深入的了解，也经常会写一些关于中国文化的诗篇并发表在学校的微信公众号上。为此，我还曾有幸被学校的宣传部采访报道过。这些都让我感到无比光荣和荣幸。我已经看到，我的理想和梦想正渐渐融入中国梦中。中国国家主席习近平曾说："实现中国梦不仅造福中国人民，而且造福世界人民。"我希望有一天，我的梦想能真正搭上中国梦这艘大船，在我的祖国和中国之间架起一座桥梁，共享发展的成果。

［韩国］　赵亨一　中国人民大学

[Republic of Korea] Cho Hyungil, Renmin University of China

My father was among the first Koreans who came to Weihai, Shandong Province for business following the launch of China's reform and opening-up policy.

At that time, under the policy proposed and led by Deng Xiaoping, China opened its doors to the world, and began to develop many industries that had long been neglected. In my father's words, "I saw that China developed into a prosperous and medium-income developing country within a short span of several decades from a poor and backward country. That is amazing. "

I went to China with my father not long after a period of schooling. Perhaps it was precisely because of China's rapid development and abundant opportunities that my father decided to bring me along. We have now been in China for ten years. During this time, I can say I regard China as my homeland. And whenever I return to Korea, I find myself trying to fit in. It seems that I am already a Chinese.

I was in second grade of elementary school when I came to China. At that time, the Olympic Games were to be held in the country. Happiness and

我的父亲是改革开放之后第一批来到中国山东威海经商的韩国人。

那时的中国在邓小平爷爷主张改革开放的带领下，打开了中国对外的大门，改革开放，百废俱兴。按我父亲的话说，就是："我看到了中国从一个贫穷落后的国家在短短的几十年时间内，发展成了一个富强的中等发展中国家，这是非常惊人的。"

我是在韩国上了一段学之后跟随我父亲来中国的。或许正是因为中国的发展如此之迅速，发展机遇如此之多，我父亲才选择让我来到中国，并一住就是十年。在这十年里，我似乎把中国当作了我的故土，回到韩国则有些不适应，好像我已经是个地地道道的中国人了。

当初我来到中国的时候，是小学二年级，那时中国举办的奥运会即将开幕，全中国都处于一片欢庆之中，所有人都迫不及待地想要迎接这一伟大盛事。那时的我，汉语水平并不像现在这么好，甚至有些许口吃，像是婴儿咿咿呀呀学语言一样，经常半天憋不出来一个字，所以我很惧怕跟别人说话。但是令我没有想到的是，在那时威海的街上经常有翻译志愿者，他们身穿印有奥林匹克五环的 T 恤衫。我跟他们说韩语他们也都能听懂，而且说得非常好，他们也非常热心地告诉我，我该去哪里。

celebration flooded every corner. Everyone could not wait to meet this great event. Back then, I did not speak Chinese so well, and would stutter like a baby with lack of command of the language. Because of this I was afraid to talk to others. To my surprise, the streets of Weihai had numerous translators, who wore T-shirts with the Olympic Rings. They could understand me and even spoke Korean well. They were very warm-hearted in giving me directions. Although that did not improve my Chinese proficiency, it made me feel hospitality and sense of safety, the likes of which I had never seen before.

Later, I made a lot of Chinese friends in school. We went to school and had fun together. They treated me as one of their own. This greatly improved my Chinese proficiency and I began to feel more confident to speak Chinese, though I still had some stuttering. They always told me, "Don't worry, and take your time. " I am very grateful for their tolerance and understanding.

When I first came to China, I was very curious about why Chinese fruits were so cheap. I remember my childhood Chinese playmates—children of my neighbors. They always gave us some fruit and meat, and said that their mother had bought too much so they would like to share some with us. Those deeds made me very curious, because in Korea, fruit was priced by pieces instead of bags, and was very expensive. Later, I realized that it was because Korea lacked in such produce, and most fruits depended on imports, while China is abundant in farming, and thanks to the reform and opening-up policy proposed by Deng Xiaoping, fruit production doubled to say the least. So at that time, I decided to live in China in the future.

Fruits aside, culture was the main drive of my decision to stay here. Another was similarities between the two nations. Moreover, this once poor

这虽然并没有让我的汉语水平提高，但是却让那时的我感到中国的温馨和极大的安全感。

后来，我在学校里交到了很多中国朋友，我们每天一起上学，一起玩乐，他们待我如同自己的同胞兄弟一样。这使我的汉语水平得到了极大的提高，我开始不那么胆怯地说汉语了，但还是会有些口吃，他们总会提醒我，慢慢说，不着急，我也非常感谢他们对我的宽容和理解。

刚来中国的时候，我非常好奇，中国水果为什么那么便宜。我记得我小时候的中国玩伴——我邻居家的孩子总会给我们送些水果和肉，总是会说他妈妈买多了要给我们家一些，而且一送就是一大袋子。这令幼小的我非常好奇，因为在韩国，我们的水果是论个卖的，而不是一大袋子，并且水果大多都非常昂贵，可以说"价格不菲"，而在中国，我的邻居一送就是一大袋子。后来我才知道，因为韩国物资匮乏，大多水果

中国人民大学提供

中国人民大学提供

and backward country, in recent few decades, has experienced dramatic changes. It is a miracle of the world. China is really fascinating, much like a paradise for those who want to make difference and realize their dreams. I think a lot of people feel the same. During my 10 years' studying in China, I have learned a lot of things, which have made me grow fond of it. I believe that China will have greater achievements in the future.

中国人民大学提供

都依赖进口，而中国物资富足，又因为邓爷爷的改革开放，水果产量更是翻番。所以那时的我就决定，我以后一定要一直在中国生活。

我来中国的原因并不只是因为这个，而是因为中国有着丰富多彩的文化，更有我的家。虽然身处异国，但仍能感受到家的温暖。虽然这个国家曾经贫穷落后，但在最近的几十年里，发生了翻天覆地的变化，堪称世界奇迹。中国更是想要实现梦想的人的乐土，如果想要大干一番事业，那么中国是不二的选择。我想很多人都会这么想吧，这着实令人着迷。在中国十多年的留学经历之中，让我学到了很多东西，这也使我更加爱上了中国。我相信，中国在未来还会有更大的成就。

你也会爱上中国
You'll Fall in Love with China Just Like Me

[韩国]　金我妍　北京师范大学
[Republic of Korea] Kim A Yeon, Beijing Normal University

When I was still in the Republic of Korea (ROK), someone who had been to China a long time ago told me that China, with a vast territory and a large population, has been a developing country for several decades and was a less advanced civilization compared to the developed world. But when I came to China, I found that China was utterly different from what I had heard. I saw many dustmen and motor sweepers cleaning the streets in the late night to keep the city clean. With dustbins placed along the streets, there was little rubbish. One day, I went to McDonald's for breakfast, I saw people standing in line and waiting to place orders or take meals. I would like to share what I have seen in China with people unaware of the changes that have taken place.

If you ask me to choose a word to describe Chinese people, my answer would be "friendly" . Since ancient times, Chinese people have been deeply influenced by Confucianism. Therefore, following the guidance of "all the people of the world are brothers" and "it is always a pleasure to have friends coming from afar" , they value interpersonal relationships and like to make friends. Chinese people are all very kind, be it taxi drivers or female staff

　　记得我在韩国的时候，就有很久之前去过中国的人告诉我：中国地域辽阔，人口众多，一直都是发展中国家，文明程度不如发达国家。但是，来到中国以后，我惊奇地发现：现实中的中国是完全不同的。我每天凌晨看到有很多清洁工和清扫车在大街上扫地，干干净净的。城市里的每个街道旁都有垃圾桶，所以大街上几乎没有垃圾。我去学校里的麦当劳，发现人们都排队点餐和取餐，井然有序的样子。在我眼里，中国人是非常讲文明的。所以，我想跟那些像几年前的我一样，不太了解中国、对中国仍有偏见的外国人说说我所看到的中国是什么样子。

　　如果让我用一个词来形容中国人，那就是"友好"。从古至今，中国人一直受到儒家文化的影响，重视人与人的关系。中国人有着"四海之内皆兄弟""有朋自远方来，不亦乐乎"的博大胸怀，喜欢与人友好相处。不管是出租车司机，还是食堂里打工的阿姨，人们都很友好。可能我说中文时会有口音，但是中国人都会热情地帮我纠正，给我解释。

　　之前，我也在韩国上过大学。现在，身为一个留学生，我感受到在中国的大学生活和在韩国的大学生活确实不同。平时我有很多课要上，所以会感到很疲倦。但是，我在这里上大学有很多好处。尤其是所有的

working in the school canteen. Maybe I have an accent when I speak Chinese, but Chinese people will kindly help me correct and explain to me.

Before I came to China, I had studied at a university in the ROK. Now, as a foreign student, I can clearly feel the differences of university life between the two countries. In China, I have many courses to take, which is a little bit exhausting, but those friendly and cordial professors help me a lot, giving me a fulfilling university life. In the ROK, teachers usually do not remember everyone's name and will not interact with students after class, while in China, no matter wherever or whenever I meet my teachers, they can always speak out my name, which is quite surprising. It is their kindness that makes me listen carefully and respond to them actively because I want to win their recognition.

Apart from my university life, what impresses me most in China is the use of QR codes. In fact, people also use QR codes in the ROK and other countries but it is not as universal. Scanning QR codes has already become part of Chinese people's lives. QR codes have occupied everywhere from computers, posts and tables or goods in supermarkets and group-buying websites. By scanning QR codes, people can complete payments, join chat groups, get discounts and get information about life. What amazes me is that in China, you just need to scan the QR code to pay your bill. In my opinion, the universal application of QR codes is related to China's social development. Now, with the changes of times and the advancement of technology, the whole society runs at a fast speed and Chinese people also want to lead a time-efficient and convenient life. QR codes completely meet their needs.

Recently, we can see shared bikes in yellow, blue and orange parked at curbs, which are another amazing service in China. Bike sharing is very

老师都很热情友好。其实，在韩国，老师几乎不会记住每一个学生的名字，课下也不会跟学生交流；而在中国，不管什么时候，不管在哪儿，我所见到的老师都会叫出我的名字，并跟我打招呼，这是非常令我惊讶的事情。就因为我身边有这么友好的老师，为了得到老师的认可，我在课堂上认真听讲，积极发言。

除了我的大学生活以外，我最欣赏中国的一点就是使用二维码。其实，之前在韩国和其他国家也使用二维码，但没有中国这么普遍。在中国，扫二维码已经是一件司空见惯的事情了。不管是在电脑、海报、餐桌上，还是在超市的商品、团购网站上都有二维码。让我感到很新鲜的是，在中国买东西结账时，扫二维码即可。我认为，二维码在中国的广泛使用和当今中国社会的发展息息相关。目前，随着时代的变化，科技的发展，中国社会也开始走上了快节奏的路线，人们开始追求高效、省

北京师范大学 / 刘艳伶摄

北京师范大学提供

convenient because people can ride shared bikes and pay the fare by scanning the QR code. Actually, there are shared bikes in the ROK too, but they have to be parked at designated positions. This inconvenience holds people back from using them. In contrast, Chinese people can even use the APP to check where the shared bikes are parked. Shared bikes free me from taking the bus which usually makes me anxious in the rush hours. Now, I can ride with classmates to see the beautiful scenery and do some exercise, all of which make me healthier and my university life wonderful.

After graduating from university, I may be unwilling to leave here. I probably will choose to stay in China to work and live with Chinese people, enjoying the colorful life here. China has become an important part of my youth. In the future, I will continue my story with China. I love China and the life here. Will you also love the life here and even China when you see this?

时、方便的生活方式。此时，二维码就满足了人们对生活的这种追求。通过扫二维码，人们可以完成支付，加入聊天群，获得打折优惠，得到有关生活的信息等。

最近，我们在大街上走路时就会看到黄色、蓝色、橙色的共享自行车停在路边，这是让我感到很新鲜的，也是我欣赏的一点。人们使用共享单车时，可以通过扫二维码的方式来支付，用起来很方便。其实，在韩国也有共享单车，可它只能停在指定的位置，这会让人觉得有点麻烦，所以人们不爱用。而在中国，人们使用共享单车时，不但用起来方便，而且还能用 APP 实时查询单车的位置。我坐公交出行时经常会堵车，弄得我很着急，现在我跟同学们一起骑单车，到很多风景好的地方走走，还能运动，使我身心健康，感觉我的大学生活是非常美好的。

我想，大学毕业以后，我会舍不得离开这里，也许会留在中国继续发展，跟中国人一起工作，一起生活，过上丰富多彩的生活。我的青春里充满着与中国的美好回忆。将来，我还会续写我和中国的美好故事。我爱中国，我爱这里的生活。看到这里，你们也会爱上中国，爱上这里的生活吗？

双城记

——似而不同中萌生的纽带感

A Tale of Two Cities

—Similar But Different Root Plants a Bond

［泰国］ 李纹 华南理工大学

[Thailand] Phoemphun Warunrat, South China University of Technology

I have been in China for almost three years. When I first came here, I felt like a fish out of water but now I am well-accustomed to life here. My story in China is not only a story of time but also a story of space.

I come from Phuket, the biggest island in Thailand. My hometown is blessed with green seawater, blue sky, and smooth sands. Time always goes quite slowly there and I, a typical Thai, favor such a slow pace of life very much. I did not take it seriously when the staff in the training institution told me about the fast pace of life in Guangzhou. Not until I came to Guangzhou did I truly understand what a fast-moving city is like. In Guangzhou, people walk fast on the streets, stay up late and get up early. In ever see such things in Thailand. But what impressed me most was the busy schedule and quick tempo in studies. I need to fully concentrate in classes during the daytime and do my homework after class to master what I have learned. This is totally different from what it is in Thailand.

从刚来时候的不适应，到现在的"如鱼得水"，我在中国已经快三年了。我的中国故事不仅是时间的故事，也是空间的故事。

我来自普吉，泰国最大的岛屿。翡翠色的海水和蔚蓝的天空，细腻的沙滩，这里是我的家乡。时间在普吉总是特别慢，而我，一个典型的泰国人，很喜欢这样慢节奏的生活。当培训辅导机构的人告诉我广州生活节奏很快的时候，我并没有怎么在意；直到我来到广州，才真正体会到生活的速度。路上行人快速地走过，大家都很早起床很晚睡觉，人们在周末也在用手机聊工作。这些都是我在泰国的时候未曾见过的。当然，对我而言，感受深刻的是学习的紧张和快节奏。白天的上课需要聚精会神，晚上回家后还要完成作业巩固学习。这与泰国的生活学习节奏完全是不同的样子。

中国的科技和交通也在支持这样的快速度，我认为方便就是快速。比如，共享单车改变了我的生活。现在我出门从我的宿舍到地铁口的话，我一般都会选择骑 ofo 单车从宿舍到地铁口；而以前，我常常因为要步

The fast pace of life is made possible by the advanced technology and transportation in China. In other words, convenience means speed. For example, shared bikes have changed my life. Generally I would ride an ofo bike from my dormitory to the subway station, which saves me the trouble of walking there. Another example is the convenience in making payments in China. People can go out without cash. All one needs is a smart phone equipped with WeChat and Alipay apps. Such convenience accelerates the pace of life and I really like such a lifestyle.

During this process of getting used to life in China, I have been changing little by little. To my delight, changes are also quietly taking place in my hometown.

I came to Guangzhou to study not only because it is closer to Thailand but more importantly, it has a favorable language environment here. However,

华南理工大学提供

行而感到麻烦。又或者，在中国付钱是非常方便的，如果有了微信与支付宝的话，不带现金都没什么问题，只要带了手机就行。生活的便利使节奏变快，而我也很喜欢这样的生活方式。

从不习惯到习以为常，我自己一点一滴在改变。让我欣喜的是，我的家乡也在悄悄发生变化。

我来广州留学，除了因为离泰国比较近，更重要的是这里的语言环境很好。不过，近几年我回家，发现家乡越来越多的人也会说汉语了。不仅是导游，还有卖东西的小贩；不仅是售票员，还有的士司机。中国游客越来越多，普吉岛也有了中国味儿。我很喜欢看中国的连续剧，也喜欢和朋友讨论。我发现，越来越多的泰国朋友也开始喜欢上中国的连续剧。比如，《致我们单纯的小美好》《三生三世十里桃花》等电视剧，在泰国也有很多的观众。以前，我只是和中国朋友聊电视剧里的故事，现在我可以和家乡的朋友聊中国剧了。当我走进普吉岛的 7-11 便利店

in recent years, when I go back to my hometown, I find more and more Thai people speaking Chinese, including guides, vendors, ticket sellers and taxi drivers. The increasing flow of Chinese tourists is making Phuket a city that caters to Chinese. I like watching Chinese TV series and discussing them with my friends. I find that more Thai friends are fond of Chinese TV shows. For instance, Eternal Love, A Love So Beautiful and many other TV series are very popular in Thailand. In the past I talked about these shows only with Chinese friends, but now I can also talk about them with friends in my homeland. When I shop in 7-11 convenient stores in Phuket, I find that Alipay is available. As several Chinese language schools have been set up in Phuket, I believe my fellowmen in Thailand will have a better command of Chinese.

China changes and develops rapidly every day. Alipay and the shared bike brand ofo have entered the Thai market. As I am acquiring more and more Chinese, I love Guangzhou and the whole of China more and more. The city's development provides me with goals and gives me confidence. I hope that I can make friends with more Chinese people and one day work here and do my bit to cultural exchanges between China and Thailand.

During my trips between Guangzhou and Phuket, I have noticed not only differences but common changes between the two cities. Guangzhou is changing, Phuket is changing and I am changing, too.

Here I extend my sincere wish for a better China.

华南理工大学提供

买东西的时候，我发现也可以用支付宝支付了。普吉岛目前也开设了好几家中文学校，我相信大家的中文水平会越来越好。

中国每一天都是新的，每天发展都非常快，比如共享单车的小黄车、支付宝现在都进入了泰国市场。因为对语言的熟悉，我越来越喜欢广州，越来越喜欢中国。城市的发展，也给我带来了目标与信心。我希望可以认识更多的中国朋友，也希望有一天可以在这里工作，加强中泰两国文化交流。

广州—普吉，普吉—广州。往返这两座城市，我感觉到的不仅是差异，还有共同的变化。广州在变，普吉在变，我也在变。

由衷祝愿中国发展得越来越好。

我的中国故事
My Story in China

[加拿大]　David Allen　上海财经大学

[Canada] David Allen, Shanghai University of Finance and Economics

It is my great honor to be funded by the Canada-China Scholars Exchange Program, which grants me the opportunity to have this incredible journey. My dream would have never been true without the scholarship.

I was asked frequently, "Why will you go to China?" When I became friends with international students studying in Fredericton, New Brunswick, my hometown, I learned many different cultures. Among them, China's aroused my interests the most. Personally, my dream has been to live abroad and experience overseas life. Shanghai University of Finance and Economics (SUFE) is the top financial university and also my top choice. The reason why I choose Finance at SUFE is that Shanghai is the financial center of China, and the major global player in the financial market.

My overall goal is to travel, socialize and gain experience as much as possible. My long-term goal is to live in China, learn Mandarin, have a go at the financial industry, and start a business.

As soon as I went to SUFE, I took Chinese courses. When I got off the plane, I felt the urgency and importance of mastering Chinese language. It is a

（前排右一为作者）

特别感谢中加学者交流项目（CCSEP）让我踏上了难以置信的旅程，没有这个奖学金，我的梦想就不可能实现。

我经常被问道："为什么要去中国？"我和在我家乡新不伦瑞克的弗雷德里克斯顿（Fredericton）学习的国际学生成为朋友后，我学到了很多不同的文化，中国激发了我的兴趣。就我个人而言，我的抱负是移居海外，体验海外生活。我的专业考量是中国作为金融市场的主要全球参与者，上海是中国的金融中心，而上海财经大学（SUFE）作为顶级金融学院，就是我想去的地方。

我的总体目标非常简单：尽可能地旅行、社交和获得经验。我的长期目标是在中国生活，学习普通话，回到金融行业，开拓创业。

一到上海财经大学，我就把我的课程改成了汉语，从我下飞机的那一刻开始，我就感受到了这一点的紧迫性和重要性。学校对我来说是一个挑战，尤其是要适应不同的教育系统的教学方式。我很熟悉以理解为关注点的西方教育体系，但中国更注重以记忆为基础的教学。两者都很重要，都有优点。

我在中国的前六个月，在学习的同时，我开始与一位拥有期货经纪

challenge for me to study at SUFE, where I need to adapt to teaching methods of a different educational system. The Western educational system I am very familiar with focuses on comprehension, while the Chinese is more based on memory. Both are important, with their own advantages.

In the first half a year in China, apart from learning, I also developed a hedge fund with a partner running futures brokerage. I studied in the morning and worked for the project in the afternoon and evening. After one year, though we had made initial progress, there was a sudden spike in the stock market by over 60 percent when we were about to launch the project. With higher stock prices, financial companies prefer going public to fund investment. Due to our slow response to the market shift, the project was abandoned, but I learnt a lot from it.

After that, I spent two years learning mandarin. After many difficulties, I obtained a job as a Chinese tutor finally. The teaching made me wonder if there was a convenient tool to link language learners. This idea gave birth to "Language Partner. " My team built an iOS app which was then launched in the Apple Store. The "Language Partner" project won awards in many Entrepreneurship contests, and also organized professional trainings on English learning. Although with the initial success, I still heard the calling from the financial industry and the investment dream I had been pursuing while the graduation was approaching.

During the start-up of "Language Partner, " I was awarded a MSc. in Finance and was qualified for Chartered Financial Analyst (CFA). During my postgraduate study, I got the chance to provide trainings for established organizations, including People's Bank of China and Amgen (China)

业务的合伙人共同开发对冲基金。我每天早上学习，下午和晚上做这个项目。一年后，我们取得了很大进展，但在我们推出对冲基金项目之前，股市上涨了 60% 以上。在高股价下，金融公司希望上市而不是投资于投资基金。总之，我们太慢了，但我学到了很多。

之后，我花了两年的时间专注于学习普通话。我经历了很多挑战终于找到了一个汉语家教，然后我开始思考是否可以建立一种便捷的方式使语言学习者联系起来。就这样，"语言伙伴"诞生了。我组建了一个团队，构建了一个 iOS 应用程序，并在苹果商店推出。"语言伙伴"项目参加了许多创业比赛，也赢得了一些比赛。除此之外，我们还举办了英语学习专业教育活动。虽然我们取得了小小的成功，但临近毕业时，我感到回到金融业去追求投资梦想才是我真正的方向。

Pharmaceutical Company, which built up my experience. Observing and comparing the internal operation of a Chinese company and a foreign invested company in China can be very intriguing.

After graduation, I found a job. It is not easy for foreigners to get a job in China, with challenging language and culture difficulties. To leverage great advantages and opportunities, you need to carry on with creativity, entrepreneurship, endurance and openness. It was finally proven that all my efforts were worthwhile.

The latest project was research on emerging technology with Guotai Junan Securities, Ltd. , China's largest state-owned investment bank and securities company, which taught me the operation of state-owned enterprise and investment banks in China.

In my spare time, I visited Taiwan, Hong Kong, Macau and many places of China, and also foreign countries such as Thailand, Laos and France. My parents also visited China and travelled around with me.

In retrospect of the passing time in China, I wondered if I really achieved what I aimed at. The answer is absolutely yes. And how far have I advanced on my way of pursuing a long-term goal? My Chinese is getting better, which will make my life here easier; my job hunting in financial industry is challenging but rewarding. I kept looking for job and start-up opportunity.

In short, I was transformed by such experience in China. I am still in China and excited for new opportunities and adventures, with growth and progresses each day.

在"语言伙伴"创业期间，我获得了金融硕士学位和特许金融分析师（CFA）的资格。在我硕士期间，我通过向一些著名的公司提供培训课程来拓展我的经验：中国人民银行和安进（中国）制药公司。学习和观察一家中国公司和一家在中国经营的外国公司的内部运作是非常有趣的。人们的行为和思维方式各不相同。

毕业后，我找到了工作。在中国找工作对外国人来说并不容易。语言和文化上都有很大的障碍。也就是说，虽然存在着巨大的优势和机遇，但你需要有创造力、企业家精神、耐心和灵活性来坚持不懈，然而我发现所有的努力都是值得的。

毕业后最近的一个项目是与中国最大的国有投资银行和证券公司国泰君安证券有限公司（Guotai Junan Securities，Ltd.）合作进行新兴技术研究。我学到了国有企业和投资银行在中国是如何运作的。

除了工作之外，我还游历了台湾、香港、澳门和中国内地。我访问过的国家还包括泰国、老挝和法国。值得一提的是我带父母来中国旅游，和他们分享我在中国的经历和对中国的爱，以及中国的文化，一切都太棒了。

反思一下，我在中国的这段时间（旅行、社交和经历），我得到了我想要的东西吗？是的，是的，是的！我在实现长期目标的路上走了多远？我仍在努力提高我的中文水平，在这里我的生活变得越来越容易，而在金融方面，也是一个极具挑战性但回报颇丰的过程，我坚持找工作，并寻求创业的机会。

简而言之，这种经历改变了我的生活。我还在中国，每天都在为新的机遇和冒险而兴奋快乐着。向前，向上！

我的中国梦
My Chinese Dream

[马来西亚] 张颖敏 上海中医药大学

[Malaysia] Teoh Ying Min, Shanghai University of Traditional Chinese Medicine

Chinese dream, my dream, guides me to the dawn. I am a Malaysian Chinese who accepts western education. My Chinese blood leads me back to China. Last year, I came back to Fujian Province to seek where my ancestors live and happened to find my aunt and uncle who were already in their nineties. Though we never knew each other, but there was a special feeling when we met, a feeling that I had come home. I can still remember the tears they shed when I had to leave, which confirmed my determination to study in China.

I am now a student of Shanghai University of Traditional Chinese Medicine. My love for Chinese culture since childhood helped me to adapt to life here very quickly. My uncle was a TCM doctor before he became an educator, and I want to continue his unfinished dream. I am keen on Chinese medicine culture, hoping to spread this culture to the world and eliminate people's misunderstanding of Chinese medicine. As Chinese medicine is the quintessence of China, we should carry it forward. I am working to realize my goal.

Every time I go out, people are surprised at my fluent Chinese as an

中国梦，我的梦，一个指引我走向黎明的梦。我是一位接受西方教育的马来西亚华裔，作为一名炎黄子孙，我骨子里的华夏血液引领着我来到中国。我在去年回到福建踏乡寻根，找到了我鲐背之年的堂伯公和堂婶婆。我们从不相识，一见面却有种特别的感觉，一种我回家了的感觉。还记得我要离开时他们不舍地流下泪水，这坚定了我要到中国留学的信念。

因为从小热爱中国文化的缘故，从来到中国留学的一开始就非常快地适应了这里的生活。我是一名上海中医药大学的学生。我的堂伯公在成为一名教育人士之前是一名中医，我想延续他未完成的梦想。我本身也十分热爱中医文化，我希望将此文化弘扬至世界，消除人们对中医的误解误会。中医是中国的国粹，我们理应将它发扬光大。这是我的目标，我也正朝着它前进。

每每出门游玩，别人都会非常惊讶我是一名留学生但中文却说得那么溜。我认为身为一名华人，学好中文是我应该做的，而且我要精益求精。在学习的过程中肯定遇到过难题，老师们也非常负责任地给我讲解，也取得了理想的成绩。在这些日子里，我感受到了这座城市，这个国家

overseas student. But for me, it is necessary to learn Chinese and I want to keep improving. In the process of learning, I certainly have encountered many difficulties, and the teachers were very responsible to solve them. Thus, I also got ideal results. In these days, I feel the passion of this city, this country. I like to take a walk whenever I am free. I saw a young man helping an elder by stabilizing his wheelchair quietly all the way in the subway; I saw a white-collar sitting on the curbside, meditating; I saw a couple who were having a argument; I saw an old woman collecting rags; I saw a handsome gentle man get off from a limo; I saw an old woman with a basket in her hand picking up a little flower and holding it to her ear; I saw a drunk tramp buying everything at an old man's stall late at night and yelling at him to hurry home and go to bed.

I have been to the downtown where I saw the dreamy neon lights at night and walked through the maze of skyscrapers. I have been to the countryside where I ate rice grown by the hard-working farmers and listened to the chorus of poultry. I have been to kindergartens where I saw sweet new lives. I have been to the emergency department of a hospital where I saw people's desperation. I have been to hospice service center where I saw the comfort and relief. I have heard many stories and met many people who have a soul of their own that no one has ever seen.

Too much has the country gone through. People bleed and sacrifice for the peace of this country. Our martyrs and ancestors would be delighted by a thriving and prosperous China. Now, this land is writing its own story. Months ago, I wanted to study in this country; while now I want to stay and live here after graduation. I am proud of myself for being a Chinese, a descendant of Yan and Huang Emperor, a child of this land. I want to kowtow in front of ancestors' graves and tell them I have come back home.

的热情。我喜欢散步，每当闲来无事时都会到处走走。我看见了一位年轻人在地铁全程默默地帮助一位坐在轮椅上的老者稳定轮椅；我看见了一个白领坐在马路边沉思；我看见了一对在吵架的情侣；我看见了在捡拾旧物的老奶奶；我看见了一位英俊潇洒的男子从豪车里下来；我看见了一个手里提着菜篮子的大妈采了一朵小花放到耳边；我看见了一个醉醺醺的人在深夜里将老人摊位上的东西都买了，还嚷嚷着让老人赶紧回家睡觉去。

我到过市中心，看见了夜里迷幻人心的霓虹灯，走过让人迷失的摩天大楼丛林。我到过乡村，吃过用汗水换来的米饭，听过家禽的高歌。我到过幼儿园，看见了许许多多懵懂的新生命。我到过医院急诊部，见过人们绝望的眼神。我到过临终关怀中心，看到了人们的释怀。我听过许多的故事，见过许多的人。他们都不像表面一般，他们都拥有一个只

上海中医药大学提供

My grandfather told me that no matter how far you go, do not forget where you came from, the way back home and your root. I have always born that in mind.

In just a few months, I learnt how to look at my own life and found contentment in it, which is much more than theories taught at school. There is still a long road ahead of me. Inheriting from the past, I look forward to the future. I have no fancy words to express my love for China. The five-star red flag flying in the air is my belief and my motivation to learn. I wish that the seed of Chinese medicine I planted will grow and deliver fruits one day, and my Chinese dream will also come true.

上海中医药大学提供

属于自己的灵魂，没人见过。

这个国家过去经历了太多太多。牺牲的先烈流过的血，换来了今天这个国家的和平。家国犹在，昌盛繁荣，不负英魂先辈。如今这片土地也正在经历着属于她的故事。我从想来这个国家到现在我想在这片大地留下。我想毕业以后仍然留在这里，伴着这亲爱的土地，在这里生活。我想要抛开一切国籍之说，磊落光明地说我是中国人，我是炎黄子孙、华夏子弟。我想到祖坟前磕头告诉先祖们我回来了，回家了。我的爷爷告诉过我，无论走多远都不要忘记自己从哪儿来，不要忘了回家的路，不要忘了自己的根本。我也一直将此铭记于心。

短短的几个月里，我学到的远不只学校的理论知识，更多的是一种人生观和知足感。路漫漫其修远兮，回溯历史，展望未来。我没有华丽的辞藻，但有着拳拳的中国心。飘扬在空中的五星红旗便是我的信仰，是我学习的动力。我期待着我埋下的中医种子有一天会茁壮成长，我的中国梦也终会实现。

体验中国高考作文
On Composition of the National College Entrance Examination

［越南］ 阮氏秋香　中国地质大学（武汉）

[Vietnam] Nguyen Thi Thu Huong, China University of Geosciences (Wuhan)

At 11: 30 am, June 7, students in Hubei Province just finished the Chinese subject of the National College Entrance Examination and left the examination hall with various feelings. At about 12 noon, the first group of foreign students from our college came to a room with tension and curiosity. This is a program well planned by Changjiang Cloud which arranged a special writing examination for our college's foreign students to learn how the foreigners view Chinese National College Entrance Examination.

The title of the composition is "A letter to 2035". That is exactly the year I heard from news last year. On the 19th CPC National Congress held in 2017, President Xi Jinping said in his report that the CPC will lead the country to basically realize socialist modernization by 2035.

China has a solid foundation to realize this strategic plan. 2018 marks the 40th anniversary of Chinese reform and opening-up, and 2019 will witness the 70th anniversary of the foundation of the People's Republic of China. Within a few decades, Chinese leaders have led the whole nation to explore a

6月7日上午11：30，2018 年湖北省高考语文科目结束，莘莘学子神色各异地走出了考场。12 点左右，我们学院的首批外国留学生，怀着紧张而新奇的心情迈进了一个特殊的"考场"，由长江云精心策划了一档栏目，安排我院外国留学生来一场说考就考的即兴高考作文，以了解外国人眼中的中国高考。

作文题目是《给 2035 年的一封信》。2035 年？这不是去年我在新闻中听到的时间吗？在 2017 年中国共产党的十九大会议上，习近平总书记在报告中提出，到 2035 年，中国将基本实现社会主义现代化。

中国能提出这样的战略构想，完全有自己坚实的基础。2018 年是中国改革开放四十周年，2019 年是新中国成立七十周年。短短几十年，新中国领导人带领国家各族人民，探索适合自己国家特色的社会主义道路，把中国从一个贫穷落后的国家建设成为世界第二大经济体。中国自己发展强大的同时，还能顺应经济全球化的趋势，愿意与世界各国人民共同分享中国改革开放的成果，中国发展的经验和教训。"一带一路"的重要平台"上海合作组织"，为了促进沿线各国人民之间的人文交流和民间往来，承诺并且落实了一系列项目。

successful road to socialism with Chinese characteristics, transforming China from an undeveloped country to the second biggest economy in the world. While developing itself, China is willing to share the successes and experiences of its reform and opening-up with the world in line with the trend of economic globalization. Shanghai Cooperation Organization, which is an important platform for the Belt and Road Initiative, promised and carried out a series of projects to promote people-to-people exchanges and nongovernmental communication among countries along the route.

It is under such circumstances that I have this great opportunity of pursuing my master's degree in public administration in China University of Geosciences (Wuhan) with the scholarship provided by the Chinese government. Before coming to China, I lived a comfortable life at home with happy family, warm-hearted friends and a stable and well-paid job in accounting. However, as a young man, I aim high. I want to see this fast-changing world. Located in the middle of China, Wuhan is a major transportation hub of airplanes, railways, expressways and rivers. It is not only home to East Lake, Sha Lake and Yangtze River, and mountains such as Luojia Mountain, Nanwang Mountain and Guizi Mountain, but also a city of delicacies. Beancurd skinsoup dumpling, hot dried noodles, and duck's neck are all worth trying. Wuchang is now the center of education and culture, and Hankou the commercial center.

In class, the teacher introduced Chinese traditional culture to us, including "Tai Chi and Tai Chi Quan", "Chinese tunic suit and cheongsam", Chinese Valentine's Day, Chinese weddings and funerals and others. Besides, we also learn about Confucius who teaches students in accordance with their aptitude, Sun Wukong who has magic power in *Journey to the West*, and *A Dream of the*

中国地质大学（武汉）提供

　　正是在这样的国际环境和背景下，我才有机会获得中国政府奖学金，来中国地质大学（武汉）攻读公共管理专业的硕士研究生。虽然来中国以前，我的生活是那样的舒适安逸，拥有幸福的家庭、热情的朋友、稳定而收入较高的会计工作，但是年轻的我，却有一颗不安分的心。世界那么大，变化那么快，我想去看看。武汉位于中国中部，是航空、铁路、公路和长江航道等的交通枢纽；有东湖、沙湖、长江等大面积水域；有珞珈山、南望山、桂子山等四季常绿的青山；有老通城的豆皮、四季美的汤包、热干面和鸭脖子等地方特色美食；有人口素质较高的教育文化中心——武昌，也有经济繁华的商业贸易中心——汉口。

　　课堂上，老师给我们讲解了"太极和太极拳""中山装和旗袍""七夕节""红白喜事"等中国传统文化；也给我们介绍了孔子是怎样"因材施教"的，还让我们喜欢上了《西游记》中神通广大的孙悟空，而对《红楼梦》中的爱情悲剧充满了同情。课外，除了学校为我们留学生组织的各项中国传统文化活动，比如篆刻、毛笔书法、中国花鸟画的学习等，

Red Mansions which describes a sympathetic love tragedy. After class, the school has organized many activities for us to deepen our understanding of Chinese traditional culture, such as learning seal cutting, Chinese calligraphy and painting. We also went to Huangshi to visit the smelting industry. Besides, there are various celebration activities and special programs held in Wuhan. All of these help us experience the ancient and mysterious Chinese culture. We wholeheartedly admire the wisdom and creativity of the Chinese people.

On the day of the Lantern Festival, a lantern show was held in the East Lake of Wuhan. There were many wonderful lanterns exhibited there. "Happy New Year" brought so much joy; "Pangu Creates the World" sent me back to the ancient times; "Chime-bells from the Tomb of Marquis Yi of Zeng" demonstrated the greatness of ancient Chinese instruments; and many lanterns in shape of dogs attracted streams of tourists to take photos. A huge lantern in shape of a lion exhibited before the Changtian Tower stole the thunder from the others. A batch of works made by successors of intangible cultural heritage with Chinese characteristics were also exhibited during the show, such as the block-printed Chinese New Year pictures, Han embroidery, paper-cutting, dough modeling and egg paintings, which brought me, a foreigner, closer to the intangible cultural heritage.

I would like to tell my fellows in 2035, "17 years ago, there is a Vietnamese girl who is as young as you. Following her dream, she chose to study in China where she became a better herself. China is now a more open, friendlier, and inclusive country developing at a fast speed. Come here and check it for yourself while you are still young. "

以及赴黄石参观冶矿工业等社会实践活动以外，武汉本地丰富多彩的节日庆祝活动和特色项目，也让我们这些年轻的"歪果仁"对传说中古老而神秘的中国文化有了最真实的体验，从心底里佩服中国人的智慧与创造能力。

2017年元宵节，武汉东湖举办了灯会，"新春吉祥"带来一片红红火火、喜气洋洋；"盘古开天"让我们穿越回到了史前人类；"曾侯乙编钟"再现了中国乐器的风采；十几只各种形态的狗狗灯组，吸引了大批游客合影留念。长天楼前的"四面狮"灯组高达七层楼，成为灯会的耀眼之星。与灯组交相辉映的是木拓年画、汉绣、剪纸、面塑、蛋画等一批独具中国特色的非遗传承人作品，与游客进行现场互动表演，一下拉近了我这个老外和"非遗"的距离。

想到这里，我不禁想对自己2035年的年轻同胞说：17年前，有一个和你们一样年轻、充满幻想的越南姑娘，她选择了去中国留学，从而成就了最好的自己。如今的中国，更加开放友好、发达包容，趁年轻，一定要亲自去看看！

火辣辣的柳州
Spicy Liuzhou

［乌兹别克斯坦］ 洪业　柳州城市职业学院

[Uzbekistan] Ostonov Okhunjon, Liuzhou City Vocational College

It has been more than a year since I came to Liuzhou. I want to use one word to describe the impression Liuzhou has on me, that is, "spicy".

But why do I say that? I remember the first time that I ate snail rice noodles. Looking at the chili sauce added on the noodles, I asked my friend, "Is this spicy or not?" My friend said with a smile that it was not and chili in Liuzhou was not spicy at all. "Snail rice noodles here are delicious!" I trusted his words and ate it in a gulp, but within two seconds, I burst into tears because the noodles were too hot for me! My friend laughed at me. From then on, I was afraid of eating chili. However, everything in Liuzhou was cooked with chili. Every time I ate chow mein, I would say, "Sir, please do not add any chili to the noodles!" But when it was served on the table, there was still so much chili, which always made me uncomfortable. I even wondered if the chili was free of charge because it was used so widely and frequently.

Besides, the weather in Liuzhou is also hot. In summer, Liuzhou is as hot as a big furnace. If one goes outside, the clothes he wears will be drenched with sweat within five minutes. When the summer came to an end, even my African

来柳州有一年多了，对于柳州的印象，我想用一个字来说：辣！

为什么这样说呢？记得第一次吃柳州美食螺蛳粉的时候，我看着螺蛳粉上的红油，问朋友："这个辣不辣？"朋友笑着说："不辣，柳州的辣椒一点也不辣。螺蛳粉，好吃！"我很相信他，于是夹了一大筷子的粉放到嘴里，可是两秒钟不到，我就被辣得眼泪流了出来！朋友在旁边哈哈大笑。从此以后，我见到辣椒就怕。但是柳州所有吃的都放辣椒，每次去吃炒面，我都说："老板，不要辣椒！"可一端上来，那炒面里还是有很多红红的，每次都辣得我泪流满面。我很想问："老板，辣椒不要钱吗？"

柳州的天气也是火辣辣的。夏天的柳州就像一个大火炉，人在外面不到 5 分钟就全身湿透了，一个夏天下来，连非洲来的黑人同学都说他们的皮肤黑了。到了冬天，虽然不下雪，可是这里没有暖气，又常常下雨，冷得人发抖，刮在脸上的风都是辣辣的。

不过，柳州人的性格很好。刚来时，我汉语不好，在路上跟一个人打听怎么去中国银行，他说的怎么走，往哪儿拐，我都听不懂，说了好久，他不但没有不耐烦，最后还亲自把我送到了银行。分别的时候，他跟我握手说："兄弟，欢迎你来柳州！"柳州人火辣辣的热情，让我十分

classmates said that they were suntanned. In addition, although there is no snow in winter, between non-heating system and frequent rain, people shiver due to the chill. And the strong wind blows on the face painfully.

However, people in Liuzhou have a very good character. When I first came here, I was not good at Chinese. I asked people for the way to the Bank of China. But I could not understand what they said. He would not be impatient even after explaining for a long time, and finally, led me to the bank. When he left, he shook hands with me and said, "Welcome to Liuzhou, buddy!" I was really moved by the enthusiasm of people in Liuzhou.

What's more, I always think that girls in Liuzhou are very beautiful. However, they are "spicy girls" as well. While eating Liuzhou snails rice noodles, they add chili; in dressing, they always dress in style and look hot; talking and acting in great hurry, they are hot-tempered. And besides these, due to their hot-tempered personality, they act like Liuzhou's weather: if you do something wrong, they shout at you in a cloudy mood despite having shown friendliness minutes before. Why do I know all that? My girlfriend is a Liuzhou native.

Therefore, I love this hot city—Liuzhou. Please remember my name: Hongye (Ostonov Okhunjon), meaning great cause. I came to Liuzhou with an ambition to achieve my own great cause. I will try harder to learn Chinese and serve Liuzhou, the hot city, with my enthusiasm.

柳州城市职业学院提供

感动！

另外，我觉得柳州女孩子很漂亮，可是她们是"辣妹子"！她们吃螺蛳粉要加辣；她们打扮时髦，身材火辣；她们说话又快又急，做事风风火火，性格火辣！不仅如此，她们的脾气也很火辣，如果你做错事，她们就像柳州的天气，刚刚还万里无云，可一转眼就"阴云密布，狂风暴雨"地对你吼起来！你们问我怎么知道？因为我的女朋友就是柳州妹！

所以，我爱这"火辣辣"的柳州！请您记住我的名字——洪业，我怀着梦想来到柳州，我要成就我的宏图伟业！我要学好汉语，我要用我的热情，回馈这"火辣辣"的柳州！

艺术无国界，艺术无障碍

——给李玉刚的一封信

Art Knows No Borders or Barriers

—A Letter to Li Yugang

[俄罗斯] 塔尼亚 沈阳大学

[Russia] Karpushina Tatiana, Shenyang University

Dear Mr. Li Yugang,

How are you doing!

My name is Taniya (Karpushina Tatiana) and I am a student at the Oriental Institute of National Research University "Higher school of economics" Saint Petersburg. I would like to pour out my heart to you: I am inspired and touched by your artistic talent, and thus I think I must introduce your works to Russians.

When I came to Shenyang in 2017, I knew you for the first time. In fact, Russians do not know much about Chinese artists, but your songs and performances inspire me a lot, from which I see the charm and beauty of Chinese culture. In order to understand more, I check relevant information on the Internet, appreciate the artistic conception of your songs with carefulness, and watch your interviews again and again. You greatly widen my horizon and introduce me into a better and richer world. You give me inspiration and serve as a mentor for me.

李玉刚先生：

　　您好！

　　我叫塔尼亚，我是俄罗斯高等经济研究大学圣彼得堡部东方学院的学生。我想向您倾诉：我被您的艺术鼓舞了，它让我感动，所以我认为一定要把您的艺术介绍给俄罗斯人。

　　2017年来到沈阳学习的时候，我第一次知道您。其实，俄罗斯人不太了解中国艺术家，但是您的歌曲和演出给了我很多启发，您让我看到中国文化是那么神奇而美丽。为了了解更多一点儿，我在网络上查相关资料，仔细体会您的歌曲的意境，一次又一次看您的采访。您让我大开眼界，带我进入了一个更美好更丰富的世界。您给了我灵感，也成为我的大师。

　　从小，我就想做一名传播者。当我了解到一种新的艺术，我就想传播给更多的人。我是这样的人，我觉得您好像也是这样的。我感受到了您的歌曲魅力，我翻译了它们，尽力符合它们的原意，选出了最合适的

From an early age, I dreamed to be a communicator. Whenever I learn about a new form of art, I am willing to spread it to more people, and I think you seem to be like this. I grasp the charm of your songs, so I translated them and tried to express their original intents. By means of the most appropriate Russian words, I retain the mood in your lyrics to finish integrated works, which not only reflects the meaning of Chinese words, but also conveys emotions and brings special touch to readers. After translation, I uploaded them on the Russian network to spread your works in Russia. Your works has struck the hearts of Russians and received a warm response. They think that some songs are particularly elegant, beautiful, and amiable.

I have carefully translated some songs, including "The New Drunken Beauty", "Just Meet You", "Good Person's Pleasant Dream", "Top of Roof Crown", "Lotus", "Gongzhuling", and "Hometown". I want to mention the last three songs in particular, which are written by yourself and embody your true feelings. Your thoughts and soul are reflected in these songs, which I dare not misinterpret. So I work hard to translate, and now Russians know what you want to express, and they will understand your inner thoughts.

Have you heard of Yesenin, a well-known poet in Russia who is loved and respected just like Pushkin by people? Yesenin lives in the silver age of Russian poetry, which is an awfully difficult period for the country. He came from the countryside like you, and in order to spread his art, he moved to the capital Moscow. Your songs "Hometown" and "Gongzhuling" especially have something in common with his works. Yesenin enjoys the simple life of country and dislikes the busyness of city. His poetry often mentions where he was born and raised. When I first heard your song, I remembered Yesenin. So, you are

沈阳大学提供

俄语的词，保留了您歌词里诗的意境，直到翻译成为一个完整的作品。不仅能够反映中文文本的意义，还能传达情感，给读者带来特别的感动。翻译完之后，我把它放在俄罗斯的网络上，把您的艺术在俄罗斯传播。您的作品冲击到了俄罗斯人的心灵，得到了俄罗斯人的热烈响应。他们觉得有的歌曲特别高雅，特别美，有的歌曲很亲切。

我已经精心翻译了一些歌曲：《新贵妃醉酒》《刚好遇见你》《好人好梦》《宝顶之巅》《莲花》《公主岭》《故乡》。我想特别提起的是最后三首歌曲，这三首是您自己写的，是您的真实感受。您把您的想法和灵魂投入这些歌里，我不敢曲解您的感觉。所以我很努力地翻译，现在俄罗斯人会知道您想表达什么，他们会明白您的内心的想法。

您有没有听说过俄罗斯诗人叶赛宁？在俄罗斯他是一位非常有名的诗人，像普希金一样获得了人民的喜爱。叶赛宁生活在俄罗斯诗歌白银时代，是国家非常困难的时期。他像您一样从农村来，为了传播他的艺术，他搬到了首都莫斯科。您的歌曲《故乡》和《公主岭》特别像他的

more welcomed to Russians than you think.

I was fortunate to attend the "Li Yugang ten-year classic concert" in Chongqing. Although I was sitting far, and I still felt excited to see your performance and hear your voice. What a wonderful feeling this is! I came to St. Petersburg from a small city because I was very fascinated by the city. Known as the cultural capital of Russia, St. Petersburg is a place with a long history and rich cultural heritage. The Mariinsky Theatre is the oldest theatre in St. Petersburg, where many important performances are held. I always imagine you standing on the stage of the Mariinsky Theatre and bringing wonderful performances to Russians. You deserve the applause of the Russians and should feel our joy. Therefore, if you plan to come to Russia to perform, I will endeavor to help you. I am ready to do that. I know what your dream is and am willing to help you achieve it. You once said, "My path is very, very long, but no matter how long, and no matter how lonely, I will carry through firmly to the end by myself, and stay true to my original aspiration. " I hope that you will receive my letter, write back and accept my proposal. If not, I will continue to do what I am doing for you. For me, the foremost thing is to spread culture.

Now I have a ticket for the Prajna Horn in Shenyang on June 10. I will be there to appreciate the performance directed by you and enjoy it. Thank you, my great master. See you there!

Karpushina Tatiana from Russia

June 1, 2018

作品。叶赛宁喜欢乡村的简单生活，不喜欢城市的忙碌，他的诗歌里经常会提到他出生和长大的地方。当我第一次听到您的歌时，我就想起来了叶赛宁。所以，您对于俄罗斯人来说比您想象得更亲切。

我有幸在重庆看到您的"李玉刚十年经典演唱会"。尽管我坐得很远，但我看到您的表演，听到你的声音仍然非常兴奋。这是特别美妙的感觉！我自己从一个很小的城市来到了圣彼得堡，因为我对这个城市非常着迷。圣彼得堡被称为俄罗斯的文化首都，圣彼得堡是一个有悠久历史和丰富文化遗产的地方。马林斯基剧院是圣彼得堡最古老的剧院，这里经常会举办很多重要的演出。我会想象您站在马林斯基剧院的舞台上，给俄罗斯的人们带来精彩的演出。您应该得到俄罗斯人的掌声和感受我们的喜悦。因此，如果您打算来俄罗斯演出，我会尽力帮助您。我已经做好了准备，我知道您的梦想是什么，也想帮您实现它。您曾经说过"我的路是非常非常漫长，但是不管多么长，不管多寂寞。一个人坚持走下去，不忘初心"。希望您能收到我的信。我真的希望您会回应并接受我的提议。如果没有，我仍然会继续做我正在为您做的事情。对我而言，为其他人传播文化是最重要的。

现在我的手里拿着 6 月 10 日沈阳站《般若号角》的票。我会来看您导演的演出并好好享受它。谢谢您，我的大师。我们不见不散！

俄罗斯塔尼亚

2018 年 6 月 1 日

[马来西亚]　吕玥卿　深圳大学
[Malaysia] Lee Yue Qing, Shenzhen University

Happy time flies. Once I was a stranger to Shenzhen when I first arrived, but now I knew every street of this city, and could talk with the Chinese people fluently. Isn't it amazing? Now, I have a new look at Shenzhen after seeing its fast-changing cityscape and its soaring development. These can only be experienced as you immerse yourself in the exploration.

Shenzhen is a city of landscaped gardens with fine sceneries, trees and

与同学们的集体照

　　时间如流水，一去不回头，美好的时光总是不经意地流逝。回首初到深圳时，我还是一个对这座城市一无所知的外国人，到现在能够自由穿梭其中，流利地与中国人交谈，这过程真是太奇妙了！在这城市留学与生活，也让我看到了深圳日新月异的面貌和叹为观止的发展速度，打破了我以往对深圳的认知。有道是"百闻不如一见"，只有亲自来到这个地方，才能领略它的魅力所在。

　　深圳是一座美丽的花园城市，这里风景秀丽，绿树成荫，鲜花盛开，夜晚华灯初上，霓虹闪烁，让这座城市显得更绚烂多彩。在这片土地上，有蔚蓝的天空，有一望无际的大海；有欢乐谷的动感激情，有锦绣中华的民族风情……其中，最让我印象深刻的就是世界之窗。它是中国著名的缩微景区，这个主题公园把世界奇观、历史遗迹、民间歌舞融合在一起，一整天游玩其中，也不一定能逛完呢！来到这里，一定会让你流连忘返！

　　最让我惊异也最能体现深圳特点的是深圳的高科技。在我留学的深圳大学北门对面就有一家鼎鼎大名的科技公司——腾讯。虽然它成立不过二十年，但如今却在中国的企业界声名鹊起。腾讯开发了很多科技软件，如众所周知的 QQ 和微信。值得一提的是，它的创始人马化腾还是深圳大

flowers everywhere. When night falls, neon lights dress it in colors. It also has blue sky and vast sea, thrilling Happy Valley, and Splendid China Folk Village. What strikes me most is the Window of the World, a famous miniature theme park in China. You will get into the thick of this harmonious blend of the world wonders, historical sites and folk songs once you come here.

High technology stands for Shenzhen. Tencent, the renowned technology company, sits opposite to the north gate of my university. It shot to fame in the business community of China within only 20 years after it was established. Tencent has created a lot of well-known software such as QQ and WeChat. Its founder Pony Ma also graduated from Shenzhen University. I am very proud to have such an alumnus.

I found mobile payment a novelty as there is not such a thing in my country. One click on a mobile phone will pay for your meal, shopping, travel, and ticket. Maybe it is as some people call it "No matter where you are and what you are doing,

深圳大学第四届国际文化节

学毕业的，有这样一位学长和校友，也让我这个留学生特别自豪。

最令我感到新奇的是移动支付。那是因为我的国家还没有这种移动支付的技术。点餐、购物、旅行、购票什么的，都不需要使用现金付款，只要拥有一部手机，就能解决一切支付的问题，这可能就是所谓的"一部手机走天下"吧。在留学生活中，大部分的留学生想必跟我一样，都喜欢叫外卖来解决一餐吧，只要有了它们，你就能点单并快速享用餐食，这种点餐方式在我们国家是可望而不可即的。这就是移动支付所带来的便利。

在深圳留学的生活中，我也习了惯用网购来解决日常生活所需。只要是我需要的，就能通过一些下载软件来获取，淘宝、京东、当当、携程等软件，里面的东西琳琅满目、应有尽有。这些软件对于我这个来自马来西亚的留学生来说，是必不可缺的。它们的使用省去了我排队的时间，大大方便了我的留学生活，提高了我生活的质量。

说了那么多，当然少不了要介绍我留学的学校——深圳大学。它创立

参加学校的活动

mobile phone is the solution to all your problems. " I guess that, just like me, many international students prefer to order takeouts to save time for their studies. With mobile payment, you can order food and enjoy your meal in no time. However, my country probably could not enjoy such convenience.

I usually shop online to buy daily groceries. Apps like Taobao, Jingdong, Dangdang and Ctrip provide a great variety of goods and services, which can meet all my needs. Such software is a must-have for an international student as it saves me the time for queuing and improves my life quality.

I would like to take a moment to introduce Shenzhen University, the university I attend. Founded in 1983, it has been known for its innovation and entrepreneurialism for decades. Many of its graduates are business tycoons such as Shi Yuzhu and Ma Huateng. It is also accredited as one of the most beautiful Chinese universities with its picturesque sceneries of beautiful beaches and red woods which earn it the worthy name of Litchi Orchard. Lush and green litchi trees can be seen everywhere on campus. You will never want to leave here once you have a taste of the red plump litchi in summer.

Shenzhen was the first city I knew upon coming to China. Although I have not explored all its beauty, my passion is just beyond words. I wish that I can experience and appreciate the city more in future.

深圳大学提供

于 1983 年，几十年来以创新、创业文化著称于世。校园坐拥天风海涛、白云红荔，被誉为中国最美大学之一。在这美丽的大学里，也孕育出不少像史玉柱、马化腾这样大家耳熟能详的人才。深圳大学也有一个别称——"荔枝园"。拥有这个美誉，绝不是徒有虚名而已。只要漫步在校园里，到处都可以见到郁郁葱葱的荔枝树。到了夏天，看到大树上结满了通红饱满的荔枝，真让人不禁长叹"日啖荔枝三百颗，不辞长作岭南人"呢！

对我而言，深圳是我踏进中国后接触到的第一个城市，属于它的美，我还没完全领略，但对于它的热爱却是难于言表的！希望在今后的日子里，我能进一步体验和挖掘深圳的另一番美！

梦想与中国同行
Dream Along with China

[蒙古] 阿木古楞 中央民族大学

[Mongolia] Azbeleg Enkh-Amgalan, Minzu University of China

I have always been fascinated by Chinese culture, watching Chinese movies and listening to Chinese songs from childhood. It is my pleasure to have the opportunity to share my life, experience and feelings in China.

As early as in middle school, I have been determined to become an ambassador, and from the time I came to China at the age of thirteen, my dream began to take root and continued to thrive.

Studying in China enriches my life. The reform and opening-up has greatly boosted China's development, which attracted the attention of the Mongolian people. My father and mother seized the opportunity of friendly exchanges between the two countries and sent me to China. I started my dream when I came to China to study as a junior middle school student. At that time, I was the only foreign student in the school, overwhelmed by expectation as well as anxiety about the future life in China as a new comer. However, in the next six months, my Chinese improved even without my awareness, which inspired and filled me with hope.

When I was in junior high school in China, through my diligence and

我从小就爱看中国电影，听中国歌曲，热爱中国文化。现在我很高兴能有机会给大家分享自己在中国的生活、经历以及感受。

早在中学时我就立志成为一名大使，而我的梦想正是从我十三岁来到中国后开始生根发芽并不断茁壮成长。

我的人生因在中国读书而逐渐变得色彩缤纷。随着中国改革开放以来的飞速发展，中国这个伟大的国家引起蒙古人民的关注，我的爸爸、妈妈抓住两国友好往来的机会把我送到中国读书。初三来中国读书是我的梦想开始的第一步，我是学校里的唯一的外国学生，对初来乍到，语言不通的小孩儿来说在中国未来的生活既充满期待又忐忑不安，但是在接下来的六个月里我的汉语不知不觉地提高了，这让我感到无比振奋，并让我对未来充满希望。

在中国读中学时，通过我的努力和我的坚持，我取得了很多引以为傲的成绩。比如我不仅成为老师们眼中优秀的学生会主席，也在毕业时考过了 HSK 六级。虽然我们外国学生申请中国的大学只要求通过 HSK 四级，但是我想挑战自己，我要做最优秀的学生，所以毅然报考了 HSK 六级并一次性通过。除此之外，我还和志同道合的好朋友们组建了自己

perseverance, I gained many achievements of which I was proud. For example, I not only became the president of the student union recognized by the teachers, but also passed the HSK (level 6) when I graduated. Although foreign students are qualified to apply to Chinese universities as long as we pass HSK Level 4, I want to challenge myself and be the best. Therefore, I registered for HSK Level 6 without hesitation and passed it at once. In addition, I also formed my own band with like-minded friends. We played a beautiful song at the high school graduation ceremony to commemorate our youth. After graduating from high school, I successfully got the Belt and Road Scholarship and was admitted to Minzu University of China. This is my story with Chinese.

From the reform and opening-up policy in 1978 to the Belt and Road Initiative at present, China has gone further and further on the road of great national rejuvenation. The Belt and Road Initiative is proposed to realize the friendly exchanges between people all over the world, to build a community of shared future, and to actively develop economic cooperation with countries along the route. The Initiative not only promotes China's development, but also helps many foreign students to study in China through the Belt and Road Scholarship. I have witnessed the miracles created by China. Meanwhile, I also embark on my own dream-chasing journey in China.

Everyone could find a place in the society, just as ancient Chinese poet Li Bai once said: "Heaven has made us talents, and we're not made in vain. " My ideal job may be ordinary, but it is not simple — I want to be the Mongolian ambassador to China. I have several uncles who used to serve as diplomats, each of whom has rich professional experience. One of them, for example, worked in the Consulate General of Mongolian in Hohhot. My visits to him,

的乐队，我们在高中毕业典礼上弹奏了美丽的华章纪念我们的青春。高中毕业后我顺利地拿到"一带一路"奖学金并且考上了中央民族大学。这是我喜欢上汉语的故事。

从1978年改革开放到现在的"一带一路"，中国在民族复兴的伟大道路上越走越远。"一带一路"是为了实现世界人民友好往来，打造人类命运共同体、积极发展与沿线国家的经济合作关系的伟大创举。"一带一路"不仅促进中国的发展，也使很多外国留学生通过"一带一路"奖学金实现了来中国学习的梦想。我见证了中国创造的一个又一个奇迹，同时我也在中国开始了自己的追梦路。

每个人都有适合自己的理想工作，正如李白所说："天生我材必有用。"我的理想工作平凡却不简单，因为我梦想成为蒙古国驻华大使，我的身边有几位当过外交官的叔叔，他们每个人都拥有丰富的专业经验。

与同学们在北戴河

though short, excited me and constantly inspired me to be an ambassador. But I also learned the bitterness and arduousness of this job. As an ambassador, he represents his country. The ambassadors should spare no efforts in maintaining good relations between two countries. On the other hand, they also need to make sure that the rights of people from their own countries living in a foreign country are guaranteed. Only an outstanding talent with excellent political capacity and stress tolerance could equal to such an important task.

Determination and diligence will make a dream come true. In order to become an ambassador, I am now studying Chinese at Minzu University of China. After that, I will continue to study international relations and international laws to enrich my knowledge. I believe that I will realize my dream as long as I stick to and make unremitting efforts for my goal.

中央民族大学 / 郭文忠摄

比如说我有一个叔叔，他在蒙古国驻呼和浩特总领事馆工作，我经常去找他，每次片刻的逗留都能让我心潮澎湃，不断激发我对大使这份职业的憧憬。但我也了解到做大使的辛酸与困难，因为一名大使代表着自己的祖国在别的国家的形象，他不仅需要努力让两国保持良好的关系，也需要让自己的国民在异国生活的权利得到保证，这个重任需要具有卓越政治能力和抗压能力的优秀人才。

　　梦想的实现需要坚定的目标和努力。为了成为一名大使，我现在在中央民族大学学习汉语，在学好汉语后我会继续

在民大国际学生趣味运动会上担当主持

攻读国际关系和国际法律这两个专业，让自己的知识储备更加丰富。我相信只要目标坚定并坚持不懈，我会抵达理想的彼岸。

陕西的面
Shaanxi Noodles

[越南] 裴玉梦 西安电子科技大学
[Vietnam] Bui Thi Mo, Xidian University

Since I came to Xi'an to study in September last year, I have had a deep predestination with it, and I also fell in love with its noodles. Being in Xi'an, you will see all kinds of noodle restaurants along the avenues and alleyways, and will be able to explore all of them. Xi'an residents indulge in noodles for every occasion. Initially, I felt a bit strange about that and wondered why they seldom eat rice. Later, I discovered that eating noodles is a habit of Shaanxi natives.

Although the traffic has developed currently and it has become more convenient to transport rice from Southern China to Shaanxi, Shaanxi people are still accustomed to eating noodles. This may be because, on the one hand, a deep-rooted diet culture has formed for the delicacy has been around for millennia, they love noodles instinctively; on the other hand, having eating noodles for such a long time, the appetite of Shaanxi natives has also become accustomed to it. Furthermore, noodles are not only easy to make, but also sustain hunger, particularly when we are hungry. I have enjoyed many kinds of noodles here, such as minced mutton noodles, minced beef noodles and minced pumpkin noodles, etc. However, what impressed me the most was the

自从去年九月来到西安留学，我便和西安结下了很深的缘分，也同时爱上了西安的面。只要你来到西安，就能在大街小巷看到各种各样的面馆，品尝到各种美味的面食。我经常看到西安人午饭吃面，晚饭也吃面，一开始觉得有点儿奇怪，为什么他们很少吃米饭呢？后来我发现，陕西人是有吃面的习惯啊。

虽然现在交通很发达，大米从南方运到陕西很方便，但是陕西人还是习惯吃面。这可能是因为陕西人做面做了几千年，吃面也吃了几千年，形成了根深蒂固的饮食文化，爱面爱到了骨子里。并且经过长期吃面，陕西人的胃口也已经适应了面条，还有如果我们很饿的时候，面条不仅做起来方便，而且吃起来也非常顶饱，所以面条这种"快餐"才被陕西人追捧和喜爱。我来到陕西享受过很多面食，比如羊肉臊子面、牛肉臊子面、南瓜臊子面……但是给我留下印象最深的还是在回民街吃到的一种面。

那还是我跟朋友第一次去回民街，我们一边聊天儿，一边惊奇着回民街的热闹。回民街是西安著名的一条小吃街，每天都很热闹，人很多，美食也很丰富。我们沿着回民街一直往前走，突然看到一个门牌上

one I ate at the Muslim Quarter.

It was my first time to the Muslim Quarter with my friends, and we chatted and marveled at the jollification of the street. As a famous snack street with abundant cuisines in Xi'an, the Muslim Quarter is always bustling with visitors. As we walked along the street, we suddenly saw a very complicated Chinese character on a door plate. It was unfamiliar to me. So I quickly picked up the dictionary and looked it up, but I could not find it at all. What a strange word, not even in a dictionary? Then we asked the waiter curiously and knew that, apart from the minced mutton noodles, it was another famous Shaanxi noodles, which is called Biangbiang noodles. Actually, the Chinese character of "biangbiang" noodles was hard to be written and remembered, so the natives record the word with a jingle:

Apex rising up to the sky,

Over Two bends by Yellow River's side.

Character "Eight"'s (八) opening wide,

"Speech" (言) enters inside.

You twist, I twist too, (幺 "tiny")

you grow, I grow (長) with you,

Inside, a horse (馬) king will rule.

"Heart" (心) down below,

"Moon" (月) by the side,

Leave a hook (刂 "knife") for Matang (Mahua, Fried Dough Twist) to hang low,

On our carriage, to Xianyang we'll ride (radical: 辶 "walk").

This is a vivid description of the character "biang" . Locals are all capable of writing it, but for foreigners, particular we oversea students in China, it is still

写着个特别复杂的汉字，这个字对我来说真陌生啊，我赶快拿起字典查了查，可是根本就查不到，真奇怪什么字连在字典里都没有呢？我们好奇地问了问服务员才知道除了臊子面，这也是一种陕西著名的面食——biangbiang 面。其实 biangbiang 面的汉字很难写也不容易记住，所以当地人用一段顺口溜把这个字记录下来：

一点飞上天，黄河两头弯

八字大张口，言字往里走

左一扭，右一扭

西一长，东一长

中间夹个马大王

心字底，月字边

留个勾搭挂麻糖

推个车车逛咸阳

这是很形象的 biang 字。在这里只要是本地人，几乎人人都会写这个字。不过对外国人，特别是留学生来说还是一个陌生字，所以我也不是例外啊。陕西的面现在有很多种制作方法，并且可以烹制出不同的风味。另外，山西刀削面、武汉热干面、韩国面、意大利面等都来到了陕西，陕西人也让这些外地面入乡随俗，在陕西的地界上大受欢迎，但是biangbiang 面还是最吸引我，所以我强烈推荐外国朋友来到陕西一定要吃上一碗 biangbiang 面。biangbiang 面不仅是一种美食，味道又酸又辣的，而且还代表着陕西乃至中国一种特有的文化，它的来历非常有趣。相传过去有一个书生，当时他穷困潦倒，饥饿难耐，走着走着从远处传来 biangbiang 的声音，他闻声走去，看到一家饭馆的厨师正提着又宽又大的面在案板上挥着，并且发出 biangbiang 的声音，不一会儿一锅面就出锅了。店家给书生盛了一碗，书生看到这碗面里有红彤彤的油泼辣子、

a new word to us. Shaanxi noodles can be made with many different methods and cooked with diverse flavors. In addition, with the introduction of Shanxi shaved noodles, Wuhan hot noodles with sesame paste, South Korea's pasta and spaghetti, Shaanxi people have adapted these exotic noodles into their own unique cuisines, which are much popularized here. Among many kinds of noodles, it is still the "biangbiang" noodles that attract me most, so I highly recommend that foreign friends to Shaanxi eat a bowl of "biangbiang" noodles. The "biangbiang" noodles are not only a cuisine with sour and spicy taste, but also a representation of the unique culture of Shaanxi and even China. Its origin is curious: it is said that there used to be a scholar who was poor and hungry, walking along the road, and being attracted by a sound of "biangbiang" in far distance. Tracing the sound, he found a chef of a restaurant pulling a thick and large noodle and slapping it on the table, which made the sounds like "biangbiang" . Soon a pot of noodles was cooked. The owner served the poor scholar a bowl of savory noodles with red chili oil and chopped green Chinese onion. So he asked the owner, "What do you call it?" , but the owner could not tell either. In order to repay the owner, the scholar called it "biangbiang" noodles. "Biangbiang" noodles are special for me. Long, wide and thick as the noodles are, they look like belts, I wonder if there is a story behind every cuisine in Shaanxi. Now I have lived in Shaanxi for one year, and I have fallen in love with it, its people, its scenery, and everything else here! I think I can no longer leave here, and I am afraid I will not taste such delicious noodles anymore if I return to Vietnam.

西安电子科技大学提供

绿油油的葱花，还带着扑鼻的香味，于是就问店家："你这面叫什么？"
可店家也说不出来，书生为了回报老板，就起了个名字 biangbiang 面。
对我来说 biangbiang 面很特别，一条面好像一根裤带一样，因为面条又
宽又长而且很厚，只吃几条就饱了。虽然只是一碗面条，但它给了我很
多知识，我在想，是不是无论在陕西什么地方，无论什么美食都会有一
个故事呢？我已经在陕西生活了一年，我真的已经爱上了这里，爱上了
陕西的人，陕西的风景，陕西的一切！特别是我在陕西学习的这段时间，
惊奇地发现我居然也深深爱上了面条，我想我已经无法再离开这里了，
如果回到越南，恐怕再也吃不到这么好吃的面了。

洛阳行
My Journey in Luoyang

[加拿大]　王周艳　河南中医药大学
[Canada] Wang Zhou Yan, Henan University of Chinese Medicine

"If someone wants to know the historical vicissitudes, Luoyang alone could tell him everything. " As the capital of thirteen dynasties, this city's rise and fall present at least half of China's history. Because of its unique geographical positon, Luoyang has been seen as the key to end turbulence. In addition, Luoyang is known as the cradle of the Yellow River civilization and the Heluo Culture. It was in this city that Confucianism originated, Taoism initiated, Buddhism first introduced and Li School—a Confucian school of idealist philosophy of the Song dynasty and Ming dynasty born.

It took about two hours to drive from Zhengzhou to Luoyang. Along the way, I racked my brain to review everything I know about Luoyang: from the Xia dynasty to the five dynasties and ten kingdoms period, Luoyang had served as the capital or a second capital. It is the first and oldest capital that served most dynasties. Even Sima Guang, a high-ranking scholar-official in the Song Dynasty could not help but exclaim "fame and fortune have all been gathered in Luoyang". For about 1, 500 years, Luoyang had been the political, economic and cultural center of China. Lu Zhaolin, a famous poet in the Tang

　　"若问今古兴废事，请君只看洛阳城"，以一城的繁荣与沧桑就可以一窥至少半个中国历史的脉络。洛阳作为十三朝古都，其特殊地理位置，有"洛阳之兴衰，天下治乱之喉"的美誉。比如它是黄河文明的摇篮，河洛文化的发祥地，儒学的奠基地，道学的产生地，佛学的首传地，理学的渊源地等。

　　从郑州出发到洛阳开车要两小时左右的路程，一路上我大脑兴奋搜肠刮肚把对洛阳仅有的浅显历史知识重温一遍：从夏朝至唐末五代，洛阳一直作为国都或陪都，是建都最早，朝代最多，历史最长的都城，所以宋朝的司马光不禁发出感叹"古来利与名，俱在洛阳城"。大约有一千五百多年的时间段里，洛阳一直是全国的政治，经济，文化中心。故而有"长安重游侠，洛阳财富雄"的繁荣昌盛。著名的丝绸之路就是以洛阳为起点的，根据史料记载：东汉时期自洛阳西行——到长安、敦煌，走北道出玉门关，沿天山西行，经新疆，过葱岭，到中亚、西亚，最后到大秦（罗马帝国）。以致有"万国趋河洛，慕名来朝圣"的繁华景象……"洛阳到了"，导游的话音刚落，也把我的思绪从千年拉了回来。白马寺广场新建石牌坊已在眼前。

Dynasty, once wrote "Chang'an is the paradise of talented swordsmen while Luoyang the capital of wealth" to describe its prosperity. The world-renowned Silk Road started from Luoyang. According to historical records, in the Eastern Han Dynasty, starting from Luoyang, in the Silk Road reached Chang'an and Dunhuang to the west, bypassed the Yumen Pass through the Northern Route, went through Xinjiang along the Tian Shan to the west, climbed Pamir Mountains to Central Asia and West Asia, and went on to the Roman Empire. "Pilgrims from hundreds of countries attracted by Tang's reputation all come to Luoyang" demonstrates how thriving Luoyang was. "We are in Luoyang now. " The tour guide's voice brought me back to reality. The newly built stone memorial archway in the square of the White Horse Temple came into view.

The White Horse Temple is where Buddhism started spreading in China. The legend of white horses bringing back Buddhist scriptures here is about 400 years earlier than that of Xuanzang. During the long years, the two stone white horses in front of the gate have been eroded, becoming a mark of history. For thousands of years, the White Horse Temple has been worshiped as the ancestral temple in East Asia, because it was built during China's first attempt in obtaining Buddhist scriptures from the West; it was the residence of the first monk who came to China to preach Buddhism; it was in this temple that the first Chinese Buddhist sutra translated and that the first Chinese monk converted. In the International Buddha Hall Garden in the west wing of the temple, there are a Thai Buddha hall, a Burmese Buddha hall and an Indian Buddha hall, presenting architectures and Buddhist statues with respective features. The tour guide only gave us one and half hour to visit. No matter how unwilling I was, I had to leave. The next stop was the Longmen Grottoes.

　　白马寺，中国佛学的首传地，白马驮经，比唐三藏西天取经要早400多年，山门前的两匹石雕白马在岁月的洗礼下棱角已不那么分明了，却也印记着历史的沧桑。千百年来，白马寺一直被东亚文化区域奉之为"释源""祖庭"。因为这里是中国第一次西天求法的产物，是最早来中国传教弘法的僧人的居所；这里诞生了第一部中文佛经和中文戒律，产生了第一个中国汉地僧人等，所以在白马寺的西侧国际佛殿苑内建有泰国佛殿、缅甸佛殿和印度佛殿，具有这些国家民族特色的建筑和佛像。导游给我们一个半小时的时间，就匆匆离开，意犹未尽却也无可奈何。下一站就是龙门石窟。

　　"九朝不改青山色，百洞斧凿佛像尊"说的就是龙门石窟，它位于伊河两岸西边的龙门山和东边的香山上，其中尤以西边的龙门山上的雕刻为主，给我的感觉就是震撼、惊叹和无比的崇敬。这些巧夺天工的精美佛像

"Greenness of hills was never faded in nine dynasties, chiseled statutes in hundreds of caves were stand divinely" described the Longmen Grottoes. The Longmen Grottoes is located on the western (the Longmenshan Mountain) and eastern slopes (the Xiangshan Mountain) along the Yi River with most of its statues done on the western slope. Looking at these magnificent statutes that were sculptured by hundreds of thousands of unnamed sculptors in several consecutive decades, no one could resist exclaiming its greatness. The nine huge carved statues in the Fengxian Temple are the most representative ones in the Longmen Grottoes. They are so gorgeous and extraordinary. It is said that the Vairocana Buddha in the center was carved to resemble the only Empress in Chinese history, Wu Zetian. Although most of caves are empty and many statutes have been destroyed, the exquisite carving skills could not be derogated by its incompleteness. Walking along the Yi River, the weeping willow, the sparkling river and the green mountains are silently telling me the city's rise and fall in the thirteen dynasties. At this moment, I could not help but improvising a poem: "As royal mausoleums in the Mangshan Mountain fade away, city walls of Luoyang erect as before; stunning peony blooms as usual, while waves surging in the long Yellow River."

The 5000-year Chinese civilization is shaped by its glorious culture and history. If I have the opportunity, I will definitely visit every site where vestiges of ancient emperors, scholars, and beauties could be found to further experience the splendid Chinese civilization.

是那些千千万万的无名雕刻天才用二三十年的时间来完成的，真是太伟大了，尤其以奉先寺的极富情态质感的九尊大佛像最具有代表性，规模宏伟、气势磅礴。中心雍容大度、气宇非凡、含笑祥和的卢舍那佛，据说是以中国唯一称帝的武则天女皇为原型雕刻的。不过这里十窟九空，很多大小佛像被破坏殆尽，残缺不全但仍然难掩精美的雕工，浑然天成。漫步伊河岸边，柳枝摇曳，河面波光粼粼，青山绿水仿佛在静静地倾诉十三朝帝王之都的兴衰史。此时此景不由得让我即兴赋诗一首：

　　　　洛阳行

　　北邙山头帝陵萧，

　　洛阳城垣如前朝。

　　绝色牡丹花相似，

　　千里黄河浪滔滔。

　　五千年的中华文明，有着厚重、辉煌、灿烂文明的历史，如果有机会我一定要带上古人的诗词歌赋寻着他们的足迹去——找寻那曾经的名士风流，曾经的帝王将相，曾经的雕梁画栋，曾经的才子佳人。

河南中医药大学提供

我的新生活
A New Chapter of My Life

[哈萨克斯坦] 迪达尔 北京理工大学
[Kazakhstan] Urynbassarova Didar, Beijing Institute of Technology

Upon my arrival in Beijing, I took a taxi to the university. A teacher at the International Student Center of the university arranged a Chinese class for me. I went back to the dormitory with a curriculum schedule, wondering what my Chinese class would be like. Would there be many students? How would the teachers teach Chinese? Where could I buy books and notebooks? This list went on and on.

What should I wear to embrace my new life? I dropped my original plan of wearing suits because they would turn out to be way too serious. "A pink dress would fit just fine," I thought, but it dawned on me that I was going to a class and not a matchmaking event. With all the indecision, I abandoned all thought and opted instead for a good night's sleep first.

On the second day, I made a makeshift decision and settled for the first thing I could snatch from the closet, which turned out to be a pair of jeans! Uh-oh, I felt uneasy about the fact that I was going to open a new chapter in my life wearing jeans. On my way to the classroom, I comforted myself, "What really matters at this point is to learn Chinese well, rather than to care

　　我来北京以后坐出租车到大学。留学生中心的老师为我安排了一个汉语班。我带课表回宿舍，然后开始想我的汉语班是什么样的，学生多不多，老师们教得怎么样，在哪儿买书本等。可是我没想多久就决定不想了，等明天看吧。

　　我穿什么迎接我的新生活呢？我先打算穿西服，可是穿西服太严肃；我又打算穿粉色的裙子变女神，学汉语又不是跟男朋友约会，我决定不穿裙子了。想了一晚上都不知道穿什么好，我决定先睡觉。

　　到了第二天，我临时决定把手放在柜子里，拿到什么就穿什么，我闭着眼睛把手放在柜子里，拿到了牛仔裤！哎呦，我得穿牛仔裤迎接我的新生活，心里有点不开心。在去教室的路上我安慰自己："穿什么衣服不重要。没事，重要的是好好学中文。所以我要坐黑板对面的第一个桌子。这样我会更努力。加油加油！"

　　到教室后发现，大部分同学都到了。倒霉！我想坐的桌子已经坐了一个男生。当然有别的空位，可是我想坐在黑板的对面。这样我就当了那位男生的同桌。我同桌有点胖，桌子有点小，有点不方便。我再安慰自己说："他有点胖我有点瘦，桌子刚刚好，没事吧。"这样我们开始了

about what to wear. It will be just fine! I need foremost to secure a seat by the blackboard."

I arrived at the classroom only to find that most of my classmates had already shown up. Alas! The seat I want had already been taken by a man. I still wanted to secure one that would at least face the blackboard directly from the first row. So this literally left me no choice but to sit beside him. It was somehow a bit inconvenient because that he was a little fat. I comforted myself once again that, "He is a little fat, but I am a little slim, so the desk is just fine. It's okay. " So we started learning and I gradually mixed with my classmates including Ali, Degema, Chen Mingming, Zhou Natai, Adinamu and others.

Every day I would always be greeted with a smile from Ali, who was sitting right beside me. One day, so flattered by a chocolate he gave me, I said to him that, "Let's share this chocolate. " He responded, "I cannot let myself gain more weight. " I looked at him and said, "You don't look fat at all because you are so tall. " We both happily shared the chocolate and have become good friends since then.

The most needed tool for learning a language is a dictionary. Degema taught me how to use a Chinese-English dictionary named Pleco, which turned out to be very useful for foreigners to learn Chinese.

One day, after Ali told me that he had bought some books on Taobao, an e-commerce platform, I went back to my dormitory and tried it as well, which made it much easier for buying books, shoes and so on. I always check the comment box on Taobao before I make my final decision, but sometimes I am unable to grasp the meaning of some characters. In such cases, Pleco comes in

学习。慢慢地认识了我的同学：阿里、德格玛、陈明明、周纳泰、阿迪娜姆等。

　　每天我来上课时我的同桌阿里看着我笑。有一天他给我巧克力。我高兴地说："咱们一起吃吧！"他回答："我已经太胖不要再胖了。"我看着他说："你不胖，你的骨头大。"我们俩高兴地分享了巧克力，成了好朋友。

　　学语言时最需要的是词典。德格玛教我用Pleco，Pleco是汉英英汉词典。对学汉语的外国人很好用。

　　有一天阿里又说他在淘宝买了书，我也回家试试淘宝，真心好，可以买书、衣服、鞋子等。我买东西之前会看评价，看评价时有的汉字我不认识，所以用Pleco词典翻译。着急要时我跟卖家约好用顺丰快递发东西，说实话淘宝帮我提高了我的中文。

　　我和陈明明一直安静地写汉字。德格玛和阿迪娜姆喜欢看书。他们俩读中文很快。我们班的周纳泰不喜欢写汉字也不喜欢看书。可是他会

在北京理工大学

handy. If it is an urgent purchase, I hit up the seller on the platform and require SF Express for delivery. Taobao did help me a lot in improving my Chinese proficiency.

Chen Mingming and I always practice writing Chinese characters quietly. Degema and Adinamu both like to read Chinese books, and they read Chinese very fast. Zhou Natai is not a big fan of reading Chinese books or writing Chinese characters, but he can sing Chinese songs. I once said to Zhou Natai, "Zhou Natai, you are so awesome. We can't even speak Chinese. But you can sing Chinese songs!" To which he replied, "It's no big deal, I just listen to Chinese songs every day on KuGoo. What's more, lyrics of all Chinese songs on KuGoo Music are available. " After that, I also started to listen to Chinese songs on KuGoo Music, a really handy platform.

For Adinamu, taxis have been the transport of choice, while I often opt for a bus. Generally speaking, people prefer taxi. But for me, taking a taxi was very troublesome at that time because I was not yet good at speaking Chinese, so drivers hardly knew where I was going. But it seemed not a big trouble for Adinamu even though his Chinese was not that fluent. So I asked him how he chatted with taxi drivers. He said that with a ride-hailing APP called Didi, he did not need to chat with drivers at all, which came as a big shock to me. Later on I also started to use Didi, which helped me a lot. I also used Qunar. com, on which I even managed to book train tickets from Beijing to Tianjin. Among all these handy apps, WeChat is absolutely my favorite! With WeChat, I can chat with friends, pay my phone bills, and even engage in video chat with my families. WeChat wallet makes it totally unnecessary for me to take a purse when I go out. WeChat is such a precious

唱中文歌。我对周纳泰说："周纳泰你真的很牛。我们都说不出来中文。可是你会唱中文歌！"周纳泰说："我不牛，我就是每天听酷狗音乐。酷狗音乐里所有的中文歌都可以看到歌词。"我以后也开始用酷狗音乐了，学中文歌酷狗音乐很方便。

　　阿迪娜姆常常打车出去玩儿，我坐公交车。一般人决定坐出租车，但是对我来说打车很麻烦。因为我的发音还不准，司机不懂我要去哪儿。我看阿迪纳姆的发音也不那么好可是他却没问题。我问他怎么跟司机聊天儿的。他说他不跟司机聊天儿。我非常吃惊！唉！他说他用一个叫滴滴打车的APP。后来我也开始用滴滴打车，很方便。我自己会用去哪儿网了，还尝试买了从北京到天津的火车票，这些APP都非常方便。我最喜欢的是微信！用微信可以跟朋友聊天，充话费。我用微信跟家人视频联系。我现在出门都不带钱包，因为我有微信钱包。微信非常好用。有

北京理工大学提供

app that I sometimes even wonder how I would live without it.

I like my Chinese class. Chen Mingming and I are good at writing Chinese characters. Degema and Adinamu read Chinese very fast and fluently. Zhou Natai knows how to speak Chinese with the right pinyin and tones. I like happy Degema, quiet Chen Mingming, tall Ali, singer-like Zhou Natai and smart Adinamu. I like Baidu, Pleco, Taobao, Didi, KuGoo Music, Qunar. com, WeChat and etc. I really enjoy my life in China! I like China very much!

北京理工大学提供

的时候就想，如果没有微信我们该怎么生活呀？

我喜欢我的班，我和陈明明的汉字比较好看，德格玛和阿迪娜姆读中文很快，周纳泰的中文很标准，我很喜欢快乐的德格玛，安静的陈明明，骨头大的阿里，唱歌好听的周纳泰，聪明的阿迪娜姆。喜欢百度，Pleco，淘宝，滴滴快车，酷狗音乐，去哪儿，微信等。我很喜欢我在中国的生活！我很喜欢中国！

中国与我，且行且体验
Understanding China in Traveling

[泰国]　周玲　大连海事大学
[Thailand] Kaipech Miss Aumpika, Dalian Maritime University

Several years ago, when I went abroad for the first time, I knew nothing about China. Thanks to the student exchange program between my university then and Guangxi University, I came to Guangzhou, my very first stop in China.

When the plane landed at the Guangzhou Baiyun International Airport, my schoolmates and I were excited and nervous as it was our first visit to China. Some students just started learning Chinese several months ago. Since I have learnt Chinese for a relatively longer time, I was entrusted with the duty of exchange for them. But who would ever think the first challenge for me, a person who had learnt Chinese for two years, is communication. What I learnt in Thailand did not work at all in practice and the most vivid example is that I could not understand what Chinese people were talking about.

Fortunately, the pick-up teacher from Guangxi University showed up timely, saving us from embarrassment. However, we soon came across another incident. When we got on the bus, it was nearing sunset. It took three hours to drive from the airport to Hezhou, Guangxi by bus. We had fallen asleep in this long journey during which we could saw nothing but dark sky. In a daze, we all

几年前，我第一次出国，那时，我还是个懵懵懂懂的大学生，借着我的大学与中国广西大学的交换生计划，我踏上了中国的土地，来到了我的第一个中国城市——广州。

飞机降落在白云机场，我和同校一起来的同学都既兴奋又紧张，因为我们中的大多数人都是第一次来中国，许多人才学了几个月的汉语，我是这些人中汉语学习时间比较长的，所以交流的任务基本落在了我的身上。可谁曾想，我这个学过两年汉语的人到了中国以后，面临的第一个问题竟然是沟通障碍。原来在泰国学的汉语真的可以称得上是"纸上谈兵"，我听不懂中国人说话。

还好，广西大学的接机老师及时出现，避免了我们的尴尬，可是紧接着我们又遇到了第二场"尴尬"。我们的目的地是广西贺州，从白云机场到那边需要乘坐三个多小时的大巴车，此时已经接近傍晚，夜幕降临，沿途根本看不到任何风景，再加上长途的飞行，我们几乎都睡着了，迷迷糊糊中，我们被大巴车的突然鸣笛惊醒了，以为发生了意外，在我们惊慌失措的时候，大巴司机却还是一副淡定自若的样子，我们开始议论，并询问来接机的老师，才知道原来在中国，行驶中鸣笛是很常见的

woke up by the honking car. Assuming that some accident happened, we were in panic. However, the driver was in perfect calm. After we asked the teacher, we learnt that it is very normal for drivers to honk in China. In Thailand, we like to do everything slowly. Even in Bangkok that is known for traffic jams, few people will beep. Therefore, we tended to relate horns with accidents.

After my first day in China filled with excitement, hopefulness, nervousness, upset and even shock, I began to worry about my study in China. At first, I only talked with others in English for fear of making mistakes in speaking Chinese. I was very lucky that I met two Chinese friends who understood me. In the first place, they tried their best to talk with me in English. Till one day, one asked me: "Why don't you just give it a try?" They told me it would be a waste if I do not make use of the language environment since I was in China now. That inspired me a lot.

It did not take too much time for me to speak fluent Chinese which encouraged me to improve my Chinese in other ways, such as watching Chinese movies and TV series. I understood the importance and necessity to learn a language in context. After I took the right direction, I found more interesting things. Playing badminton is my favorite sport since childhood. Joining in the badminton club brought me more Chinese friends. We played together and sometimes compete with each other. Gradually, I had my own friend circle and became a participant of social activities rather than a bystander, which gave me the simple pleasure of being involved. Interaction with Chinese friends also enabled me to experience different culture and local customs in Hezhou. For example, you should tap the table to express thanks when someone pours tea for you and hold your wine glass lower to show respect when someone come to

行为，而在泰国，我们喜欢什么事都"慢慢来"，即使在曼谷这种"堵车大城"也基本没人会鸣笛，导致我们每次听到鸣笛都会觉得是有意外发生。

这样说吧，我到中国的第一天，兴奋、期待、不安、沮丧，甚至是惊吓，这些情绪充满了我的内心，对于未来在中国的学习生活，我开始忐忑不安，我越来越不敢说汉语，明明学过，却只敢用英语和别人交流。庆幸的是，我认识了两位中国朋友，他们非常理解我的处境，开始时，他们也尽最大的努力和我用英语沟通，直到有一天，其中一个朋友问我，为什么不尝试用用汉语呢？他们还告诉我，既然来到了中国，有了这么好的语言环境，如果不好好利用，那就白白浪费了这次好机会了。这对我来说真的是一语点醒梦中人了。

从磕磕巴巴到流利表达，我并没有花费太多的时间。我决定再尝试一下其他的提高汉语的方法，我看汉语电影，看中文电视剧，我体会到在语境中学习语言的必要性和有效性。而且一旦我的思路打开了，我发现了更多有意思的东西。我从小喜欢打羽毛球，通过加入羽毛球社团，我认识了更多的中国朋友，我们一起打球，一起比赛，渐渐地，我发现我有了一个属于我的朋友圈。我不再是一个"旁观者"，而是一个"参与者"，这种参与感和体验感真的太棒了——在与中国朋友的交往

toast with you.

When I got another chance to further my study in China, I chose a different city, Dalian. This northern city exposes me to the differences between the south and the north and between the coastal areas and the inland. Indeed, in summer, it is much cooler in Dalian than in Guangxi. I had never been stroke by the sea breeze in Guangxi. When it snows in winter, my friends and I often take pictures and send them to families and friends. The Dalian cuisine is a little bit spicy and salty to me and its buildings sometimes remind me of those in Russia.

The biggest change I have observed in China is the convenience brought by Taobao, Alipay, Wechat Pay, and all kinds of food delivery apps. In my visit, I understand more about China. As my story with China continues, I expect to find and experience more surprises in this booming country.

大连海事大学提供

中，我体验到了不一样的文化氛围和贺州当地的习俗，例如，当有人给你倒水时，你要拍打桌子以示感谢；喝酒碰杯的时候，你的杯子要比对方的杯子低以示尊敬，等等。

　　现在，我又有机会来中国读研究生了。我来到了中国的另一个城市——大连，我故意选择了一个北方城市，就是想体验一下中国人常说的"南北差异"，想看看沿海和内陆的不同。的确，大连的夏天比南方凉快多了，时不时的大海风确实是我在广西没体验过的，冬天下雪时我和朋友们会在外面拍好看的照片给国内的家人朋友看，大连的菜对我来说又辣又咸，建筑的感觉有时会让我觉得自己是在俄罗斯。

　　而这一次来中国，我感觉到中国最大的变化就是淘宝、支付宝、微信支付、外卖 APP 等新鲜事物的普及以及它们为生活带来的诸多便利。我在中国学习着，生活着，行走着，我和中国的故事还在继续着，我期待着发展中的中国还能带给我更多的惊喜和体验。

乘着改革开放的东风
Riding on the Wind of Reform and Opening-up

［韩国］ 金兰一 东华大学
[Republic of Korea] Kim Ranyi, Donghua University

It is my second time to study in China since I first came here 13 years ago. During the decade, astounding social changes have taken place.

It was a hot summer in 2005 when I, as a kid, set foot on the country with my parents for the first time. The city transportation of Shanghai was not as advanced as it is today. However, the metro lines of Shanghai today extend in all directions like a complex spider web, which is amazing. After 13 years, besides transportation, spectacular development and changes impressed me.

In 2016, I came to study in China again. One day, I went to Hangzhou with my university friend. Upon arriving at the West Lake, we took a boat ride into the wind. After then, I couldn't help admiring the vastness of it. The pagoda on the other side towering over hills sets off the lake even more elegantly. I thought to myself, "I must see every corner of the city before going back to Shanghai. "

It could be time-consuming and tiring to walk around in the city for cash-strapped university students like us. As taking a taxi neared luxury we decided to ride a shared bicycle. I often ride ofo in Shanghai, but I did not expect to

　　这是我第二次在中国留学，距离第一次间隔 13 年，而正是这 13 年的社会变迁让人震惊，也令人钦佩。

　　最初是 2005 年炎热的夏日，年幼的我和父母一起第一次踏上中国的土地。当时的上海城市交通不像现在这样发达。然而，现在上海的地铁线路复杂得像蜘蛛网似的，令人感叹。时隔 13 年，除了交通，中国的发展变化引人注目，给我留下了深刻的印象。

　　2016 年，我再次来到中国留学。有一天，我跟大学朋友一起去杭州旅游。抵达西湖，迎着风环绕一圈后，不禁赞叹西湖的辽阔。对岸矗立着一座宝塔，映衬着凹凸不平的低矮山峰，西湖变得更加清雅。所以我想："回到上海之前，非要感受这座城市的每一处不可。"

　　坐出租车对贫困的大学生来说是奢侈的，而不大不小的这个城市走起来也会很吃力。因而我们决定骑共享单车徜徉。我在上海经常骑 ofo，可根本没想到在杭州也能使用 ofo。穿行于杭州的大街小巷，虽然汗水沿着我的脸颊流下来，但心情却很舒畅，一边蹬着自行车，一边欣赏这座城市的独特魅力与曼妙情调。这样的体验，不仅让我摆脱日常生活的单调与专业学习的压力，还使我享受难得的闲暇与源自内心的愉悦。想

use it in Hangzhou. Riding across the streets and alleys of Hangzhou, I was more than happy even with sweat dripping down my cheeks. Immersed in the graceful atmosphere of this city, I appreciated its unique charm while riding a bike. Such experience not only freed me from the monotony of daily life and the pressure of learning, but also allowed me to enjoy rare leisure and inner pleasure. You can use the shared bikes across China just with your mobile phone scanning the QR code. How convenient!

Nowadays, few people in China pay in cash. The mobile payment system has integrated into every aspect of Chinese people's daily life. Now it seems that you can do anything with a mobile phone in China. Hailing taxi of Didi, ordering take-away food, paying for electricity and water bill, and even sorting and recycling garbage can be done by mobile phone. Obviously, these diverse systems have made my study life abroad more convenient, modern and cutting-edge. The Republic of Korea is one of the countries with the highest internet connection speeds and availability rate in the world. However, the depth and scope of Internet application pales in comparison to those of China. Why?

Forty years of reform and opening-up has made China the world's second major economy, which rides on the wind of reshape and the wave of the scientific and technological revolution. Among all changes, chief of them is the spiritual change of the Chinese people. We are inspired and touched by the openness, tolerance, self-confidence and enthusiasm we have seen. Today's China has really become what Confucius once said, "When there are adequate stores, people will know what is decorum; when the people have enough food and clothing, they will know what is honor. " As a result, they have the ability to

在乌镇

一想，只要用手机扫描二维码，就能使用全国各地的共享单车，这多么方便！

　　如今，在中国很少有人使用现金来购物，移动支付系统已渗透到中国人日常生活的方方面面，现在好像在中国没有用手机做不到的事情。滴滴打车、外卖、缴纳水电费，甚至可以用手机分类回收垃圾。显然，这些多种多样的系统确实让我的留学生活变得更加方便，更加具有现代感和科技感。韩国是世界上网速最快、互联网普及率最高的国家之一，不过互联网应用的广度与频度远不及中国。为何如此？

　　四十年的改革开放，中国不仅成为世界第二经济大国，乘着改革开放的东风，踏着科技革命的浪潮，中国人精神上的变迁才是最大的变化，中国普通民众身上洋溢的开放、包容、自信、上进让人羡慕，也让人感动。现在的中国真正如孔子所说的"仓廪实则知礼节，衣食足则知荣辱"，

update their thinking and the power to adapt to the changes of the new era.

It can be predicted that in the world of dramatic changes, this capacity will become a huge driving force for China's rejuvenation. In the near future, China will surely shake the world again!

东华大学提供

其结果，他们具有了更新思想的能力和更快适应新时代变化的能量。

可以想见，剧变的世界形势下，这种力量将成为中国希望再次崛起的巨大动力。不久的将来，中国必将重新震撼世界！

东华大学提供

白驹过隙，匆匆七年
——我在中国留学的美好时光

Seven Years Fly in a Twinkling
—My Best Time of Studying in China

[孟加拉国] 胡赛因 西北工业大学

[Bangladesh] M Shakhawat Hussain, Northwestern Polytechnical University

I am Husaiyin (M Shakhawat Hussain) from Bangladesh.

I will never forget the day, August 29, 2011, when I began my life of studying in China. I vaguely remembered reading in my book as a child: China is one of the world's four ancient civilizations, with a history of 5, 000 years, and is a dazzling oriental pearl. A saying goes in my country: "If you want to learn knowledge, go to China. " Since then I have had a keen interest in this mysterious and ancient country. In August 2011, I was fortunate to be a member of the Bangladeshi government-sponsored student to China which has haunted me for a long time. Because of this, I have the opportunity to appreciate the time-honored oriental pearl.

As we all know, language is closely related to history and culture. To appreciate China's long-standing history and splendid culture, I must learn Chinese well first. Time flies, and a year of Chinese learning at Tianjin University has passed away. After that, I came to Xi'an, a famous historical city, and the

我叫胡赛因，来自孟加拉国。

我的留学生活始于 2011 年 8 月 29 日，我永远也忘不了那一天。依稀记得小时候在书中读到：中国是世界四大文明古国之一，有五千年的文明史，是一颗璀璨夺目的东方明珠。在我的国家有一句话："如果你想学到知识，那就去中国吧。"从那时起我就对这个神秘而古老的国家产生了浓厚的兴趣。2011 年 8 月，我有幸成为孟加拉国公派留学生中的一员，来到这个令我魂牵梦萦的国家深造，正因为如此，我才有机会欣赏这颗历史悠久的东方明珠。

众所周知，语言与历史文化有着密切的联系。想要了解中国悠久的历史，灿烂的文化，就必须先学好汉语。光阴似箭，在天津大学一年的中文学习随着时光悄然而逝。之后，我来到历史名城、十三朝古都——西安。在西工大期间我参加了很多丰富的校内外的活动，其中印象最深的是去年的暑假参加的铜川市政府的见习实践，在这里我认识了我的队长，已经在此岗位认真负责工作二十余年，为人亲切真诚的一名政府工

ancient capital of thirteen dynasties. During my days at the Northwestern Polytechnical University (NPU) , I participated in a lot of activities on and off campus. The most impressive one was the probation in Tongchuan Municipal Government during last summer vacation where I met my captain, who has been earnestly working for more than 20 years at his post and is a friendly and sincere government worker. We have accomplished a number of tasks together, the most of which are food and drug safety inspections, the places we inspected includes supermarkets, drug stores, restaurants, eateries and small shops on the roadside. The work seems to be boring, but in the real practice, the careful inspection, patient communication, and strict execution are all indispensable. I have learned a lot in the real work, and I feel that Chinese government staff enforced the law in an amiable manner while taking into account rules and regulations.

What made me most memorable was the poverty alleviation work in the rural areas of Tongchuan. What happened during the period remains fresh in my memory. Although I have been in China for more than seven years, I have always lived in cities. I still remember the old lady who has experienced hardships but was full of energy. She was optimistic and staunch and full of appreciation in her eyes, and kept showing her thanks to the Communist Party of China, with her hands shaking. I was deeply touched by the fact that the government has been helping her who has nothing to depend on over the years. Just like a wooden barrel, its success is always determined by the shortest board. A country is truly powerful only if it does not give up the vulnerable group at any time.

My footprint has covered more than 20 cities during summer and

作人员。我们一起参加了多项工作，其中最多的是外出检查食品和药品的安全和各方面的合格性，大到超市、药店、餐厅，小到路边的小饭馆和小商店，这项工作听起来很枯燥，实际工作的过程中，需要细心地检查，耐心地沟通，严格地执行，在实际的工作中我学到了很多，感受到了中国政府工作人员的亲切执法，同时兼顾着严格的规章制度。

让我最难忘的是那次在铜川农村参加的扶贫工作。期间发生的事情让我现在还记忆犹新。虽然我到中国已经七年多了，可是一直都是在城市里面，我还记得那个历经生活困苦却精神抖擞的老奶奶，她乐观而坚强，眼里满是感动，嘴里不停地说着感谢共产党，双手颤抖着。从聊天中得知，这些年政府一直在帮助着年老无依无靠的她，这让我深受感动，就像一个木桶，决定它容量的永远是最短的板，一个国家不管在什么时候都没有放弃困难群体，才是真正的强大。

这七年我利用寒暑假的时间，去过二十多个城市，在上海感受国际大都市的繁华，在济南品味它的文艺，在青岛享受它的活力，在武汉体

winter vacations over past seven years. I feel the prosperity of Shanghai, an international metropolis, savour the ambience of art in Jinan, enjoy the vitality in Qingdao, experience the swelter in Wuhan, relish the spicy foods, slow-paced life and the cute giant panda in Sichuan, and experience the romance in Dalian, which have made me perceive the beautiful scenery and rapid development of China.

I have witnessed the rapid development of Xi'an for these years, especially the railway tracks, subways, bullet trains, and other roads building. The easily-accessible transportation will surely drive positive growth in trade. For example, the Xi-Xian Free Trade Zone and the Chan'ba Inland Port will certainly boost the economic growth of Xi'an. In sum, as the starting point of the "Belt and Road", Xi'an will surely surprise others with even more amazing development speed. I was chosen as a "Belt and Road" international young reserve talent this year. I will go to Beijing for relevant training in this August, and my country is an important hub of the "Belt and Road". All of this makes me feel proud and full of expectations for the "Belt and Road".

Seven years fly in a twinkling. When I first arrived, I could not say any Chinese and now I become half a China hand, but can I say that I understand everything? No. After learning more about Chinese culture, I have an even more deep feeling that I need to work hard to learn more professional knowledge and practical skills, and I am also willing to learn from the diligent Chinese people's the philosophy—"never too old to learn". I had a happy life at NPU. Finally, I would like to express my heartfelt thanks to the Chinese government and NPU for giving me the chance to study and live here.

验它的闷热，在四川品尝到了麻辣和城市的慵懒，还有见到了可爱的大熊猫，在大连体会它的浪漫，这些都让我感觉到了中国秀丽的风景和快速的发展。

在西安的这些年，我亲眼见到了西安各方面的快速发展，尤其是铁路轨道、地铁、动车，还有各种道路的建设，而交通的便利必然带动贸易方面的正增长，如陕西西咸自贸区，浐灞内陆港一定会拉动西安经济的增长。总而言之，作为"一带一路"的起点，西安一定会用更惊人的发展速度艳惊四座。我今年参加了"一带一路"国际青年后备人才选拔并成功入选，今年的八月即将去北京参加相关培训，而我的国家作为"一带一路"的一个重要的节点，这一切都让我觉得非常的自豪，对"一带一路"充满着期待。

时间如白驹过隙一般，七年匆匆而逝，初来乍到时那个一句汉语都不会说的我俨然成了半个中国通，但我能凭此就说我什么都了解了吗？不能。了解了更多中国文化以后我便更加深刻地感受到，我需要努力学习更多的专业知识和实践技能，并且，我还要向勤奋的中国人学习"活到老，学到老"的精神。西工大的每一天我都过得很开心很充实，最后我想真诚地说：感谢中国政府，感谢西工大，让我可以来到这里学习和生活。

［俄罗斯］ 热尼亚　哈尔滨工业大学

[Russia] Kozhevnikov Evgeny, Harbin Institute of Technology

Every story has a beginning. The story between me and the Harbin Institute of Technology began far back in 2013. The past half decade has been of mixed memories to me. And I would like to take this opportunity to share with you some of my experiences, and everything they have taught me as well as how my character has, to a certain point, been reshaped.

In August 2013, I took the train and set out for Harbin. While leaving my family, I was sad and reluctant. But a new chapter was about to begin and I was the leading role.

Once arrived in Harbin, I buried up in Chinese learning immediately. Honestly, the first term was not easy at all. I could have never imagined that studying could be so hard and tiring. At the end of the term, I found that classmates neither did their homework nor memorized new words. I can remember perfectly well the times I told myself to "try and make my life easier, and not exhausting". One day, I left my glasses in the classroom. When I came back I found that a teacher was marking my homework carefully. She looked so tired. I was sympathetic to her. Unlike students who only need to go back to

　　每个故事都有自己的起点。我与哈工大的故事在 2013 年就开始了。现在想一想，不知不觉已经过去五年了。这五年对我来说发生了好多事情，好的不好的什么都有。而此刻，我想跟热心的读者们分享一下我在哈工大学到的三个重要的经验。如果能够为看到的朋友们提供些许帮助，那将是我的荣幸。

　　2013 年 8 月，我坐上火车从我的家乡向哈尔滨出发了。离开家人的时候心里酸酸的，很舍不得走，但是我想：中国哈尔滨的哈工大是我的下一个目的地，我必须得去。

　　到哈尔滨之后我就开始埋头学习中文。说实话，第一学期过得太不容易了。我从来没有体会过学习是那么辛苦那么累的一件事儿。快到学期末的时候，我看大家都不怎么想写作业，也不怎么想背生词。当时我记得特别清楚，我一直对自己说：我也想轻松一点，为什么让自己累成狗？有一天我把眼镜儿忘在教室里了，回去取的时候发现一位老师用心地检查家庭作业，特别累的样子。那个时候我好心疼她，因为她不像学生回宿舍写完作业就可以了。她回家还需要准备明天的课程。再说，老师是女性，回家得做饭、收拾屋子、陪孩子写作业或者做游戏，还得听

the dormitory and finish their homework, she had to prepare for the next day's class. As the breadwinner in her family, after going home, she had to cook, clean up the house, help her children with homework, bond with them, and even listen to her husband's complaints. After thinking about all her hard work, I made up mind that no matter how tired, I could not let my teachers down or let their work be in vain. So I started to do my homework carefully every day, memorize new words patiently, and kept getting up early every morning. The effect was obvious. I easily finished all the test questions and passed the HSK. So the most important experience I learned in the first term was endurance. No matter what you do, when there is endurance, there are results.

The second lesson is the perseverance I learned from academic courses. To be honest, after learning that my thesis supervisor had some different ideas on my dissertation, I felt very bad about myself and thought I would never graduate. Until one day, on my way home, I suddenly recalled a statement I had learned in the first term— "Perseverance prevails. " So, I set myself a goal to do my best regardless of the promises of graduation. Now I have published an SCI paper, the second one has also been contributed, and the third is still in writing. In addition to publications, I also registered a patent in China. Hence, the lesson I share here is perseverance.

The third lesson is actually known to everyone and very important. My major in Russia was healthcare instrument technology and studies on medical equipment. After I came to the Harbin Institute of Technology for a PhD program, I suddenly realized that my previous knowledge and skills were far from enough since here I had to do experiments on my own, such as animal anesthesia surgery and cell culture. Through such experiments, I also realized

老公讲这一天发生的乱七八糟的事情。考虑完这些之后，我默默地告诉自己：不管我多累都一定要让我的老师们高兴，让她们感觉到她们的辛苦与付出不会白费。然后我开始每天认真地做作业、耐心地背生词、坚持每天早起去上课。效果很明显，考试的时候我轻轻松松地搞定了所有的考试题，还通过了 HSK 考试。所以，第一个学期我掌握的最重要的经验便是"耐心"。不管做什么事必须有耐心，有耐心才会有好的结果。

第二个经验是我刚刚上专业课的时候学到的，它叫作"坚持"。说实在的，我跟导师关于论文的构思上有些分歧。那时我产生了一个很可怕的想法：我是个失败者，毕不了业。有一天，我在回家的路上突然想起了第一个学期学过的一个句子："坚持就是胜利。"后来我又给自己定了一个目标：不管能不能毕业我都要坚持我应该做的事。现在我已经发表了一篇 SCI 文章，第二篇也投出去了，第三篇还正在写。除了发表文章，我还申请了中华人民共和国的专利。所以现在我想对大家说：如果想要一个好的结果，必须得耐心地坚持做下去。

第三个经验其实每个人都知道，而且很重要。在俄罗斯我的专业是

that confidence is the key to do things well. Confidence can help people succeed in a range of fields. Nevertheless, people with no confidence may not only be ill-trained in professional knowledge but often fail in their career.

A period of five years has taught me invaluable lessons, which drove my progress. These three lessons can not only be applied in study, but also be practical in daily life. Do everything with endurance, confidence and perseverance, you will find that nothing is impossible in the world.

Although each story has its beginning and end, the story between the Harbin Institute of Technology and me has not yet concluded. There will be more experiences for me to accumulate. Life is limited, but learning and thinking will never stop. The story never ends, and the future is promising.

哈尔滨工业大学提供

哈尔滨工业大学提供

医疗仪器技术和设备研究。来哈工大读博士后，我才突然发现我之前的知识和技能根本不够用。因为在这儿我得自己亲手做动物麻醉实验的手术，自己培养细胞等。通过做实验我突然发现了：得有"自信"，才能做事儿并且做好。其实我觉得人有自信会在很多不同的事情上获得成功。没有自信的人不仅专业知识不过关，而且还会常常失败。

　　五年之后，能够毫不迟疑地说出这三个经验，我想这已经是成长对我的褒奖。这三个经验不仅仅可以应用在学习上，在生活中也特别实用。做任何事情都要有耐心，有自信并坚持去做，这样大家一定会发现，世界上没有搞不定的事情。

　　虽然每一个故事都有自己的起点和终点，但是我与哈工大的故事还并未结束，还有更多的经验等待我去积累，还有更多风景等待我去亲历。人生有涯，学习与思考却永远不会停止。终点未至，未来可期。

我的收获在华工
Gains in SCUT

［越南］ 黄氏美幸　华南理工大学

[Vietnam] Hoang Thi My Hanh, South China University of Technology

Last September, I arrived at South China University of Technology (SCUT), starting my study here. As to my first impression here, "hot" was the only word in my mind. Although autumn had been here for some days, high temperature still lingered on. When I was trying to find the B1 building of School of International Education to get registered, I got lost. A gentleman helped me to find the right office. On the way, I asked him: "Is Guangzhou always so hot?" He laughed and said: "It is not hot at all! July here will tell you how hot it could be. In Guangzhou, you can only experience two seasons. " I was shocked then and thought that studying in such a high temperature city might make my tan skin darker. I even worried about it for a period of time, but later I gradually got used to the climate in Guangzhou and my study and life in SCUT.

The most important thing I have harvested in SCUT is teachers' love and care. Their passion and patience could be seen in every class. They warm our hearts by encouraging smiles, boost our morale by hortative remarks, take us into the palace of knowledge with only some pieces of chalk, and correct our mistakes and give us hope by short comments. Dear teachers! On behalf of all

　　还记得我来华工留学的第一天，最初的印象就是"热"。那是去年的九月初，已到了秋季，但气温还很高，真是"秋老虎"！去华工国际教育学院 B1 办公大楼报名的时候，因为不认识路，就请一位男生为我们带路。路上我问他："同学，广州一直这么热吗？"他大声地笑着说："这不算热啊，七月才热呢，在华工两件衣服穿一年啊。"那时候我愣住了。糟糕！我本来就黑，来这么热的地方留学会更黑的。我还为了这件事情发了一段时间愁呢。渐渐地，我适应了广州的气候，适应了华工的学习，适应了华工的生活。

　　我在华工的重要收获就是得到了老师们的关心与爱护。每一节课，我都能感受到老师们的热情、辛劳与耐心。几次鼓励的微笑，将我们的心灵温暖；几句鼓励的话语，将我们的斗志激起；几行朴素的粉笔字，将我们带入知识的殿堂；几句短短的评语，让我们改正缺点，看到希望。老师！您为我们的将来操心，作为班里的一员我代表全班同学向您表达谢意与敬意；您为了我们付出多少心血与汗水，我们都看得到，虽然没有说出来，但在心里我们都很感动，能作为你们的学生就是我们的骄傲。我想真诚地跟你们说：老师，谢谢你们，你们辛苦了！"一日为师、终

the classmates, I would like to express our gratitude and pay our tributes to you for your efforts and devotions. We know your love and care clearly and are deeply moved, but we have never told you that we are really proud to be your students. Thus today I want to tell you once again: "Dear teachers, thank you for all the devotions! " I will never forget the proverb "A teacher of one day is a father of a lifetime. " All the courses you once taught us, be it about Chinese characters, Chinese literature or Chinese folk culture, have brought us valuable knowledge and great experiences, purifying our minds and souls. Thank you, teachers from SCUT, for giving us a lot of knowledge and moved stories.

Another precious thing I have harvested is the friendship with my dear classmates. They make up my wonderful school life here. Sometimes, I would be sad when the thought that I will leave one year later comes up. Dear classmates, I would like to tell you that all the time I spend with you, having classes, hanging out, eating and singing, is the best in my youthfulness. You often ask why I like to take photos for you. Actually, I am very afraid of forgetting you when we could not stay together in the future. Although we have not known each other for a very long time, you are already my family members in my mind. In the big family of SCUT, teachers play the role of parents while we are each other's brothers and sisters. Destiny ties us together. Therefore, we will always be friends and share one heart wherever we will be and whatever will happen in the future. I hope all of us can achieve our common goal, which is our promise too: graduate on time. Besides, I wish all of us could realize our dreams and ambitions. Regardless of the result, we can say to ourselves: I have tried my best and I have nothing to regret. Thank you, dear classmates, for giving me friendship and happiness.

身为父"这句话我一辈子都不会忘记。你们给我们上的每门课,不管是汉字课、中国文学、中国民俗文化还是其他课程,都给我们带来很多宝贵的知识与体验,让我们的心情更加纯净,让我们的灵魂得到提升。感谢您,华工的老师们,您让我们收获了知识与感动!

对我来说,最珍贵的收获还有班上同学之间的友谊。跟他们在一起的时候让我觉得学生生活真的很美好,偶尔也会想到一年后大家都不能在一起的时候,突然觉得很难过。我们班里的同学,我很想跟大家说,跟你们一起上课、一起去玩、一起吃饭、一起唱 K,都是我青春里最美好的记忆。你们问我为什么喜欢偷拍你们,我在这里告诉你们:"因为我怕以后,我们不能在一起的时候,我会把你们忘记。"我们相处的时间虽然不长,但在我心中已经把你们当作家庭成员,老师们就是我们的父母,而我们就是家里的兄弟姐妹。缘分让我们相遇,尽管以后距离遥远,天各一方,但无论世界发生什么变化,我们的心永远在一起,我们永远

放学后的我和我的朋友们

华南理工大学提供

I do cherish every second I spend with my teachers and classmates. Guangzhou carries my unforgettable memory of them. Now, I really fall in love with Guangzhou and SCUT.

华南理工大学提供

是朋友。我希望我们都能达到共同的目标，这也是我们的承诺：按时毕业；我也希望大家能够实现自己的抱负和梦想。不管以后结果如何，我们也可以跟自己说，我已经尽力了，我们问心无愧！感谢您，华工的同学们，你们让我收获了友谊与快乐！

我很珍惜跟老师和同学们在一起的每一刻，每一秒。广州，有我的一片记忆，这里有我的老师、我的同学和很多令我难忘的回忆。现在，我真的爱上了广州，爱上了华工。

我的中国日志
My Journal in China

[巴基斯坦] 那西 中南财经政法大学

[Pakistan] Nazir Muhammad Imran, Zhongnan University of Economics and Law

It has been two years since the day I left Pakistan for Wuhan to learn and experience Chinese culture in 2016. For me, this experience will be unforgettable all my life. I would like to thank the Chinese government scholarship for making my dream come true and helping me study as a doctoral student in finance at Zhongnan University of Economics and Law in Wuhan, Hubei Province. I think Wuhan is one of the best cities in the world with beautiful natural sceneries and numerous outstanding students.

During my two-year study as a doctor, I have gained a lot of wonderful memories that I have never had before, which I call "My Journal in China". A single article is far from being able to sum up all those priceless memories and experiences I have had in China.

I can still remember the struggle I faced when I started to learn Chinese, the bonds that international students forged between each other, and gratification of our teachers when they saw us achieve our goal of studying in China. Of course, it was also a wonderful experience to make new friends who helped me understand some Chinese knowledge which I could not learn in

2016 年我离开巴基斯坦来到武汉学习并体验中国文化，我现在已经在这里居住了两年。对我来说，这段经历将是终生难忘的。感谢中国政府奖学金让我实现梦想，成为湖北武汉中南财经政法大学金融专业的博士生。湖光山色，莘莘学子，我认为武汉是世界上最好的城市之一。

在两年的博士学习时光中，我收获了很多以前从未有过的美妙回忆，我把它叫作"我的中国日志"。一篇文章远远难以概括我在中国得到的所有无价的回忆和经历。

我还记得刚学习中文时的挣扎，各国留学生们之间建立起的感情纽带，以及我们的老师看到我们实现来中国学习的目标时的欣慰。当然，认识新朋友并帮助我了解课堂上学不到的中国知识也是一段美妙经历。我也还清楚记得孩子们和他们的祖父母们一起外出时的其乐融融，广场舞大妈们伴随着传统音乐翩翩起舞时的怡然自得。

今天的中国依旧没有舍弃传承悠久的古老文化和习俗，但同时也是一个充满新奇想法和创新精神的国家。尽管一些事物看起来似乎经久不变，像美味的饺子和茄子，但也有很多东西以不可思议的速度在持续更新着。

class. I also remember how happy the children were when they were out with their grandparents, and how delighted the old ladies were when they danced with the traditional music in the square.

Today's China is a country full of new ideas and innovative spirit while carrying forward its time-honored culture and customs. Although something remains unchanged, like delicious dumplings and eggplant, there are also many things that keep updating at an incredible pace.

Taking part in marathon and mountain climbing are precious experiences for me during my study. Although I win no champion of the marathon, the scenery along the way was enough for me to cherish. I find hiking is one of the most popular leisure activities in China. It is also a way to travel, to maintain physical and mental health, and to enjoy the natural scenery. I had a wonderful experience of hiking with foreign friends and local Chinese. In the activities organized by the Wuhan Student Travel Club, I visited Purple Mountain, Mufu Mountain, Fangshang Geopark and Yinshuidong Geopark with other international students.

Hiking turns me into an adventurous man, which brings me a life that is totally different from the monotonous one I lived before. Hiking for several hours brings me an endless passion, but what struck me more is that even elderly Chinese would brave it out to climb to the top. Now, I prefer to climb mountains rather than going to the beach, because climbing guides and motivates people to achieve their goals, no matter how difficult and distant they may seem.

China leads the world in infrastructure development. It has made great contributions to the world's renewable energy technology. I am also amazed by

中南财经政法大学提供

　　参加马拉松和爬山都是我在学习期间的珍贵经历。尽管我并没拿到马拉松的冠军，但参赛时沿途的美景已经值得珍藏。我发现远足是中国人最喜欢的休闲活动之一。它不仅仅是一种休闲，也是旅游、保持身心强健、欣赏自然风光的方式。我和外国朋友们以及中国当地人一起远足的经历非常美好。在武汉学生旅行俱乐部组织的活动中，我和其他国际学生参观过的地方有紫金山、幕府山、房山地质公园和隐水洞地质公园。

　　远足使我变成了一个勇于探险的人，这和来中国以前单调的生活完全不同。持续几小时的远足带给我无尽的激情，更使我震撼的是，那些上了年纪的中国人也不甘示弱地往顶峰攀登。现在，我更喜欢爬山而不是去海滩，因为爬山带给人一种方向感，给人达成目标的动力，不论目标看起来是多么困难和遥不可及。

　　中国的基础设施发展世界领先。除此之外，我个人对于中国的认知

the convenience of going to another city by high-speed trains, which I cannot experience in my country. I also saw something special on my train journey — solar panels in huge open spaces. Although it sounds incredible, it was at that time that I really understood China's efforts to improve people's lives and combat climate change.

With China's rapid economic growth, we have more reasons to believe it will provide more ideas and technology to deal with climate change. China now has the most cyclists in the world. The convenient bike-sharing system encourages more Chinese to ride bicycles instead of gas-guzzling cars. I believe that riding electric bicycles and electric cars is an effective way to reduce pollution, and it is necessary for other countries to do the same thing. It is reported that the Chinese government plans to introduce new buses and cars powered by hydrogen.

I believe that China has done more than its part in combating climate change. Through the window on the high-speed train, I can see the hope right in front of me — the hope that we can succeed in creating a sustainable and cleaner environment. China's economy is booming and its people are living a richer life. During my two-year stay here, I have witnessed China's potential. And in the future, China will definitely become a world leader.

Now, I am glad to say: "I'm Chinese, not a foreigner. "

还有它对世界可再生能源科技方面做出的巨大贡献。还有，我深深被乘坐高铁去另外一个城市的便利性所倾倒，这在我的国家是体验不到的。此外是我在乘坐火车旅行时看到的特别景象：透过车窗，可以看见很多太阳能板建在巨大的空地上。尽管听起来不可思议，但的的确确就在那个时候，我才真正体会到中国在提高人民生活水平以及对抗气候变化上做出的努力。

随着中国经济的飞速增长，我们有更多理由相信这个国家会提供更多创意和技术来对抗气候变化。现在中国拥有最多的骑自行车出行的人。方便的共享单车系统鼓励更多中国人使用自行车而不是耗油的汽车出行，我本人非常确信电动自行车和电动汽车是一个减少污染的有效方法，其他国家也有必要采取同样的行动。也有新闻称，中国政府计划引进以氢气为燃料的新型公交车和汽车。

我相信在和气候变化做斗争时，中国确实尽到了责任，而且采取的行动远比报道出来的多。通过高铁的车窗，我仿佛看见希望就在我眼前——当前这辈人成功创造的可持续的、更干净的环境的希望。中国经济正在繁荣发展，人民生活更加富裕。我在中国的两年里目睹了中国的潜力，在未来，中国一定会成为世界领导者。

现在，我可以很高兴地说："我是中国人。我不是外国人。"